LITERATI AND
SELF-RE/PRESENTATION

*Autobiographical Sensibility
in the Eighteenth-Century
Chinese Novel*

Literati and Self-Re/Presentation

AUTOBIOGRAPHICAL SENSIBILITY
IN THE EIGHTEENTH-CENTURY
CHINESE NOVEL

Martin W. Huang

Stanford University Press
Stanford, California

Stanford University Press
Stanford, California
© 1995 by the Board of Trustees of the
Leland Stanford Junior University

Printed in the United States of America

CIP data appear at the end of the book

Stanford University Press publications are distributed
exclusively by Stanford University Press within
the United States, Canada, and Mexico; they are
distributed exclusively by Cambridge University Press
throughout the rest of the world.

To Yi

ACKNOWLEDGMENTS

The completion of this book gives me an opportunity to express my appreciation to those who have helped me over the years. First of all, I feel extremely fortunate to have Robert Hegel as my mentor. Enthusiastic, patient but always demanding, he has been the first judge of almost every piece of my work. I continue to benefit from his advice and help now that I have begun my own academic career. Without his help I could certainly not be where I am now. I am also indebted to William Matheson, Joseph Allen, Beata Grant, and Emma Kafalenos for their advice and help during the time of my graduate study. My research has also benefited from the stimulating conversations with Yang Shuhui (now at Bates College), Xiao Chi (now at Singapore National University), and Guan Daoxiong (now at the University of California, Santa Barbara). I thank Elsie Pettite and Marianna Brittis and their families for their help and compassion. All these people made my days as a graduate student a fond memory that I will always cherish.

Andrew Plaks patiently read my Ph.D. thesis as well as the book manuscript and offered helpful suggestions; Paul Ropp not only read the entire manuscript and made many suggestions but also generously offered to share with me many of his own research results; David Rolston, despite his busy schedule, read the manuscript carefully and spared me many errors; Zhou Ruchang (Chou Ju-ch'ang), a widely respected *Honglou meng* scholar whose monumental works are indispensable to the writing of this book, read the chapter on *Honglou meng* and shared with me his thoughts on various interesting and important issues. Those who have read portions or the entirety of the manuscript include Theodore Huters, Michael Fuller, Ellen Widmer, and Stephen Roddy. I am grateful to all the people mentioned above for their suggestions and help, although I have not been able to implement all their suggestions. Needless to say, the remaining errors are my responsibilities.

The present study was developed from some ideas in my Ph.D. thesis. The bulk of the manuscript was written during the spring and summer of 1992. I am grateful to the University of California at Irvine and the Department of East Asian Languages and Literatures for teaching relief during the spring quarter of that year. The Faculty Career Development Grant provided by the University greatly facilitated my research. I would like to thank Pauline Yu, the former chair of the Department (now the Dean of the School of Humanities at UCLA), for her support and encouragement.

Professors Sun Xun of Shanghai Normal University and Wang Lixing of Nanjing University helped me gain access to various research materials, for which I am deeply thankful to them. My gratitude also goes to my editor, John Ziemer, for his critical insights and meticulous editing, which have greatly improved this study.

Finally, I want to thank my parents and my wife, Yang Yi, for their caring and help. I am grateful to Yang Yi for having faith in me when I needed it most. Without her constant encouragement and support, this book could never have been completed. To her this book is affectionately dedicated.

M. W. H.

Contents

Note on Citations and Abbreviations   xi

Introduction   1

1   The Problematic Literati Self and Autobiographical Sensibility in the Novel   15

2   The Self Masqueraded: Auto/Biographical Strategies in *The Scholars*   45

3   The Self Displaced: Women and Growing Up in *The Dream of the Red Chamber*   75

4   The Self Reinvented: Memory and Forgetfulness in *The Humble Words of an Old Rustic*   109

Conclusion   143

Notes   155
Selected Bibliography   203
Character List   223
Index   231

NOTE ON CITATIONS AND ABBREVIATIONS

The following texts are used in citing the three novels that are the focus of this study. For *Rulin waishi* (The scholars), Li Hanqiu, ed., *"Rulin waishi" huijiao huiping ben*; cited as RLWS, with chapter (*hui*) and page numbers given, separated by a colon. English translations, unless otherwise noted, are from Hsien-yi Yang and Gladys Yang, trans., *The Scholars*; cited as S, with page number given. For *Honglou meng* (The dream of the red chamber), Cao Xueqin, *Honglou meng*, in 3 volumes, edited by the *Honglou meng* yanjiu suo (Institute for *Honglou meng* study); cited as H with chapter and page numbers given. English translations, unless otherwise noted, are from David Hawkes and John Minford, trans., *The Story of the Story*, in 5 volumes, referred to as SS, with volume and page numbers given, separated by a period. For *Yesou puyan* (The humble words of an old rustic), Xia Jingqu, *Wen Suchen* (an alternative title), published by Wenyuan shuju; cited as W, with chapter and page numbers given; occasionally the 1881 edition of *Yesou puyan* is cited and referred to as Y, with chapter and page numbers given.

In addition, the following abbreviations are used throughout this study:

CLEAR	*Chinese Literature: Essays, Articles, Reviews*
DMB	Goodrich and Fang, *Dictionary of Ming Biography, 1368–1644*
ECCP	Hummel, *Eminent Chinese of the Ch'ing Period (1644–1912)*
HJAS	*Harvard Journal of Asiatic Studies*
HXK	*Honglou meng xuekan*
HZJL	Zhu Yixuan, *"Honglou meng" Zhiping jiaolu*
LZW	Guo Dengfeng, *Lidai zixuzhuan wenchao*

MXLC   *Ming Qing xiaoshuo luncong*
MXYJ   *Ming Qing xiaoshuo yanjiu*
RLYZ   Li Hanqiu, "*Rulin waishi*" *yanjiu ziliao*
SBBY   *Sibu beiyao*
XWJ   Yuan Mei, *Xiaocangshangfang shiwen ji*
ZHJ   Feng Qiyong et al., *Zhiyan zhai chongping "Shitou ji" huijiao*
ZMTY   *Zhongguo tongsu xiaoshuo zongmu tiyao*
ZXLX   Huang Lin and Han Tongwen, *Zhongguo lidai xiaoshuo lunzhu xuan*

For complete bibliographical data for these works, see the Selected Bibliography, pp. 203–21.

LITERATI AND
SELF-RE/PRESENTATION

Autobiographical Sensibility
in the Eighteenth-Century
Chinese Novel

Introduction

Students of Chinese cultural history have often been fascinated by the historical period spanning the late Ming and early Qing (approximately from the early sixteenth century to the late seventeenth century). It has been described as "the most creative and stimulating period in the history of Chinese thought" and a time of "lively controversy and intellectual diversity."[1] It produced such intellectual giants as the philosophers Wang Yangming (1472–1528) and Li Zhi (1527–1602). Above all, it was an age when the individual was probably valued more highly than at any other time during the long history of imperial China. Many have considered Li Zhi the most radical champion of the individual in traditional China.[2] In his recent study of autobiographical writings in traditional China, Pei-yi Wu attributes the flourishing of autobiography during this period to this late Ming obsession with the individual. Wu considers the period from 1565 to 1680 the golden age of Chinese autobiography.[3] According to him, however, this golden age came to a sudden end because of the drastic dynastic transition and the changed intellectual atmosphere.

Manchu rule, now fully consolidated, was efficient and vigilant. There was little tolerance of the sort of reckless behavior and bold experimentation that had thrived under the disintegrating Ming. Censorship and literary inquisition were carried out on a scale unsurpassed until recently. The Wang Shoujen [Wang Yangming] school, which could claim most of the autobiographers during the genre's golden age, was now out of favor. . . . Scholars in the next and subsequent generations turned away from ontological questions to matters of philology and textual criticism. If there was still any secret longing for the blooming of a hundred flowers that had been nourished by the rank but fertile late Ming soil, the elevation of Chu Hsi [Zhu Xi] to the Confucian pantheon by an imperial edict in 1712 signified to all that the court would not suffer any dissension from orthodoxy. Gone were the spiritual fervor and restlessness, the earnest belief in self-transformation, and the burning urgency in the search for ultimate truth. To a combination of all of these factors we must attribute the cessation of [the golden age of Chinese autobiography].[4]

The reasons for this conservative turn in the early Qing are complex. Never before in Chinese history were rulers so anxious to establish themselves as the sole guardian of or authority on "truth" as these Manchu monarchs, a phenomenon that may be related to their eagerness to claim legitimacy for their foreign rule by embracing the dominant native orthodox ideology.[5] There was a certain measure of truth in the otherwise overly flattering remarks made by the famous minister and proponent of the Cheng-Zhu wing of neo-Confucianism (*lixue mingchen*) Li Guangdi (1642–1718) that the Dao and government had been separated for a long time in Chinese history and that only now were the two reunited in the person of the sagely Kangxi emperor (r. 1662–1722). Probably because of the arrival of this sage-king, the emperor began to lecture the ministers and censors, rather than they lecturing the emperor as they would have done in an age such as the late Ming when "men of learning restrained the throne."[6]

Evidence of the initial tightening of control over the literati by the new regime can readily be seen in a series of imperial edicts issued in the early Qing. For example, an edict of 1653 reads:

Discussions of the Classics ought to be based on the editions and interpretations of the Sung dynasty. In official documents, clarity and correct citations of classical precedents are most important. . . . Those works that stealthily advance strange principles or heterodox theories, or which self-consciously set themselves apart [from the Classics], even though their prose is artful, should not be copied out by students. Bookstores should be allowed to print and circulate only books of [the Sung School of] principle, works on government, and those books that contribute to literary enterprise. Other works, with petty concerns or immoral language, and the publication of all literary exercise books or collections sponsored by literati associations are strictly forbidden. Those who violate this prohibition will be punished severely.[7]

No wonder that Mao Qiling (1623–1716), an ardent follower of the Wang Yangming school of neo-Confucianism, reluctantly destroyed his study of the errors in Zhu Xi's (1130–1200) commentaries on the *Four Books* when he learned of the favor the teachings of Zhu Xi were receiving in the imperial court.[8] Mao's fear was certainly justifiable in view of the many literary inquisitions that would soon be launched by the government. These later escalated into a large-scale campaign of political persecution and intellectual terrorism after the middle of the eighteenth century. Intellectual dissent became more difficult than ever.[9]

Another important and probably more relevant factor was the tendency within a large group of early Qing literati thinkers to blame various late Ming ideologies (especially those associated with the Wang Yangming school of neo-Confucianism) for the collapse of the Ming dynasty. Figures such as Li Zhi and various "individualistic" ideologies became the scapegoats.[10] The intellectual independence demonstrated by many radical followers of Wang Yangming was now thought to be one of the main causes of the factionalism that had plagued imperial politics and the intellectual world in the late Ming. Thus, the revival of the more conservative Cheng-Zhu neo-Confucianism in the early Qing could be considered part of some Confucian thinkers' reaction to the painful reality of "a fallen country," in addition to being a result of deliberate policies of the new Manchu regime. Some scholars have characterized this "conservative" retreat as a "purist" movement within the development of Confucianism.[11]

All these trends were inimical to the development of formal autobiographical writings, which, in the late Ming, had often tended to focus explicitly on the meaning of one's individual self, a focus inspired in part by the more individualistic tendencies of the left wing of the Wang Yangming school, as Pei-yi Wu has argued in his study.[12] Although we may question the accuracy of Wu's designation of 1680 as the specific year ending the golden age of traditional Chinese autobiographical writings, it is undeniable that the eighteenth century compares unfavorably with the previous two centuries in terms of the number of impressive autobiographers.[13]

Wu does not discuss any autobiographical works produced after the seventeenth century. Here, a brief comparison of autobiographical writings by two writers, one who lived in the seventeenth century and the other in the eighteenth century, should help us see how this genre underwent a decline that may reflect the changing cultural milieu of this period.

The late Ming writer Zhang Dai (1597–1676?) left several remarkable pieces of autobiographical writing characteristic of the late Ming temperament.[14] Zhang Dai begins his "Ziwei muzhiming" ("Self-written tomb inscription") by presenting his past self as a playboy obsessed with various materialistic pursuits, such as fine clothes, beautiful women, and delicate food. However, the sudden fall of the Ming and the resulting destruction of his family changed everything. Hiding in the distant mountains, he was now an old man living in destitution. This drastic change of fortune forced him to ask serious questions about the meaning of his past existence and the nature of his present self.

Examining my past life frequently, I have found there are seven things about myself that I cannot understand. Before I was always treated like a nobleman even if I was dressed plainly, but now I am looked down on like a beggar even though I have an illustrious pedigree to claim. This is a confusion of the highborn and the common, and the first thing I cannot understand. The value of my property was below average, but I wanted to live like a rich person. Although there were many ways to get rich quickly, I chose to remain a recluse. This shows that I could not distinguish what was "poverty" from what was "wealth." This is the second thing I cannot understand. As a scholar I participated in various military activities, but when I was engaged in literature I acted as if I were a general. Here I did not maintain the distinctions between the civil and the military [wenwu] properly. This is the third thing I cannot understand. While I wouldn't even fawn on the Jade Emperor, I was never haughty before peasants and beggars. I ignored the distinctions between the noble and the humble. This is the fourth thing I cannot understand. I wouldn't take offense if a meek person spat on my face, but, when offended by a powerful man, I would confront that man single-handedly. Here I misconstrued what was "forgiving" and what was being "vindictive." This is the fifth thing I cannot understand. I was always behind other people when it came to fame and profits while letting others go ahead of me when playing games or watching a performance. This was a wrong judgment of what was important and what was not, and the sixth thing I cannot understand. When playing chess or gambling, I didn't not know who was winning and who was losing, but when tasting tea or judging the quality of spring water I was always very perceptive. This is where stupidity and intelligence became all mixed up. This is the seventh thing I cannot understand.

If I cannot explain these seven things about myself, how can I expect others to understand [me]? That is why you can consider me rich as well as poor, smart as well as dumb, strong as well as weak, overenergetic as well as indolent. I have tried to improve my calligraphy and swordsmanship, to learn to be virtuous, to write good essays, to be a Daoist immortal or a Buddhist monk, a farmer, and even a gardener, but I have succeeded in none of them. People can call me a profligate, a good-for-nothing, a fool, an unruly commoner, a dumb scholar, a drowsy guy, or a damned old devil.[15]

This "autobiography" starts out as a self-indictment but soon becomes a self-celebration. Beneath the apparent rhetoric of self-critique, there is a persistent emphasis on Zhang's uniqueness. The so-called seven things he cannot understand about himself are actually incomprehensible only in the eyes of the conventional. Obviously, Zhang Dai does not think there is anything about himself that is inherently "contradictory." Rather, it is the environment that is contradictory. What appears to be incomprehensible to others may well be the very thing he considers unique about himself and, therefore, worth celebrating. Social alienation is applauded here as an ultimate symbol of one's uniqueness.

Immediately following this passage of seeming self-debasement, Zhang begins to list all the books he has written and indulges in the endearing memory of his childhood: how he impressed an important cultural figure of his time, Chen Jiru (1558–1639), with his literary talent when he was only six years old. The conventional self-humbling rhetoric of traditional autobiography is used here to serve the purpose of self-celebration.[16] Throughout this autobiographical narrative, Zhang never feels the need to apologize for his act of discoursing on his own self, as prescribed by the autobiographical conventions.[17] This is a sample of the unapologetic obsession with the individual self typical of the late Ming that produced some remarkable autobiographical writings during that period.

Another self-written tomb inscription, by the eighteenth-century literatus Zhang Junmin (1696–1780), is an interesting contrast to that of Zhang Dai. This autobiographer starts his "tomb inscription" with a lengthy observation that only a man of great achievement is worthy of the honor of having his tomb inscription written by others. Because he has led a mediocre life and is reluctant to bother others with the request for a tomb inscription that might exaggerate or glorify his humble career (thus becoming a laughingstock for future generations), he has decided to take the liberty of writing one for himself.

Even after this apology, however, the author feels obligated to further justify his autobiographical venture: Why should he write about himself if that self is not that great? Zhang Junmin argues that if a life not worth being recorded in a tomb inscription is nevertheless accurately recorded, then the record can at least warn others against following the example of the deceased. In other words, they could at least know what kind of life does not merit a tomb inscription. However, the rest of this self-written tomb inscription makes no mention of any wrongdoing committed by the "dead" serious enough to serve as a warning to the future generation. Instead, it is a pedestrian narrative about an uneventful life, and the autobiographer never ventures to expose his private self.[18] This overwhelming "Confucian sense of decorum" (to use Pei-yi Wu's phrase) seems to have prevented Zhang from discussing any aspect of his self that could be considered unique (if there were any). The author constantly apologizes for his past life and for producing a record of such a life. As a result, throughout the narrative, the autobiographical self, under the constant pressure to be "humble" and "discreet," is never allowed to take a recognizable form. The more orthodox aspects of Confucian ideology—the tendency to de-emphasize the "individual" and the longing for uniformity and order—seem to have received an extra boost in the conservative milieu of eighteenth-century China, a phenomenon certainly not conducive to the development of an autobiographical tradition that stressed self-expression and self-assertion. An eighteenth-century autobiographer apparently could no longer talk about himself without apologizing and without trying to convince others of his absolute worthlessness as an autobiographical subject.[19]

But the age that witnessed the decline of formal autobiographical writings also saw a steady rise of autobiographical tendencies in the novel. Two of China's best-known novels, *The Dream of the Red Chamber* (*Honglou meng*; also known as *Shitou ji*, or *The Story of the Stone*) and *The Scholars* (*Rulin waishi*) were produced around the middle of the eighteenth century, and both are marked by explicit autobiographical concerns.[20] In fact, many features familiar from Zhang Dai's autobiographical writings re-emerged almost a century later in *The Dream of the Red Chamber* (hereafter *The Dream*), such as deep regret for one's past life and nostalgia for it, bitter memories of a drastic decline in personal fortunes, the celebration of a unique self, open admiration for eccentricity, a fascination with the reality of dreams, and, above all, an acute sense of the multiplicity of the self. In the novel, however, these are represented in a much grander and more complicated form behind the mask of a fictional other (or others), a testament to a changed cultural environment that made open assertion of the individual self increasingly difficult.[21] Later in the eighteenth century, another full-length novel, *The Humble Words of an Old Rustic* (*Yesou puyan*; hereafter *Humble Words*), was even more audaciously autobiographical. Generally, there was a rise of what has been called "subjectivism" in many literary works, especially in fiction, during the Qing dynasty,[22] although it would be inaccurate to characterize many of them as formally or explicitly autobiographical (see Chapter 1 for a more detailed discussion of the rise of autobiographical sensibilities in the novel during the seventeenth and especially the eighteenth centuries).

Thus we confront a somewhat perplexing phenomenon: the novel was becoming increasingly autobiographical during a time when the late Ming individualist mode of thinking had fallen from favor and autobiography as a nonfictional genre had lost its creative momentum.[23] A student of traditional Chinese fiction has to ask two questions: Why do some Qing novels exhibit a persistent concern with the individual and search more deeply into private experiences when the general intellectual atmosphere of the period was turning increasingly orthodox and repressive? And why was fiction almost the only art form during the period that continued to explore, with even more subtlety than late Ming autobiographies, many aspects of the individual, while other arts such as painting showed a quick, conservative retreat?[24] Although the answers to these questions are complex and must await other occasions, suffice it for now to say that the reasons for this migration of autobiographical sensibility lie, at least partly, in the historical development of the Chinese novel and in this narrative genre's unique position in the general cultural matrix of the period.

That autobiography and fiction (such as the novel) are particularly congenial is an interesting fact already widely acknowledged.[25] The compatibility between autobiography and fiction becomes even more significant when we consider the burden of traditional historiography that both autobiography and fiction had to carry, as well as the need on the part of both genres to move away from that tradition in their respective developments.[26] It is probably no coincidence that the late Ming writer Li Zhi figured so prominently in the development of both vernacular fiction and autobiography.

Autobiography could find a new ally in vernacular fiction, which had reached full maturity only one generation earlier. The alliance was now possible because the best representatives of the new fiction were, in the words of Andrew Plaks, "literati novels." They were written and read by the same group of people who might try their hands at autobiography. Li Chih [Li Zhi], for instance, was at once an autobiographer and a pioneer in developing a critical literature for the great novels. The popularity of this new genre must have shown autobiographers the possibility of breaking away, even if only in a limited and sporadic fashion, from the rigid exigencies of historiography that had prevailed for centuries. In telling their life stories some of them did display a willful embellishment and a sheer inventiveness that seems to disdain credibility.[27]

The increasingly fictional nature of some formal autobiographical writings of the seventeenth century, such as those by Mao Qiling and others, helped facilitate the "intertraffic" between autobiography and fiction.[28] Even as formal autobiographical writings were becoming increasingly fictionalized during the seventeenth century, the tendency of some works of fictional narrative toward the "autobiographical" was rising, a trend that accelerated in the following century as some novels began to demonstrate a persistent and sometimes complicated autobiographical agenda.

One general observation that can tentatively be made here is that as the cultural milieu of the eighteenth century became increasingly conservative, the late Ming consciousness of the individual found new modes of expression in fiction. The rise of the autobiographical sensibility in the novel, whose avowed fictionality seems to have provided a safer medium for continued exploration of the self, should be understood in the context of the repressive cultural atmosphere of the eighteenth century, when formal autobiography suffered far more restraints than previously for its lack of fictional "disguise."[29] To put it differently, when direct self-presentation was no longer tolerated, indirect self-re/presentation in the form of representation of an explicit *other* (or others) offered itself as an attractive alternative for the autobiographical urge.

Another factor contributing to this migration of autobiographical sensibility was the relatively marginal status of fiction in late imperial China. Radical sentiments or heterodox ideologies manifested in a fictional work were apparently less likely to invoke censorship because of fiction's relatively low cultural status and because of fictional "masquerading," although, as I shall discuss later, beginning in the late sixteenth century the prestige of fiction as a literary genre rose considerably among a quite large group of literati. The kind of radical self-obsession and self-celebration found in autobiographical writings by writers such as Zhang Dai and Mao Qiling reappeared a century later in eighteenth-century novels like *The Dream* and *Humble Words*, albeit behind a much more complex and elaborate fictional mask. The same concerns continued to be explored and were further complicated in these long fictional works. In a word, the late Ming autobiographical urge appears to have survived and even thrived under the license of fiction or the cover of *xiaoshuo* (literally, "small talk") in the eighteenth-century novel.

This turn to the mask of a fictional "other" for self-presentation is also related to the new strategies adopted by some eighteenth-century literati to deal with their increasingly complex self-identity. An important argument of this study is that with the rapidly diminishing opportunity for governmental service, the decline in the appeal of the lofty neo-Confucian ideal of sagehood, the ever-increasing social mobility (for example, the rise of the merchant class), and the professionalization and fragmentation of the field of learning, the literati as a social group in the eighteenth century were experiencing a profound identity crisis (see Chapter 1 for further discussion of this issue). The novel as a narrative genre seems to have provided them extra opportunities to explore the multiplicities of their selves at a time when some of the more sensitive minds were beginning to question the conventional concept of a stable and unified self. That is to say, the increasingly ambiguous and complex sense of self-identity many literati authors were experiencing made the novel an especially welcome medium for self-examination as well as self-representation (a task greatly facilitated by the assumed otherness of fictional discourse).

This emphasis on the fictional other highlights the paradoxical nature of autobiographical writing in general, a question that will come up again and again in the detailed discussions of the novel in subsequent chapters. It may be helpful to outline the general characteristics of autobiographical writing here before we consider its various specific manifestations in the eighteenth-century Chinese novel.

Autobiographical writing is generally understood as an author's writing about himself or herself. In that act of writing, the "I" who writes coincides with the "I" who is being written about. Strictly speaking, however, these two "I"s are not identical. The German philosopher Immanuel Kant (1724–1804) detected the paradox in the act of self-knowing: the knowing "I" cannot be identified with the known "me." In the effort to know herself, the knower (subject) has to become the known (object). Thus what the knower knows is not the knower but the known. In other words, the "I" can only know "me" but not "I."[30] By the same token, in order to write about oneself, one has to treat one's self as an other. Self-writing is by definition self-othering.[31] The distance between the "I" who writes and the "I" that is being written about is absolutely necessary (as well as unavoidable) for any meaningful autobiographical act to become possible. In fact, the potential for becoming an other or the possibility of self-othering is an important factor motivating an autobiographer to write about his or her own "self." Consequently, an author of self-writing starts out with the intention to write about his or her "self" but always ends up creating an "other."

In traditional China, writers appeared to be particularly conscious of this "othering" nature of self-writing (including poetry). It was a well-established rhetorical convention in literati literature that an author described himself through elaborate comparisons of himself to a specific other—often a historical figure for self-judgment, or a frustrated figure, such as an abandoned woman—to draw attention to his own plight. Self-expression and self-analysis are often achieved through such comparisons. This need for an other figures even more significantly in formal autobiographical writings. The eighteenth-century writer Wang Zhong (1745–94), for example, wrote his well-known autobiography ("Zixu") in the form of a detailed comparison of his own life with that of Liu Xiaobiao (462–521). He claimed to have adopted this form of "comparative autobiography" mainly because his model had successfully written his own autobiography by comparing his own life with that of a historical figure from the Latter Han dynasty (25–220).[32] The story did not end here, however. Almost a century later, still another writer, Li Xiang (1869–1931), decided to follow Wang Zhong's example and wrote an autobiography comparing himself with Wang Zhong for exactly the same reason as Wang.[33] Thus, discoursing on one's own self often became a permanently regressive referral to an other in the past.

This example highlights the rather unusual intimacy between self and other in the discourse of self-writing in traditional China. Self-expression is always achieved through reference to an other. That is to say, the self is presentable only as a metaphor in terms of an other. Here James Olney's observation on "self as metaphor" may be pertinent.

> The self expresses itself by the metaphors it creates and projects, and we know it by those metaphors; but it did not exist as it now does and as it now is before creating its metaphors. We do not see or touch the self, but we do see and touch its metaphors: and thus we "know" the self, activity or agent, represented in the metaphor and the metaphoring.[34]

This understanding of the autobiographical enterprise as a metaphoring process of the self, despite its strong phenomenological undertones, comes close to the concept of *jituo* (self-allegorizing) or *zikuang* (self-comparison) in traditional Chinese self-writings (a point to be discussed further in Chapter 2).

In the case of the novel, which makes "fictionality" one of its most important claims, this strategy of self-metaphoring (as others) becomes even more crucial, and as a result the potential for self-othering is dramatically enhanced. The novel's open claim of fictionality enables the author to explore and self-consciously dramatize this paradoxical nature of self-writing. In some of these autobiographical novels the necessity of writing about an other is turned into a virtue of self-othering or self-invention: writing about explicit others becomes an autobiographical strategy. When carried to the extreme, however, this self-masking strategy of writing about others also creates problems. Sometimes, a novelist, such as the author of *The Scholars*, has to struggle to prevent his autobiographical self from being overshadowed by the opaque presence of all those others he has created for the purpose of discoursing on that very "self" (a result of the strategy of excessive dependence on others). Of course, if we accept that the self is accessible only as an other, or a metaphor, as James Olney has argued, then this becomes a problem of the tension between the metaphoric and relatively non-metaphoric natures of these different others (i.e., characters in the novel) in their relation to that infinitely elusive self—the self-image the author tries to reconstruct in the text.[35] This problem becomes even more interesting when an author of a self-writing makes it into a virtue by pretending that he is dealing with many "actual" others. For example, in *The Dream*, the young girl Tanchun is so successful as an independent character that the reader tends to ignore her simultaneous significance as a metaphoric displacement of the autobiographical self (the emphases on her sharing with the author the fate of being an "unrecognized talent" and "being born at the wrong time," a point to be discussed in detail in Chapter 3).

The problem of writing about the self (which, by definition, cannot be written about *directly*) by claiming to write only about "actual" others while, at the same time, insisting on the function of these others as metaphors of the self becomes a nagging question some novelists have to face in their autobiographical endeavors. As previously mentioned, an autobiographical act starts out as a discourse on the author's self but often ends up creating an "other." Here, we might say that, at a different level, the reverse was also true of many works of self-writing in traditional China: they start out as writings about other(s) but often end up with using these others as metaphors for the authorial self. Here the discursive boundaries between self and other are anything but stable. This is another aspect of the *jituo*, or self-allegorizing, rhetoric that we will explore in the following chapters.

In this study I will examine various strategies of appropriating others for the sake of writing indirectly about the self (e.g., the autobiographical self is displaced in the representation of other selves or independent characters in a novel) and, what is more interesting, how sometimes the presence of these others becomes so dominant and even so oppressive that the sheer existence of the autobiographical self in the novel is threatened—the others tend to lose their function as metaphors for something or someone else while demanding more independent (non-metaphoric) status for themselves. This study will concentrate on three novels—*The Scholars*, *The Dream*, and *Humble Words*—in order to examine the special nature of the autobiographical discourse embedded in these eighteenth-century novels, to evaluate its significance in the larger cultural context of late imperial China, and to explore its implications for the history of the Chinese novel.

Chapter 1 attempts to examine in more detail why this migration of autobiographical sensibility from formal autobiographical writings to fiction happened at this particular historical juncture, namely, during the late seventeenth and eighteenth centuries; it discusses this migration in terms of its possible relationship to the changing social roles of the literati during that period, which may have contributed to the rising autobiographical urge in their literary (especially fictional) works. That is to say, it examines each novelist's autobiographical endeavor in terms of the collective literati self-image during the eighteenth century. The next three chapters are individual studies; each focuses on one novel in order to examine how different autobiographical strategies of appropriating others are employed to address its literati author's particular autobiographical concerns.

This study explores the autobiographical in the broadest sense of the word. Each novel is considered to be autobiographical in the sense that its author attempts to come to terms with his own personal dilemma as a member of the literati class, which as a whole was experiencing a profound identity crisis at the time. I will argue in particular that what makes these eighteenth-century novels so significant in the history of the traditional Chinese novel is, to a large extent, their unprecedentedly persistent focus on the question of "literati self-re/presentation." The autobiographical sensibilities of these eighteenth-century novels will be explored in terms of various expressions of their authors' profound anxiety over their identity as literati. What differentiates these particular novels from other literati novels (such as those produced during the late Ming) is their consistent and sometimes intricate autobiographical agenda.

This study is not intended to be a conventional exercise of finding correspondences between the biographical facts of the author and what is described in his novel (as some scholars have done in their studies of *The Dream*). Nor is it to be regarded as an attempt to establish a subgenre of "autobiographical novel" within the tradition of the Chinese novel (for reasons to be explained at the end of this study). Instead of reading these novels as romans à clef, I focus on how these literati authors tried to *re*construct or *re*invent their "selves" through various strategies of fictional narrative in order to come to terms with their increasingly problematic self-identity as literati. One point that I would like to emphasize at the beginning of this study is that the following readings are not presented to prove that these novels can only be read autobiographically (there are many ways of reading them). What interests me in this study is the question of how the assumption of an author/novelist being the subject of his or her own writing shapes that work and how the autobiographical works itself out in these novels. I hope that this study will contribute to our understanding of some of the representative Chinese novels of the eighteenth century in terms of their unique autobiographical features (an important issue in the history of the Chinese novel that has yet to be adequately studied) and to the forming of a broader picture of literati culture in eighteenth-century China.

1
The Problematic Literati Self and Autobiographical Sensibility in the Novel

In order to discuss the nature of the rise in autobiographical sensibility in the eighteenth-century Chinese novel, we must first look at a major development in this narrative genre during that period—its "literati-ization" (*wenren hua*, a process in which literati became more directly involved with the production and consumption of the novel).[1]

Historiography and folk literature are usually considered the two major predecessors of the traditional Chinese vernacular novel.[2] Because of the novel's substantial borrowings from folk literature (both in terms of narrative formula and story materials), the emphasis in literary studies has traditionally been on its popular nature, almost as if the novel were merely a major genre of folk literature.[3] Recently, however, several important studies by scholars of the Chinese novel (mainly in the West) have demonstrated that, despite significant amounts of material derived from the folk tradition (often presented in parodic and ironic modes), the aesthetics of the major novels produced after the fifteenth century differs substantially from that of folk literature largely because of the sophistication of their *wenren* (literati) authors. These artistically sophisticated works have been appropriately designated as the "literati novel."[4] In his monumental study *The Four Masterworks of the Ming Novel*, Andrew Plaks has meticulously demonstrated how the basic values of popular literature (aesthetic as well as ethical) are purposefully subverted in such late sixteenth-century masterworks as *The Journey to the West* (*Xiyou ji*) or *The Plum in the Golden Vase* (*Jin Ping Mei*; also known in English as *The Golden Lotus*) and how literati authors manipulated various narrative strategies to elevate their works to a much higher level of literary sophistication. It may be appropriate to say that the development of the traditional Chinese novel, to a significant extent, was also a process of its becoming increasingly "literati-ized" (being increasingly assimilated into the elite culture), a process paralleling the development of traditional Chinese drama.[5]

After the literati novel reached maturity during the sixteenth century, its literati-ization seems to have quickened. In the sixteenth century few literati novelists would claim credit for their works, but this began to change in the next century.

The tradition of scholar-novelist begins in earnest during the seventeenth century. This is not to say that Chinese novelists writing earlier in the Ming did not include literati, but by this time members of the scholar-gentry not only wrote novels, they also willingly took credit for doing so. With the exception of Lo Kuan-chung [Luo Guanzhong], early in the fourteenth century, most novelists are either anonymous, disguised behind untraceable pseudonyms, or unknown because nothing is recorded about named authors or compilers. . . . But some seventeenth-century writers were overtly proud of their creations in fiction; Chang Chu-p'o [Zhang Zhupo] wished he could have written a novel himself.[6]

The author of the novel *A Sequel to the Water Margin* (*Shuihu houzhuan*), Chen Chen (b. ca. 1614) identified his own fate with that of his novel: "Those who know me will know me for *Shui-hu houchuan* and those who blame me will blame me for *Shui-hu houchuan*."[7] This remark is modeled on a remark attributed to Confucius in the *Mencius*: "It is the *Spring and Autumn Annals* which will make men know me. It is the *Spring and Autumn Annals* which will make men condemn me."[8] Although throughout the history of traditional China many literati authors had employed this famous saying to emphasize how much they had invested in their works and how seriously the reader should take them, Chen Chen is one of the earliest novelists to refer to a novel in this way in order to put his work on a par with a Confucian classic.[9]

It is also during this time that some literati readers began to read the novel with a seriousness previously reserved only for the Confucian classics. The seventeenth century saw the flourishing of criticism of fiction, such as the sophisticated works produced by the well-known commentators Jin Shengtan (1608–61) and Zhang Zhupo (1670–98).[10] In his influential commentaries on *The Water Margin* (*Shuihu zhuan*), Jin Shengtan attempted to explain away some of the contradictions in this work by reconstructing a consistent authorial presence and a strong authorial personality. In Jin's criticism the intention of the "novelist-author" assumed an unprecedentedly important significance in interpretation, even though the "author" may well have been a figure of his own creation rather than the historical person who wrote the novel.[11] In his commentary on *The Plum in the Golden Vase*, Zhang Zhupo emphasized the novel's "autobiographical" dimension and even read one character as the author's self-metaphor.[12]

As the literati appropriation of the novel continued, some important concepts regarding literary writing from the high literati tradition began to be associated with the novel. In the literati tradition, for example, the theory that "one takes to writing to express one's anger" (*fafen zhushu*) was extremely influential. It was formulated by China's most famous historian, Sima Qian (b. 145 B.C.), in his much-admired "Letter in Reply to Ren An." Sima Qian used this idea to justify his choice of the punishment of castration over the death penalty (for having displeased the emperor) by emphasizing his determination to finish his *Records of the Historian* (*Shiji*).

Confucius was in distress and he made [wrote] the *Spring and Autumn*; Ch'ü Yüan [Qu Yuan] was banished and he composed his poem "Encountering Sorrow"; after Tso Ch'iu [Zuoqiu] lost his sight, he composed the *Narratives from the States* . . . ; most of the three hundred poems of the *Book of Odes* were written when the sages poured forth their anger and dissatisfaction [*fafen*]. All these men had a rankling in their hearts, for they were not able to accomplish what they wished. Therefore they wrote about past affairs in order to pass on their thoughts to future generations.[13]

Since then, many traditional Chinese writers and critics have taken anger to be the most important motivation in a writer's creativity. Han Yu (768–824) asserted that "those who are happy can hardly produce good writings, whereas those who suffer from sorrow and frustration can easily write well."[14] Later Ouyang Xiu (1007–72) put forward the famous formulation "Great literature is the result of great suffering" (*qiong er hougong*), which subsequently became a cliché in literary criticism.[15] In this theory, the success of a literary work is attributed to the personal experiences of the author. That is to say, to be successful, a literary work has to be autobiographical to a certain extent. This may explain why most belletristic writings by literati authors (i.e., poetry) were always read autobiographically.[16]

The first critic who used this theory to account for a novelist's creative efforts was probably Li Zhi. In a preface to *The Water Margin*, Li Zhi invoked Sima Qian's canonical idea of *fafen zhushu* to interpret the author's motivation:

Sima Qian once said: "*The Difficulty of Persuasion* [*Shuinan*] and *A Loner's Anger* [*Gufen*] were works written by a virtuous man who wanted to express his anger." Thus we may say that the men of virtue in ancient times could not have written those wonderful works had they not experienced great sufferings and frustrations. Had they written them without suffering, hardship, and frustrations at first, they would have acted like someone who groaned when he was not sick or who trembled when he was not cold. Even if he did write something, what would be the value? *The Water Margin* is a work written as a result of great anger.[17]

Since then, many novelists and novel commentators have followed Li Zhi (including Jin Shengtan and Chen Chen) in appealing to this theory to emphasize the seriousness of their works or of the works on which they were commenting.[18] Consequently, Li Zhi's association of the novel with this canonical idea was extremely significant in the development of the traditional Chinese novel. It signaled that the novel as a narrative genre, at least among some literati, was beginning to be admitted to the pantheon of high literati literature, thus far dominated by lyric poetry (which was always cherished partly because of its autobiographical possibilities). Moreover, this was the first time that the expressive aspect of the novel—the relationship between a novelist and his works, particularly how the author's personal views found expression in the novel—was explicitly addressed. Previously such issues had been addressed only in discussions of belletristic writings (such as poetry criticism). To a limited degree, beginning in the seventeenth century, fiction writing also became an autobiographical adventure for some literati authors, just as writing poetry had always been. It became a means of *liyan* (seeking cultural immortality through writing). In a preface (dated 1775) to his novel *The Plum Under the Snowy Moon* (*Xue Yue Mei*), the author Chen Lang (Jinghu yisou) openly acknowledged that he had resorted to writing fiction as a means of seeking cultural immortality (*liyan*).¹⁹ This elevation of fiction among some literati, coupled with the decline in formal autobiographical writings that began in the late seventeenth century, contributed to the rise of autobiographical tendencies in the novel.

From the Literati Novel to the Novel of the Literati

There were also significant changes in the nature of the authorship of the novel. In the seventeenth century some novels, such as *A Marriage That Awakens the World* (*Xingshi yinyuan zhuan*), were written by individual novelists without substantially relying on previous written sources. Unlike the four well-known novels of the Ming, *The Romance of the Three Kingdoms* (*Sanguo yanyi*), *The Water Margin*, *The Journey to the West*, and, to a large extent, *The Plum in the Golden Vase*, which all underwent a relatively long and complicated process of deriving their story materials from previously existing sources, *A Marriage That Awakens the World* was apparently written by a single author (though the identity of its author remains controversial).²⁰ In fact one characteristic of all three eighteenth-century novels examined in this study (*The Dream*, *The Scholars*, and *Humble Words*) is that each was the product of an individual literati author (of course, in the case of *The Dream*, we are dealing only with the first 80 chapters; see Chapter 3). In fact, it was during the seventeenth and eighteenth centuries that the writing of a novel generally became the individual project of a single literati author; previously it had been largely a collective enterprise, involving many hands (scholars are still undecided whether *The Plum in the Golden Vase* was written by a single author or was a product of many hands). In the preface to *The Footsteps of an Immortal in the Mundane World* (*Lüye xianzong*), an eighteenth-century novel, the author, Li Baichuan (ca. 1719–71), gives a relatively detailed account of his frustrations in life, his liking for ghost stories, and a history of how the novel came to be written. This is probably the first "authorial preface" (*zixu*) to be attached to a novel emphasizing the novel's intimate relationship to the author's own personal experiences.²¹

Although it is difficult to determine the exact autobiographical significance of this novel, critics have pointed out the possible connections between the author's personal frustrations and those of Wen

Ruyu described in the novel.[22] I believe that another main character, Leng Yubing, is a more elaborate displacement of the autobiographical self in the novel. The detailed account of this character's frustrations in the civil-service examinations early in the novel, which are largely due to his moral uprightness, may be the author's attempt at self-vindication. Leng's later phenomenal successes as a Daoist immortal are apparently a fantasized "solution" that the author uses to relieve his own anxieties over his failure to pass the examinations. The "dialogue" between these two characters, Leng Yubing and Wen Ruyu, who contrast with each other so neatly in terms of salvation versus entrapment and success versus failure, constitutes the main autobiographical dimension of this novel.[23] This example demonstrates that single authorship is crucial for a novel as a narrative form to be able to accommodate its author's autobiographical concerns.

The changing nature of authorship—from "collective/public" to "individual/private"—paralleled the changing thematic concerns of the novel. The seventeenth-century novel was becoming increasingly "private" in content, a trend already begun in the sixteenth century. This can best be seen in the privatizing process demonstrated in the development from *The Romance of the Three Kingdoms*, a historical novel about the political struggles among three states, to *The Plum in the Golden Vase*, a novel mainly about the changing fortunes of a private family and the fate of its individual members. The dominant locale of court (where various political plots or military plans are set up) in *The Romance of the Three Kingdoms* is replaced by that of bedroom (where sexual encounters and voyeurism are the most common activities) in *The Plum in the Golden Vase*.[24]

Equally perceivable in this development is that the novel was becoming more concerned with contemporary life. Although set in the Northern Song dynasty (960–1127), *The Plum in the Golden Vase* obviously describes people living in the late Ming, contemporaries of its author(s). In this regard, this novel paved the way for many later novels that purport to deal with the "contemporary."[25] With the emergence of the so-called *caizi jiaren xiaoshuo* (scholars and beauties novels) in the seventeenth century, this focus on contemporary life received another boost. Almost for the first time in the history of the Chinese novel, a long vernacular fiction, free from the burden of a historical past, could unabashedly describe what was happening at present, thus dramatizing a literatus's concerns with his own present self. Considering the dominance of various premises of traditional historiography in the development of the Chinese novel, we should not underestimate the significance of this shift in focus from the past to the contemporary in a fairly large number of novels produced during the seventeenth century.[26] This new emphasis on contemporaneity helped to enhance the autobiographical potential of the novel as a genre of fictional narrative. Without the support of a historical past, the novelist is more likely to rely on personal experiences as sources. In this respect it is interesting to note that at the beginning of *The Dream* (H, 1: 4; SS, 1.49), the reader is specifically told that the story "has no discoverable dynastic period" (*chaodai nianji wukao*), a calculated gesture of defiance toward the historiographical convention of earlier novels. *The Scholars*, although paying token references to the previous Ming dynasty, apparently speaks about its author's contemporaries. The case of *Humble Words* is a bit more complicated: to protect his much bolder autobiographical agenda, the author carefully follows the chronology of the Ming dynasty and even has many well-known historical figures appear in the novel. All these claims to historicity are meant, however, to shield the work's direct concerns with the author's present self from possible "censorship" (a point discussed further in Chapter 4).

This shift in focus to the private/contemporary in the seventeenth-century novel was accompanied by what has been described as an "inward turning"—an increasing preoccupation with individual responsibility, personal guilt, and human fallibility. This can be seen in a number of works, such as *A Marriage That Awakens the World*, *A Sequel to the Plum in the Golden Vase* (*Xu Jin Ping Mei*), *The Romance of the Sui and Tang* (*Sui Tang yanyi*), and *A Tale of Redemption due to the Teachings of the Three Religions* (*Sanjiao kaimi guizheng yanyi*). Another important seventeenth-century novel, *A Supplement to the Journey to the West* (*Xiyou bu*; also known in English as *The Tower of Myriad Mirrors*), exhibits an unprecedented fascination with subjective experience and the psychology of dreams.[27] All these works anticipated in one way or another the autobiographical turn in the literati novel of the next century.

Simultaneously with this inward turn, the literati and their lives also became the main subjects of the novel. In "scholars and beauties" novels, literati and their aspirations or frustrations became the main narrative focus. Writing fiction became a special means of self-vindication or self-healing for those literati frustrated in the examinations. Works in this genre now almost exclusively concern a literatus's career successes and failures (mainly in the civil-service examinations) and his romances. Later in the eighteenth century, the novel would devote even more space to the description of specific aspects of literati life: education, the pursuit of scholarship, life in a literati garden, and other cultured activities.[28] Another important development from "the literati novel" to "the novel of the literati" is discernible during the seventeenth century, a development that reached its apex in the following century.[29] Not only were the literati deeply involved in the production and consumption of the novel as authors and readers, but their lives and concerns became the main topics of the novel. In their novels the literati became the object of their own observation and scrutiny. In other words, the main characters in a seventeenth or eighteenth-century novel were much more likely than before to be literati like the author himself.[30] What was being described in a novel was sometimes so close to the author's own personal experiences that "autobiographical consciousness" (or subconsciousness) became inevitable.

In Pu Songling's (1640–1715) famous collection of short stories, *Strange Stories from the Studio of Leisure* (*Liaozhai zhiyi*), the many pieces about literati frustrations in the civil-service examinations bear a great resemblance to Pu's own experiences. Here metamorphosis (a human being becomes a fox spirit or vice versa) is an important strategy of "autobiographical redemption," a tactic that allows the author to enable his fellow literati (characters in his stories) to achieve the very successes he himself was denied in his life. In these stories a literatus is often able to achieve success by transforming into another being, by being reborn in another life, or by gaining the superhuman help of a fox spirit.[31] In the works of another seventeenth-century writer, Li Yu (1611–79), various carefully manipulated personae become vehicles for voicing the author's own personal opinions; some of his short stories can even be read as wish-fulfilling attempts to "forget" his own unhappy experiences in life.[32] This interesting presence of the author could also be witnessed in many dramatic texts written by the literati during the same period. Liao Yan (1644–1701), for example, wrote several plays whose protagonists were named after himself.[33] Lacking elaborate plots, these short plays were extremely lyrical. Here the *zaju* plays became a direct autobiographical outlet for their author's pent-up emotions over his career failures, just as poetry had always been for many frustrated literati. This direct "autobiographical" appropriation of drama by a literati author was rather unprecedented in the history of traditional Chinese theater.

For a full-fledged novel that emphasizes the literati author's personal experience, however, we have to wait until the eighteenth century. Almost all the major novels produced then concentrated on the lives of the literati. One important eighteenth-century novel not treated in this study, Li Lüyuan's (1707–90) *Warning Light at the Crossroads* (*Qilu deng*), is a meticulously detailed narrative about how a young student overcomes various obstacles to mature and achieve success in the examinations. No earlier full-length novel focused so intently on a young man's personal journey to adulthood. The maturing process delineated in the novel, probably the first Chinese bildungsroman, is a feature one would normally expect in an autobiographical fiction, although there is little evidence to suggest that *The Warning Light at the Crossroads* consistently exhibits autobiographical concerns. However, *The Dream*, which was probably completed a bit earlier, contains a different version of *bildung* in which the male protagonist refuses to grow up into the role of a typical literatus. The private experiences of an individual's maturing, or, rather, the difficulties of growing up, are explored with unprecedented depth in *The Dream*. The facts that by the eighteenth century literati life had become such an important thematic concern of the novel and that the lives of the fictional characters and the life of the author had become so similar reveal some of the reasons behind the steady rise of an autobiographical urge in the novel.[34]

Before moving to the question of the literati's identity problem in the seventeenth and eighteenth centuries, which helped shape the autobiographical sensibilities of the contemporary novel, we should look briefly at the issue of pseudonymous authorship. Almost all traditional Chinese novels were written pseudonymously. This anonymity, at first glance, may appear to have been inimical to this genre's becoming more autobiographical. But the relatively "private" way in which most literati novels were produced and consumed in the eighteenth century leads to a different conclusion. For an eighteenth-century literati novelist, the likelihood of having a novel published was extremely slim. Few authors expected to have their manuscripts published, and even fewer actually saw their works published in their lifetime. All three novels examined in this study, *The Scholars*, *The Dream*, and *Humble Words*, were published posthumously; *The Warning Light at the Crossroads*, a novel finished in the 1770's, was not published until the twentieth century. The main means of reception for a literati novel was "reading and transmission by copying the manuscripts" (*chuanchao*). Thus, the readership of a literati novel could be very small. Another possible factor in limiting a literati novel's "public" appeal was its encyclopedic claim to embrace the whole of literati culture; appreciating a novel demanded a lot from the reader.

In short, at least during the initial stage of circulation, reading a novel was a much more private act than it is for the modern reader. In the eighteenth century a typical early reader of a literati novel would be one of the author's close friends or relatives (this was especially true for *The Dream*). The readership of a novel was a small private circle, many of them known to the author personally. Reading a novel by a contemporary literati author was often a private and dilettantish activity for a literatus. The sometimes intimate nature of the reception of the eighteenth-century literati novel must have increased the autobiographical possibilities of this genre; "pseudonymity" would have become a significant factor only when the work began to circulate among a much wider circle in the form of printed editions. Consequently, the circulation of a literati novel in eighteenth-century China, at least initially, resembled the circulation of a literatus's personal poems or essays, both traditionally hospitable to autobiographical agenda. It took a rather private form, a unique phenomenon of elite culture in late imperial China in comparison with the situation of the novel in the West.

Furthermore, because of the enormous length of most novels, writing one took a fair amount of time. Due to the lack of financial rewards, the motivation for writing a novel must have been something other than commercial concerns, especially since it was the publisher rather than the author who reaped the profits for publishing a best-seller in an age without copyright laws. In other words, no author could expect to earn a lot of money by writing a novel.[35] The glaring disparity between what a novelist could gain materially from his work and the amount of energy and time he had to invest in writing (few eighteenth-century novelists produced more than one novel) calls attention to the special gratification that a novelist must have derived from this otherwise unrewarding labor.

A literatus often turned to writing a novel after he had suffered many, perhaps traumatic, frustrations in his career or life. In several cases, it was primarily a vehicle for self-healing. This may partially account for the appeal to so many novelists of the theory that "great literature is the result of great suffering." Because of this genre's potential for self-healing (writing a novel could help the author forget or "misremember" his frustrations and achieve a narrative self-transformation), many literati were willing to commit themselves to an enterprise that promised little material reward, and some never even thought of publishing their manuscripts. This healing potential helped elevate the status of the novel, at least in the eyes of some literati, to that of belletristic writings, which had always accommodated autobiographical concerns. One common phrase these novelists used to describe their motivation for writing novels was "to write [a novel] to amuse oneself" (*zhushu ziyu*).[36] Li Yu was probably one of the first literati authors to comment explicitly on the healing benefits of writing a play:

> If the genre [drama] did not exist, men of talent and heroic action would die of frustration. I was born amid disaster, and have lived a life of poverty; from childhood to maturity, from maturity to old age, I have scarcely known a moment of success. When writing plays, however, I not only gain relief from my depression and resentment, I lay claim to the title of happiest man between Heaven and Earth. I feel that all the joys of rank, riches, and glory are no greater than mine. If one cannot fulfill one's desire in real life, one can produce an imaginary realm in which to do exactly as one wishes. If I want to be an official, then in a flash I attain honor and rank. If I want to retire from office, then in the twinkle of an eye I am among the mountains and forests. If I want to be a genius among men, then I become the incarnation of Du Fu and Li Bai.[37]

According to Li Yu, the greatest value for an author in writing plays or any fictional narratives lay in the opportunities for anxiety relief and fantasy fulfillment (Freud would have agreed). In a preface attached to the seventeenth-century "scholars and beauties" novel *The Flat Mountain and the Cold Swallow* (*Pingshan lengyan*), Tianhuacang zhuren made a similar observation:

> Frustrated in trying to find a use for one's talent in the public service but not willing to be content to be a failure, one cannot but resort to fabricating a

fictional character in order to envision a grand fulfillment of a thwarted ambition. . . . All those happy and unique events described in the novel are actually what made the author sad and cry tears in his real life.[38]

The personal as well as the self-healing nature of the enterprise of writing a novel was an important factor in the eventual rise of autobiographical sensibility in the eighteenth-century novel.

Simultaneously with this significant change in the nature of the novel in the eighteenth century, the literati, the most important social component of traditional Chinese society, were experiencing a profound identity crisis. The next question we shall ask is what characterized the literati as a social group during that period and which of their concerns might have found expression in their writings (particularly fictional narratives). In the following pages I argue that this identity crisis was crucial in shaping some aspects of autobiographical sensibility in the novels of that period.[39]

The Problematic Literati Self

Shi, which is usually translated into English as "literati," originally referred to knights and men with specialized knowledge (about history, ritual, and astrology), who were generally at the bottom of the hierarchy within the aristocratic class during the Spring and Autumn period (770–476 B.C.). Immediately below them were the commoners (*shuren*). Later, during the Warring States period (475–221 B.C.), their social position was lowered to that of the commoners, the so-called *simin zhishou* (the head of the four commoners), the other three groups below them being *nong* (farmers), *gong* (craftsmen), and *shang* (merchants). Thus, on the social scale they were situated somewhere between the ruling and the ruled. Because of their unique social position, members of the *shi* class were often those commoners most motivated to change their position by finding service in the government of a state (*shi*) so that they could become members of the social elite. It is probably no exaggeration to say that throughout the long history of imperial China, a most important goal in a *shi*'s life was to be able to offer his services to the government (becoming an official); this is why one Western scholar renders *shi* in English as "men of service."[40] Whether one found employment in government became nearly the sole test of a *shi*'s worth.

Beginning with the Sui dynasty (581–618), an elaborate system of examinations was established to facilitate the process of selecting *shi* for governmental service. With the establishment of this system, the emphasis on a *shi*'s learning began to be institutionalized, and gradually learning became the most important factor in defining one's identity as a *shi*. By the Southern Song dynasty (1127–1279), a *shi* was primarily perceived to be a man of learning, hence, a *literatus*.[41]

This emphasis on learning would become more significant as opportunities for a governmental career became increasingly limited in late imperial China. Since there were always more literati than official positions, many literati found themselves excluded from officialdom. Being unable to find employment in the government thus became the major source of disappointment and frustration for a large proportion of the literati.

Thwarted in their pursuit of governmental service, more and more literati confronted the task of finding a desirable alternative to government service. Becoming a sage through self-cultivation (*neisheng*) became a viable alternative to governmental service (*waiwang*) for literati disillusioned with or denied access to a public career; indeed, self-cultivation "offered a vision of learning that helped the shih [*shi*] learn to survive without office."[42] Learning had to be *re*justified as relevant and useful outside the realm of governmental service. It is within this context of redefining learning that neo-Confucianism or the *daoxue* school began to gain popularity among the literati in the Southern Song. Many *shi* began to emphasize self-cultivation (*xiushen*) as the long-cherished vision of being a "sage within and king without" (*neisheng waiwang*; i.e., achieving success both in self-cultivating and in governmental service) became only an unattainable ideal.[43] There was a gradual split between the realms of "within" and "without": one could not be a sage and an able official at the same time, and the unified image of *shi* began to fragment. The grand failure of Wang Anshi's (1021–86) political reforms may have contributed to this turn inward.[44]

By the late seventeenth and early eighteenth centuries, however, with the enthusiasm for self-cultivation advocated by Ming neo-Confucianism being discredited as "Buddhist fervor" and "empty talk," "sagehood as a goal of spiritual attainment had become almost as rare as had sainthood in the twentieth-century West."[45] According to Benjamin Elman, for many Qing literati "cultivation was no longer the primary road to knowledge" and "had become epistemologically suspect."⁴⁶ A more profound implication of the diminishing appeal of Confucian sagehood was the crumbling of the ideological foundation on which the authority of the literati as the moral arbiters of the society had long been based. By emphasizing ethical responsibility and the need for moral self-cultivation, neo-Confucianism seems to have laid unprecedented emphasis on the literati's mission as the natural moral leaders of society.⁴⁷ With the rapid decline of enthusiasm for moral self-improvement in the Qing, many literati began to feel a moral void, and some even felt that their social identity as well as respectability was under threat. Here the famous eighteenth-century painter and writer, Zheng Xie's (1693–1765; also known as Zheng Banqiao) complaint about the moral poverty of his literati peers is illustrative.

I think the best class of people in the world are the farmers. Scholars should be considered the last of the four classes. . . . Were it not for the farmers, we should all starve. We scholars are considered one class higher than the farmers because we are supposed to be good sons at home and courteous abroad, and maintain the ancient tradition of culture; in case of success, we can serve and benefit the people, and in case of failure, we can cultivate personal lives as an example to the world. But this is no longer true. As soon as a person takes a book in hand, he is thinking of how to pass the examinations and become a *chüjen* [*juren*] or *chinshih* [*jinshi*], how to become an official and get rich and build fine houses and buy large property. . . . Those who are not successful at the examinations are still worse; they prey upon the people of the village, with a small head and thievish eyes. . . .

The artisans make tools and turn them to good use, while the business men make possible the exchange of goods. They are all of some use to the people, while the scholars alone are a great nuisance to them. One should not be surprised to find them considered the lowest of the four classes of people, and I doubt that they are entitled to even that.⁴⁸

Of course, in *The Scholars* we find many examples of how the literati's self-image was troubled by this sense of moral inadequacy, and in *Humble Words* there is a tremendous—and desperate—effort to reassert or regain the moral authority that had been taken for granted for so long by the literati but was apparently undergoing a rapid decline.

This profound sense of moral inadequacy was made even worse during the eighteenth century by the virtual impossibility of an official career for most literati. With the rapid growth of population, the establishment of a new quota system for the examinations, and the dwindling number of official positions available, competition for elite status became ever fiercer.[49] As a result, the separation between those literati kept outside the official world and those allowed in was increasingly discernible.[50] The "outsiders" could no longer depend on the *shidafu*'s (scholar-official's) traditional status and social role for their sense of public identity; direct involvement in state politics was no longer an immediate concern for many literati, who were perforce becoming "depoliticized." The traditional Confucian ideal of *zhiguo pingtianxia* ([to help] put the state in good order and pacify the world) was almost entirely irrelevant. The literati desperately needed to find new qualifications that allowed them to remain members of the elite.

One alternative to governmental service remaining to a literatus in the eighteenth century was the pursuit of the life-style of *wenren* (man of culture), a life-style that emphasized literary or artistic tastes but had little interest in Confucian moral issues. Here the term *wenren* is to be understood in a narrow sense. In the Tang and the Northern Song periods, the distinction between *wenren* and *shidafu* (scholar-official) was not particularly significant because most *wenren* were in one way or another admitted into the official world and many of them were members of the *shidafu* class (e.g., Su Shi [1037–1101]). This situation began to change dramatically in the Yuan dynasty (1271–1368) when the Mongol rulers ranked the literati almost at the bottom of the scale of social classes and restricted their role in politics. A huge number of literati became disenfranchised. Among those unenthusiastic about pursuing sagehood, some turned to literary learning to assert their status as *shi*. Although with the Ming dynasty the social position of the literati improved drastically, the intensified competition in the civil-service examinations kept most of them out of officialdom. According to Yoshikawa Kōjirō, it was during the Yuan dynasty that *wenren* was first used to describe those literati who were not officials and who devoted themselves to literature and art while often displaying a degree of eccentricity or deviation from accepted norms.[51] Here, learning was redefined as "literary learning," concerned mainly with poetry, painting, and other cultured activities.

Whereas the choice of being a "man of culture" in the Yuan dynasty might often be interpreted as a political gesture (a refusal to serve the foreign dynasty), the continuing as well as increasing popularity of this life-style in the Ming and Qing (except for the early Qing when loyalty to the old dynasty and opposition to the newly founded foreign regime might be an issue of urgency) has to be explained, at least partly, as a result of many literati's attempts to cope with their failure to attain an official career.[52] However, this kind of withdrawal (*yin*) was not blessed with the usual Confucian justification of *wudao zeyin* (withdraw from government service when the Way does not prevail), because in most cases there was no convincing political reason for such withdrawal.[53] Consequently, there was always an aura of moral uneasiness surrounding the image of a man of culture. Feeling the pressure to defend the *wenren* image, the eighteenth-century poet Yuan Mei (1716–97) tried to emphasize that literary writing and other cultural activities associated with *wenren* were as important as public service.

> It is often said that contributing to society lies in one's achievements in public service [*gongye baoguo*]. However, good literary writing is also a contribution to society [*wenzhang baoguo*]; sometimes good writing is even more difficult to achieve. . . . Of course, contributing to society by means of literary writing does not mean that one has to produce distorted writings for the sake of adulation. If someone can produce a superb literary piece that is unprecedented so that people would later say that someone in certain dynasty was good at literary writing, then one cannot say that he has not brought glory to his family as well as to his country.[54]

These defensive remarks reflect the persistent pressure to exclude *wenren* from the circle of the social elite.

In fact, many early Qing thinkers, trying hard to account for the seemingly sudden collapse of the Ming monarchy, also considered the excessive life-style of *wenren* in the late Ming one cause of this tragedy.[55] Indeed, the Manchu conquest seems to have further problematized the self-identity of many literati. On the one hand, because of their traditional Confucian sense of loyalty, they felt they should not serve the new, foreign regime; on the other hand, this "barbarian" monarchy with all its vitality and impressive achievements did appear to come much closer to the Confucian ideal of sagely governance than had the corrupt Ming regime. A profound ambivalence troubled the literati. Some began to rethink the literati's traditional advocacy of *wen* (belles lettres) while underscoring the importance of pragmatic knowledge (*jingshi*, or statecraft). This contributed to the eventual rise of a new intellectual movement that would reach its apex in the eighteenth century—the so-called *kaozheng* movement—during which many literati found their self-perception changed significantly.[56]

Moreover, by the eighteenth century the alternative of being a *wenren* was further challenged by the gradual blurring of distinctions among the social classes, especially those between literati and merchants. The rise of the merchant class and the elevation of their social status can be traced to the fifteenth and sixteenth centuries.[57] But it was during the eighteenth century that merchants achieved phenomenal success. The most representative example is the well-known case of the salt merchants of Yangzhou. Ping-ti Ho notes that prior to the nineteenth century, "the salt merchants of Yang-chou boasted of some large individual fortunes and certainly the largest aggregate capital possessed by any single commercial or industrial group in the empire."[58] With the dramatic increase of their economic power, however, their social status began to improve as well. The traditional hierarchy of the so-called four classes of society began to be disrupted. One telling factor that shows how dramatically the social status of merchants improved in the eighteenth century is property holding: even as recently as the late Ming the law did not allow merchants to own large houses because of their low social status, but the eighteenth-century Yangzhou merchants built and purchased many of the famous gardens in the city.[59] This rise was also reflected in policies of the Manchu monarchy: "Unlike merchants of the pre-Yüan China who suffered from sumptuary laws and who were deprived of the right to civil-service, salt merchants were particularly favored by the Manchu government. . . . Salt merchants' children were given special quotas for district studentships, a privilege which better enabled them to become degree-holders and members of the ruling class."[60]

No wonder the Qing writer Shen Yao (1798–1840) even went so far as to say: "In ancient times the distinctions among the four classes of commoners [*simin*] were clear, but recently the members of four classes cannot be distinguished from each other; in ancient times the son of a literatus would be a literatus without exception but now often only the son of a merchant can become a literatus."[61] The period witnessed a significant "social metamorphosis." Many sons of prominent merchant families became high officials or well-known scholars by adopting the strategy of "family division of labor" (one son in a merchant family worked in business to provide financial support for the whole family, and the other sons studied for the examinations to become officials or degree holders); other merchants simply purchased offices or degrees without taking the examinations.[62]

The aggressive infiltration of merchants into spheres traditionally occupied by literati made the defining (or redefining) of the identity of a literatus an extremely problematic issue in the eighteenth century. Among the traditional elite, the *wenren*, because of their relatively low economic and social status, seemed to have felt more vulnerable to the advances made by merchants. In a study of the eighteenth-century Yangzhou painting, Vicki Weinstein argues that what frustrated many literati was the gap between "the reality of downward socioeconomic mobility of the poor scholars from commoner backgrounds" and "the myth of upward mobility perpetuated by Confucian orthodoxy of the Qing period."[63] This downward mobility forced many *wenren* to turn to merchants for patronage, an action that seriously compromised their image as independent men of culture. Zheng Xie complained bitterly that some literati had compromised their integrity by allowing their taste to be dictated by merchants.

A scholar should follow his own opinion. He might listen to the merchants' advice for dealings in daily business, but I have never heard that he should ask for their opinions about scholarship and literature. Scholars in Yangzhou are now flocking to the merchants' homes and showing utmost respect for their words. I cannot overemphasize how this has compromised their status [*shipin*] and spirit as literati [*shiqi*].[64]

This is reminiscent of a passage from *The Scholars*:

[Mr. Chin said:] "Not long ago Mr. Fang from down river asked me to write a couplet for him—twenty-two characters altogether. When he sent a servant over with eighty taels to thank me, I called the fellow in. 'Go back and tell your master that a price was fixed for Mr. Chin's calligraphy in the prince's palace in Peking,' I said. 'Small characters cost a tael apiece, and big ones ten taels. At this standard rate, these twenty-two characters are worth two hundred and twenty taels. You can't have them for a cent less!'

"After the men delivered this message, that swine Fang, to show that he had money, called in his sedan-chair to pay me two hundred and twenty taels.

But when I gave him the scrolls, he simply t-t-tore them up! I flew into such a rage, I broke open his packets of silver and threw the money in the street for salt-carriers and dung-carters to pick up! I ask you, gentlemen, aren't scoundrels like that beneath contempt?" (RLWS, 28: 381; S, 306)

Weinstein believes that the eccentricity usually associated with the eighteenth-century Yangzhou painters was actually a desperate attempt on the part of these *wenren* artists to cope with the harsh social and economic reality they were facing. "The fact that these artists sometimes had to sell their work in exchange for rice was more a matter of economics than eccentricity."[65] Traditionally, literati involvement in art and literature was considered strictly of "amateurish nature." Being an amateur by no means implied a lack of sophistication; rather, it was a symbol of aesthetic aspirations at a higher level: painting for profit or money was incompatible with a literatus's interest in cultural self-cultivation.[66] Yet this amateurism was possible only among scholar-officials because as officials with a secure income, they did not need to rely on their art for a living. As more and more literati were excluded from officialdom, however, the amateurish stance became increasingly difficult to maintain. By the eighteenth century, under the enormous pressures of commercialization (the need of merchants to appear cultured and the need of many *wenren* artists to make a living), many artists concluded that the *wenren* tradition of amateurism was an ideal too high to fulfill: "The ideal of a true *wen-jen* was no longer possible in a society in which 'vulgar' people demanded 'scholar-type paintings.'" Hence, the distinction between scholar-amateur and professional painter seems to have become blurred.[67]

This professionalization of the literati in the eighteenth century was further complicated by a new trend in the world of learning. A significant number of literati were turning to scholarship as a way of living. In a study of intellectual and social changes in eighteenth-century China, Benjamin Elman finds a "rise of professional scholars who rarely held official positions." "Teaching and secretarial services were important sources of income for the literati."[68] He further observes that in "the move from the Ming 'amateur ideal' to the Ch'ing specialist, we discern a major change in the definition and role of a Confucian scholar."[69] Here learning was further redefined as "scholarship," a new important quality with which many tried to maintain their identity as literati. Furthermore, the increasingly finer divisions of learning contributed to the fragmentation of the literati as a harmonious social group. Many literati were involved in much more precise and specialized fields of learning that might not seem directly relevant to the traditional concept of learning based on a more general belletristic education.

Evidential scholars were participants in a specialized occupation based on prolonged study and intellectual training that supplied skilled service and advice to others for monetary support or patronage. . . . The transformation of occupational criteria from possession of a broadly based range of intellectual and political concerns to possession of expertise in precise fields of evidential scholarship signals a movement toward professions.[70]

Like the alternative of being a man of culture, however, being a professional scholar (dedicated to scholarship) was an alternative some literati took only after they had failed to become an official through the examinations. Thus, this choice, too, always implied failure. It was a different matter if one could demonstrate that he had refused a proffered position. There was no lack of scholar-officials in the eighteenth century who retired early to devote themselves to scholarship or to being a *wenren*, for example, Zhao Yi (1736–1820) and Yuan Mei.[71] But for the many literati who never had a chance to be an official, the decision to be a *wenren* or a professional scholar was an unpleasant reminder of their failure, no matter how satisfying that choice turned out to be. These choices were always alternatives to a more desirable but unavailable choice (not careers valued merely for their own sake), a result of unwilling compromise.[72]

Serving as a secretary on the staffs of several different officials for many years, Liu Dakui (1698–1779), a well-known writer of the eighteenth century, complained bitterly that he could identify himself neither as a *shi* nor as a *min* (commoner).[73] By the eighteenth century, a career as a *mufu* or *muyou* (a literatus serving as a private secretary or clerk on the staff of an official) had become a rather common choice among the literati. The semi-official status implied by the profession of *mufu* further problematized the identity of many literati as *shi*. In many of his personal letters, Gong Weizhai (fl. 1800) protested that he could not earn a living practicing traditional literati skills such as essay writing, calligraphy, and painting. Having no land to farm or other skills to offer (such as medicine and fortunetelling), he had to serve as a clerk for an official.[74] The author of *Humble Words*, Xia Jingqu (1705–87), worked as a *mufu* for several important officials for a long period of time and had to sell his skills for a living. He was apparently troubled by the fact that he was so close to power but was forever barred from exercising it in his own name. This certainly was an important reason behind his feelings of frustration (see Chapter 4).

The blurring of the distinctions between a *wenren* who was supposed to cherish the ideal of the amateur and a professional who sold his skills to support himself, together with the ever finer divisions within the world of learning, further undermined the traditional identity of a *shi*. During the eighteenth century, a literatus denied the precious opportunity for "service" had, in order to continue to be considered to be a member of the elite, to constantly redefine or re-justify his learning while simultaneously being forced to play different roles that themselves lacked clear definition.

The ambiguities of literati identity, consequently, were complicated by the constantly changing standards used to judge membership in the elite. As intellectual historians have demonstrated, being a *shi* in the seventh century was quite different from being a *shi* in the Southern Song. It is both this relative fluidity of the makeup of the *shi* and the persistent linkage between the symbol of elite status and recognition as a *shi* during the long span of traditional China that added to the problematic nature of *shi* identity. Too many people who were too different from each other claimed to be the same thing. As a term of social identification, *shi* was a concept largely related to the self-perception of those who tried to maintain their status as cultural elite: "'Shih' as a concept was a socially constructed idea that those who called themselves shih held. The transformation of the shih thus can analytically be separated into changes in the way shih conceived of being a shih and shifts in the social makeup of the men who called themselves shih."[75] That is to say, members of the *shi* class tended to be more self-conscious of their social identity than members of other social groups. The literati appear by nature to have been autobiographers when they wrote, a fact confirmed by the large number of autobiographical poems. This fact become even more interesting when we learn that in traditional China nearly all those who could write belonged to the *shi* class (except for a small group located at the very center of imperial power).

During the seventeenth and especially the eighteenth centuries, the kinds of roles theoretically available to a literatus became more diverse: official, Confucian sage (no matter how impossible in reality), man of culture, professional scholar, teacher, private secretary, and even well-educated merchant. The diversity of roles and the resultant subtle divisions, however, only added to the fragmentation of the literati as a social group and to the confusion of their self-identity as *shi*.[76]

Between Masks and Roles:
New Autobiographical Strategies

To this point the discussion has treated the literati identity crisis from the late Ming period through the eighteenth century basically as a continuum. In fact, there are certain significant discontinuities detectable in the differing responses by the literati of these two periods. Li Zhi's angry condemnation of "phoniness" (*jia*) prevalent in the literati culture of his time is symptomatic of the more general anguish over the problematic nature of literati self-identity during the late Ming.

No matter how clever the words, what have they to do with oneself? What else can there be but phony men speaking phony words, doing phony things, writing phony writings? Once the men become phonies, everything becomes phony. Thereafter if one speaks phony talk to the phonies, the phonies are pleased; if one does phony things as the phonies do, the phonies are pleased; and if one discourses with the phonies through phony writings, the phonies are pleased. Everything is phony, and everyone is pleased.[77]

This uneasiness with inauthenticity was explored with a special self-consciousness by a group of seventeenth-century painters, among whom Chen Hongshou (1598–1652) is probably the most representative. A theatrical tone dominates many portraits by Chen, and his subjects' facial expressions are often "drawn into a masklike exaggeration" characterized by a "quality of psychological isolation."

The very confusion of roles is evocative of the implied psychological state of many such figures: Abstracted, dreamy, absent, they exist in a blurred realm of reverie, listening to distant music or inhaling the aroma of flower blossoms. The mental states evoked are congenial to day-dreaming, identification, or projection. The figures in these images seldom acknowledge the presence of their companions, as if to do so would too firmly fix a defined illustrative role.

The literati figures in his paintings often "look anxious about their roles . . . trapped by the weight of their roles."[78] The comments of art historian James Cahill on the presentation of the subjects in Chen's portraits are equally illuminating: "They typically appear more like people who have taken refuge in the realm of art from a world in which they have no secure place, and who find that the realm of art does not receive them comfortably either. They look out at us as if compelled by some need to assert their existence as individuals, to communicate some sense of their situation."[79]

It was exactly this sense of anguish over one's problematic identity and the need to (re)assert one's self as an authentic literatus that prompted Chen Hongshou's contemporary Fang Yizhi (1611–71) to write an interesting pseudo-autobiography. At the age of 27 Fang wrote a prose piece entitled "Seven Solutions" ("Qijie"). In this highly autobiographical work, a young man named Baoshu Zi (apparently the author's alter ego) is deeply depressed and feels at a loss as to what he should do with his talent and ambition. The frustration over one's unrecognized talent, long a main topic in literati literature, underlies every line in the piece. Seven men offer advice on his alternatives, such as seeking a career by taking the examinations, becoming an official to advise the emperor, withdrawing to become a recluse, making money as a merchant, and practicing Daoism to become an immortal (*xian*). Most of these are possible roles for a literatus (the fact that business is also suggested indicates that becoming a merchant was no longer considered an impossibility for a literatus), but none excites Baoshu Zi. "Seven Solutions" ends on a positive note. Baoshu Zi is no longer depressed, and he has finally decided to do something—but what remains unclear.[80] Indeed, the final relief appears "to be achieved merely by default."[81] The whole piece is dominated by a profound depression, the cause of which is attributable to the general literati identity crisis.

Andrew Plaks offers this general characterization of late Ming literati culture:

The entire constellation of literati culture often becomes something of an affectation, a rather self-conscious attempt to fulfil a notion of what *wen-jen* should be. . . .

38   *The Problematic Literati Self*

This groping for identity as *wen-jen* runs through the full range of late Ming cultural life, with the attempt at self-definition more often than not leading only to uneasy compromises. Thus, we see our literati artists playing the game of self-realization from behind a screen of detachment not quite substantial enough to be called alienation, but sufficient to fuel sarcasm and ironic perspective—now coming across as playful bursts of wit, now sinking into rather heavy, even bitter musings.[82]

This "ironic perspective" or self-conscious "sarcasm," already prevalent in the late Ming, would later develop into an unprecedented cynicism in the eighteenth century. By that time, although the problem of inauthenticity and the sense of self-inadequacy continued to plague many literati, the anguish over such inauthenticity or inadequacy typical of the late Ming seems to have subsided significantly, at least on the surface. Instead, cultural cynicism and skepticism began to emerge.[83] Some literati even evinced a sense of pleasure in playing with "inauthenticity" by manipulating masks and personae in art and literature. According to art historian Richard Vinograd, eighteenth-century figural and portrait paintings were "characterized by a more equable awareness of the pleasures and opportunities of fictional devices . . . manipulations of presentation, voice and persona."[84]

The most illuminating example of the eighteenth-century literati's response to the question of ambiguous self-identity is probably Yuan Mei's well-known comment on a portrait of him done by Luo Pin (1733–99). The portrait, when finished, was returned to the painter because Yuan Mei or his family did not like it. Here it is worthwhile to quote Yuan's inscription for the portrait at length:

The lay Buddhist Liangfeng [Luo Pin] painted this portrait of me. At least, Liangfeng takes it to be me, but my family members take it not to be me, and the two views seem impossible to reconcile. I only laugh and say: "The sage has two selves: the without-origin and self-less self is one self, and the self-that-is-different-from-that is another self." I also have two selves: the one in the eyes of my family is one self, and the one in Liangfeng's painting is another. Men suffer from not being able to know themselves. My not being able to know what I look like is like Liangfeng's not being able to know his own picture. When all is said and done, is it the viewer's mistake, or is it the painter's mistake? Perhaps my appearance originally ought to have been like this, and at the time in question, the mistake was made by Heaven [that which is responsible for innate qualities]. Again, perhaps although the me

The Problematic Literati Self   39

of this life is not like this, the me's of former or future lives—how does one know that they are not like this? And that therefore Liangfeng for the time being abandoned what was near at hand to depict the distant; harmonizing the former and future natures he painted the result. In that case, this picture can simultaneously be me and not-me—it doesn't matter.[85]

What is revealed in this inscription is not only a subtle awareness of one's multiple selves (the ambiguities of self-identity) but also an almost cynical pleasure apparently derived from such an awareness, a willingness to explore the multiplicities that had caused so much anguish in the late Ming to someone as sensitive as Li Zhi.[86]

The eighteenth century also witnessed a surge of enthusiasm among the literati for the theater, not only as a passive audience but more significantly as actors in the capacity of amateurs. Traditionally, acting had always been looked down on as one of the lowest of callings, almost as low as prostitution (the son of an actor was barred from taking the civil-service examinations). Attitudes remained almost the same in the eighteenth century, yet the conventional contempt for acting in general and Qing legal regulations specially designed to outlaw amateur acting (*chuanxi*) failed to dampen many literati's passion for acting. Quite a number of them even went bankrupt sponsoring or participating in amateur acting. Even the Qianlong emperor sometimes indulged in playing a role. Sometimes the distinctions between acting and living became difficult to maintain.

Many factors contributed to this rather strange literati passion. One that is most relevant here is the increasing awareness of the ambiguities of the self and the simultaneous cynical delight in manipulating personae and masks and in impersonating others to find an outlet for these identity-related anxieties. For many deeply repressed literati, masking and impersonating presented rare opportunities for role switching and self-healing. For example, the eighteenth-century poet Huang Zhongze (1749–83; also known as Huang Jinren) was notorious for his penchant for amateur acting. Impersonating became his special means of maintaining the equilibrium of his precarious self in his short but frustrated life as a *wenren*.[87]

Interpreted in this context, Zheng Xie's outrageous act of publicly offering a list of prices for his paintings can be seen as another theatrical gesture on his part to deal with the serious challenge to his identity as a literati painter (amateur) posed by the rapid commercialization of art in his times. This dramatic as well as playful act (playing with his own inauthenticity) was also intended as a declaration that a painter's status could no longer be defined in terms of traditional standards of distinguishing the professional and the amateurish.

This profound awareness of one's ambiguous and multifaceted self as well as the willingness to explore those very multiplicities or ambiguities made the novel, with its flexible form and explicit claim of fictionality, an especially favorable autobiographical outlet for some eighteenth-century literati authors. The novel provided the maximum potential for manipulation of various fictional devices, such as the creation of multiple personae or metaphors, to explore the ever-elusive self when the distinction between real and fictional was becoming increasingly blurred, as eloquently demonstrated in *The Dream*. This may also help explain why the novel was becoming significantly autobiographical just at the juncture of the eighteenth century when formal autobiographical writings as a genre were rapidly declining—the increasingly complex self seems to demand a more complex form of presentation.

The exposure of the inadequacies of conventional literati roles in eighteenth-century China is certainly a main feature of *The Scholars*. Throughout the novel the roles a literatus is supposed to play or the alternatives he can choose are carefully paraded forth one by one, and each is in turn shown to be either totally inadequate or without authenticity: examination candidate, official, recluse, *wenren*, and even knight-errant. All these were the roles the author, Wu Jingzi, himself had tried or could try in his life. This parading strategy bears a great resemblance to that in Fang Yizhi's "Seven Solutions," in which seven people suggest different options to the autobiographical protagonist. Both Wu's novel and Fang's pseudo-autobiography are a personal search for proper literati roles to play, although *The Scholars* is far more complex and its autobiographical implications more subtle. Read as a whole, *The Scholars* can be seen as a retrospective account of the journey the author had taken as a literatus in search of a proper literati "self" in relation to the various public roles available at the time. However, the critique of the inauthenticities of these roles is problematized by a reluctant realization that the practical necessity of these roles in society is indicative of the limits enclosing the pursuit of authenticity. It is partly due to this appreciation of the complexities of the self that Wu Jingzi resorts to the specific strategies of self-re/presentation used in his novel in which the different characters function as metaphors for different aspects of his own complex autobiographical self (see discussions in Chapter 2). This choice of narrative rhetoric also contributes to a profoundly pessimistic impression that the possibilities for reconstructing a coherent autobiographical self are always slim. Consequently, the novel's implied pursuit of authenticity is brought into serious doubt: we find that the author often has to rely on masking for his autobiographical presentation (representing himself through various personae or metaphoric devices) even though the novel itself is intended to be a critique of the practices of masquerading and impersonation prevalent among the literati.

In *The Dream* role-playing, at least on the surface, is not the main pattern of the action. Instead, the protagonist Jia Baoyu seems especially reluctant to play any role associated with a literatus (with the exception of writing poetry). In sharp contrast to the obsession of many characters in *The Scholars* with their self-image, Jia Baoyu appears to be particularly indifferent in this regard (this could be interpreted as a calculated gesture of excessive concern). This gesture is certainly made easier to accept because Jia Baoyu remains a teenager through most of the novel. He seems particularly bothered by the idea of growing up. The anxiety about adulthood is an important reason for his idiosyncratic behavior in the novel (a point I develop later in this study). It is precisely Jia Baoyu's wish to remain a "child," however, and his refusal to assume adult responsibilities that call attention to the question of the problematic literati self as it is depicted in this extremely complex novel. Autobiographically, this certainly reflects the author Cao Xueqin's (ca. 1715–63) own experience. The Cao family's drastic decline began when the author was young. As a member of a powerful family that had benefited from imperial favors, Cao Xueqin probably felt no pressure to follow the normal route up the social ladder as a common literatus (such as taking the examinations) till that favor was suddenly taken away.[88] He probably did not begin to (or did not have to) consider the question of how he could maintain his elite status (as a literatus) until the bankruptcy of the family forced him to suffer hardships, the kinds of hardship typically experienced by someone whose career or livelihood largely depended on recognition of his learning. In other words, the dilemma of being a future literatus as experienced by Jia Baoyu in the novel is closely associated with the fate of the whole family (the theme of being born at the wrong time—being born into the family in decline).

Moreover, this feeling of inadequacy and the resultant rejection as unworthy find subtle expression in the characterization of many female figures in the novel. This displacement of the author's male literati anxiety to the female characters, who are presented partly as metaphors for the author's own tragic self in actual life, is an important aspect of the autobiographical signification in *The Dream*. The interplay between the description of the apathy of Baoyu and that of the relatively more active attitudes represented by those female metaphors dramatizes the author's own autobiographical quandary—the often contradictory aspects of his own complex self. The high "gender fluidity" (the interchangeability between the feminine and masculine) underscored in the novel further enhances this impression of an ambiguous self. The novel's unprecedented emphasis on the relations between the real and the unreal as well as between the realms of dream and waking and the various intricate plays of doubles certainly complicate the attempt to represent a coherent autobiographical self. If we can still detect traces of bitterness and anguish over the frustrations of groping for a coherent self in *The Scholars*, what dominates *The Dream* is a profound skepticism that probably cannot be characterized simply as cynical.

In *Humble Words* almost everything, at least at first glance, is reversed. The protagonist, Wen Suchen, is successful in every role he chooses: Confucian scholar, mathematician, poet, medical doctor, knight-errant, and most important, top adviser to the crown prince and later to the emperor. The dilemma many characters face as literati (or as future literati) in *The Scholars* and *The Dream* seems to have disappeared completely. Wen Suchen is not only a devoted neo-Confucian good at self-cultivation but also, and more important, a great success in public service, a perfect paradigm of the ideal of sage within and king without. The author must have had in mind the question of a literatus's proper role posed in *The Scholars* as he was writing *Humble Words*. Consider Chi Hengshan's dismay at the disintegration of a unified literati identity in *The Scholars*: "Scholars should stick to scholarship without trying to become officials, and officials should stick to officialdom without trying to be scholars too. A man who wants to be both will succeed in neither!" (*RLWS*,

49: 662; S, 540) What is ostensibly proclaimed in *Humble Words* appears to be just the opposite: a literatus can be a scholar and a great official at the same time, as demonstrated most impressively by Wen Suchen. A comparison with *The Dream* highlights a special autobiographical feature of this novel: childhood is described as if it were an experience not that different from adulthood. Wen Long, the son of Wen Suchen, becomes a *zhuangyuan* (the candidate ranked first in the palace examination) at the tender age of eight and is later appointed regional inspector of a province; in *The Dream* Baoyu at this age is still playing with his cousins under their grandmother's supervision. What is despised or feared (adulthood) in *The Dream* becomes the very thing celebrated in *Humble Words*. Although thwarted earlier in the examinations, Wen Suchen later becomes the top official in the country. It is as if the author were trying to tell the reader a literatus can hope to be successful in public office even if he fails the examinations.

The incredibly brilliant successes of Wen Suchen become all the more autobiographically revealing when we learn how miserable the life of Xia Jingqu was. Here the novel becomes the author's autobiographical redemption through an act of "imaginative forgetting." In contrast to the earnest but often frustrating searches and personal struggles in *The Scholars* and *The Dream*, wish-fulfilling fantasizing becomes the ultimate solution to all the problems a literatus is facing in this novel. What is particularly significant about *Humble Words* with regard to the issue of the problematic literati self, however, is that the novel also invites a different reading: the ostensible claim that the protagonist is capable of playing all literati roles (conventional or unconventional) is shown to be a *calculated* exaggeration. The reading reveals how the novel carefully invalidates many of its own apparently exaggerated claims and eventually points to the opposite conclusion: the protagonist assumes so many different and even conflicting roles that he no longer presents a coherent and convincing identity. The final dream scene at the end of the novel further confirms this reading because it suggests that the protagonist's achievements as a super-literatus are just a wish-fulfilling dream.

Read together, the three novels represent the authors' different responses to the dilemma of being a literatus in eighteenth-century China and the attempt of each to cope with that dilemma. Throughout the detailed discussions of each novel's unique autobiographical strategies in the following chapters, we must keep in mind this obsession with finding alternative "qualifications" to sustain the claim to be a member of the cultured elite (an obsession that consumed all three authors for most of their lives) and the simultaneous anxiety over inauthenticity, which may have resulted from attempts to (re)define such qualifications.

2

The Self Masqueraded: Auto/Biographical Strategies in 'The Scholars'

Man is least himself when he talks in his own person.
Give him a mask, he will tell you the truth.
—Oscar Wilde

In his study of traditional Chinese autobiography, Pei-yi Wu attributes the apparent underdevelopment of the genre in early China to the tyranny and influence of the biographical format of traditional history—in which accounts of the private and emotional were usually excluded—and to the prevalent Confucian sense of decorum, which militated against self-disclosure.[1] According to Wu, the biographical conventions were so powerful that many autobiographies had to be disguised as biographies. For example, Tao Qian's (365–427) famous autobiographical narrative "The Biography of Master Five Willows" ("Wuliu xiansheng zhuan") took the form of a biography written in the narrative mode of third person: "If they could not unabashedly and boldly write about themselves in good earnest, they could at least create an alter ego, a persona like the Master Five Willows, behind whom a version of their selves could emerge."[2] Tao Qian's autobiographical strategy later became the prototype for a series of autobiographies; the famous Tang official and poet Bai Juyi (772–846) wrote one entitled "The Biography of Master Drunken Singer" ("Zuiyin xiansheng zhuan") in the same fictive fashion.

The late Ming writer Li Zhi even wrote an autobiography (entitled "A Brief Comment on Zhuowu"; "Zhuowu lunlüe") as if it were a biography written by another person. In that disguised autobiography, he created a fictional biographer/narrator named "Kong Ruogu," who narrates Li Zhi's life.³ By virtue of this device, Li Zhi was able to venture into "what had hitherto been forbidden ground in Chinese biographical literature, the domestic scene not screened by pious generality nor adorned by exemplary acts."⁴ All these autobiographies in the disguise of biography fulfill their autobiographical purport—"historical" self-presentation by virtue of "fictional" self-re/presentation (*re*presenting the self as an other).

This autobiographical strategy of self-re/presentation is by no means confined to prose narrative. The important poetic rhetoric of *jituo*, which is often translated into English as "allegorizing" for lack of a better word, is a common practice. This is especially significant because traditional Chinese poetry had always been considered autobiographical (written and read autobiographically). This autobiographical dimension of poetry was enhanced by the traditional belief in the historicity (or nonfictionality) of poetic discourse.⁵ A compiler of a literatus poet's biographical chronology (*nianpu*) often relied on the poems written by his subject for biographical data; their historical validity was rarely doubted.

However, the autobiographical significance of a traditional Chinese poem does not necessarily have to be gauged with reference only to the poet's direct self-presentation. More often the discourse of self-re/presentation is mixed. Bai Juyi's well-known "The Song of the *Pipa*" ("Pipa xing") is a long narrative poem (at least by Chinese standards) about the life of a *pipa* (lute) player. This representation of an other is transformed into a *re*presentation of the poet's own self by virtue of the direct self-presentation by the poet at the end of the poem, where he identifies himself with the *pipa* player directly, and the contextualizing preface to the poem, which places the representation of the *pipa* player within the referential frame of the poet's own life experiences—self-presentation:

In the tenth year of Yuan-ho (815), I was banished to Chiu-chiang County to be an assistant official there. In the autumn of the second year, I was seeing a friend off at Pen-pu at night when I heard someone play the *p'i-p'a* with the touch and style of the Capital. I asked about the player and found that she was from Ch'ang-an and was once a student of Masters Mu and Ts'ao. Aging, her beauty declining, she married herself to a merchant. I ordered . . . wine and food again and asked her to play a few tunes. Afterward, she looked sad and started telling us about the happy days of her youth and how she became haggard, drifting along rivers and lakes. It is now two years since I left the court to come here. I have felt content until tonight when her words made me realize the very meaning of my banishment. I wrote this long poem of eighty-eight lines for her and titled it "Song of the P'i-p'a."[6]

Here the empathy between the once glamorous *pipa* player and the poet banished from the capital is much emphasized. Consequently, the detailed account of the *pipa* player's frustrated life becomes an allegory of the poet's equally frustrated political career. What concerns Bai Juyi in this poem nominally about a *pipa* player is the *re*presentation of his own self rather than an "objective" *re*presentation of an other. Read in this light, the poem is more autobiographical than biographical, and its representation of the other becomes partly an excuse for self-*re*presentation, although most readers would not consider it an explicitly autobiographical poem.

Due to the hybrid nature of self-re/presentation inherent in traditional Chinese poetic discourse, autobiographical reference or self-presentation, which often takes the form of the representation of others, can be found in almost every poem.[7] Most poems in the popular poetic genre of *yongshi shi* (poems on history) are considered to be "representations" of the past (a recalling of a historical past). Their lyrical value (the implications of *yong*) is, however, often judged in terms of the poem's relevance to the present—how the poet/self is *re*presented. Thus in the Chinese poetic tradition a good *yongshi* poem must also be a *yonghuai* poem (poem on the poet's inner thoughts); this is exemplified in many historical poems by Zuo Si (252–306). The subject of his poems, always a well-known historical figure, is presented as a tropical projection of his own self, just as in Bai Juyi's "Song of the *Pipa*" the tragic *pipa* player is presented as a trope for the frustrated literati poet. The meaning of the subject of the poem has to be mediated through the references to the poet. In other words, in an autobiographical reading of the poem, the first is mainly a metaphor for the second (there are, of course, other ways of reading such poems). The device of self-presentation via self-re/presentation is a common practice in traditional Chinese literature, and in a literary work the autobiographical and the biographical are often not easy to distinguish.

Pei-yi Wu deplores this "submission" to the tyranny of biography as detrimental to the development of Chinese autobiography: "T'ao Ch'ien as well as his followers paid a heavy price for disguising autobiography as biography, for adopting for the self a guise too narrowly designed. What they achieved is not a portrait but a pose; they conceal more of themselves than they reveal."[8] Although Wu is probably correct that this inclination to present one's self through the representation of other(s) was not conducive to the development of formal autobiography as an independent genre, it did provide fiction writers with an alternative model. Writing a pseudo-autobiography or novel allowed them to explore under the guise of fiction (which explicitly claims to be about others) their own personal experience much more deeply, an endeavor probably more difficult to accomplish in a formal and straightforward autobiography.[9]

Some of the advantages of writing an autobiography in the form of a biography of someone else can readily be seen in Fang Yizhi's "Seven Solutions" (see Chapter 1). The fictional strategy of self-re/presentation enables Fang to dramatize his personal dilemma of being unable to choose the proper literati role(s) to play and allows him to question forcefully the validity of each role without provoking accusations of self-indulgence from his contemporaries.[10] Commenting on "Seven Solutions," Fang Yizhi acknowledged that "I wrote the 'Seven Solutions' as an allegory on myself [*zikuang*]."[11] The Chinese word *zikuang* (allegory on oneself or self-comparison) used by Fang here, which is close to the meaning of *jituo* in the sense of autobiographical signification, is probably the most appropriate term to describe this kind of self-re/presentation (auto/biography).[12]

A few clarifying remarks about the definition of the term *self-re/presentation* as it is employed in this study are in order before we embark on an examination of autobiographical signification in *The Scholars*. "Self" refers to both the revealed self (the version of the authorial self revealed in a novel or a literary work) and the created self (character).[13] The term *self-re/presentation* is specially employed to emphasize what I perceive to be the intimate relationship between self-*presentation* (the author explicitly discoursing on his own self) and self-*representation* (the author discoursing on other selves—characters) as manifested in a work. *Self-re/presentation* refers to the way in which different selves (those of the author as well as those of the characters) are presented and to the complex relationship between self-representation, as in the case of the representation of the *pipa* player in Bai Juyi's poem, and self-presentation, as in the presentation of his own self by Bai Juyi in the poem. Here the slash between "re" and "presentation" is meant to underscore the indirect manner by which the author tries to *re*present a version of himself through the representation of those *other* selves (characters); for example, Bai Juyi's own self is *re*presented through the representation of the *pipa* player. In the case of *The Scholars*, the representation of characters (other than a character, such as Du Shaoqing, who is presented as the alter ego of the author) is seldom completely innocent. The so-called autobiographical dimension that some readers have found in the novel should be understood in the light of this narrative rhetoric of self-re/presentation, which is not confined to a single character as we would expect of a typical autobiographical novel in the West. This strategy of self-re/presentation is particularly effective for an autobiographical agenda that emphasizes the intricate relationships between self and other through an exploration of the dilemmas of role playing.

Strictly speaking, the authorial self can never be directly revealed; rather, it is presentable only as metaphor. Consequently, direct self-presentation is possible only to a *relative* degree. In other words, self-presentation always has to be mediated through the representation of others because the moment one thinks or writes about one's self, that self has already become an "other" (a character), a phenomenon that arises from the paradoxical nature of self-writing (see the Introduction). Thus, the distinction between self-presentation and self-re/presentation can be only relative, and as critical terms they are employed here merely for the sake of analysis. What is unique about *The Scholars* and the other two novels discussed here is their willingness to dramatize and highlight this hybrid (as well as paradoxical) nature of self-writing. A discussion of the strategy of self-re/presentation calls attention to the conscientious effort in these novels to *mask* self-writing as writing about others or as writing about the intricate relationships between self and others by exploring the dilemma of role playing and the unstable boundaries of the self. This willingness is certainly related to the realization on the part of many eighteenth-century literati of the multiplicities of the self.

Structural Restlessness and the Autobiographical Movement

Many readers of *The Scholars* are troubled by the novel's apparently loose structure. The novel is made up of accounts (or biographies) of many different characters,[14] and the reader is ushered from the story (or biography) of one character to that of another, or from one episode to another, with no apparent explanation by the narrator. For example, early in the novel, in chapter 3, the narrative focus shifts from Zhou Jin to Fan Jin when the former as an examiner meets the latter, and Zhou almost immediately disappears from the scene. This pattern of transition is repeated throughout the novel. The narrative movement of the novel is in fact sustained by constant shifts of focus from one character to another as they meet on the road or in someone's house. Characters arrive and depart so fast that a reader relying on the high frequency of the appearance of a character he or she expects from an ordinary novel is often unable to follow the unfolding plot. This movement gives rise to a "decentering" narrative structure within which no single character assumes the position of protagonist for more than a few chapters. Thus, the author's well-known alter ego, Du Shaoqing, never dominates the novel long enough to enable us to say that it concerns mostly the authorial self.

To put it simply, at least on the surface, *The Scholars* as a novel is not about any single one person but about many different people—many "others"—a self-evident fact apparently confirmed by the novel's title, which literally means "an unofficial history of Confucian scholars," a collective history. All this seems contrary to what we would expect from a typical autobiographical novel, such as Charles Dickens's *David Copperfield* or James Joyce's *Portrait of the Artist as a Young Man*, which usually concentrates on a single autobiographical protagonist. If, however, we take into account the hybrid nature of the strategy of self-re/presentation or the mixed mode of autobiography in the guise of biography so common in the Chinese autobiographical and poetic tradition, the autobiographical imperatives in *The Scholars* may turn out to be much more subtle than usually assumed.

On the other hand, since the novel consists of a series of linked but sometimes independent biographies of different characters, it seems to have rendered itself more susceptible to the constraints of biographical practice in the historiographical tradition, which was characterized by its anti-autobiographical proclivity to suppress the private and the emotional, its impersonality, and its sense of public decorum.[15] In fact, Wu Jingzi has often been compared to a detached historian for his adoption of the pose of an impersonal narrator and for his sketchy narrative style.[16] In a sense, to be autobiographical,

Wu has to rely more on the *zikuang* (self-comparison or self-re/presentation) strategy to circumvent the anti-autobiographical constraints of the biographical convention he apparently chose to follow in his novel. The autobiographical significance of *The Scholars* has to be examined with this fact in mind.

Several hundred characters appear within the relatively short space and time span of the novel (the English translation runs to some 600 pages, and the novel covers a period of just over a century). However, the work unfolds thematically along a fairly clear pattern. Following the prologue to the novel proper in chapter 1, the first section is dominated by those obsessed with success in the civil-service examinations (roughly chapters 2–7). The second section (chapters 7–30) is concerned mainly with those trying to achieve success and fame by becoming a *mingshi* (a romantic or self-styled man of culture), such as the Lou brothers, Niu Buyi, and Du Shenqing. Du Shenqing later passes the metropolitan examinations and becomes an official, thus showing that the difference between a careerist, as exemplified in the first section, and a self-proclaimed recluse, as shown in this section, is not significant. The third section (chapters 31–46) presents the reader with several characters of integrity, such as Du Shaoqing, Zhuang Shaoguang, and Yu Yude. As independent individuals, they show concern for social reform (promoting the ideal of the so-called *li yue bing nong* [the promotion of ritual, music, military training, and farming]). Their efforts culminate in the grand sacrificial ceremony in the Taibo Temple in chapter 37. The last section (chapters 47–55) largely concerns the tragic denouement of a generation of literati (*yidai wenren*) pervaded with a sense of profound despair.[17] Consequently, the narrative movement of the novel suggests a sequential process from "social satire" (*fengshi*) to "social reform" (*kuangshi*) or a development from a literatus's concern for *wenxing chuchu* (the qualities of a literatus: solid learning, correct behavior, and the right choice between public service and withdrawal) to that for social harmony (the promotion of ritual, music, military training, and farming). However, this process finally leads to poignant disappointment or total disillusionment.

Significantly the unfolding of the stories in the novel corresponds roughly to the development of the author's thinking as well as to the ups and downs of his personal life.[18] The first section of the novel reflects an early stage in Wu's life when he was attempting to pass the civil-service examinations. He was apparently proud of the examination successes many members in his family had achieved. He was even said to have once knelt and begged an examiner not to flunk him in a qualifying test for the provincial examination (*pufu qishou*).[19] Although much of the first section, which is known for its scathing satire of examination candidates, was probably inspired in part by contemporary anecdotes and even historical records, when read with reference to the author's personal experiences, the section amounts to a self-critique. Writing about an obsession by projecting it onto others probably makes self-critique less painful as well as more possible. The second section of the novel can be read in a similar manner: here various alternatives to the examinations are presented as ways of procuring fame and social success, some of which Wu had tried. Furthermore, Wu Jingzi experienced some aspects of the life of a *mingshi* or a recluse described here after he moved to Nanjing. Sometimes the distinction between authentic recluse and fake becomes thin. This probably reflects Wu's own efforts to keep a strict division between the two when he was pursuing the life-style of a man of culture (*wenren*).[20] In the third section, which is obviously the most autobiographical, appear the author's own alter ego, Du Shaoqing, and other characters, such as Zhuang Shaoguang and Yu Yude, modeled on friends or relatives. All of them share the ideal of *li yue bing nong* to a different degree. The section ends with the disintegration of this group of men of integrity and their disillusionment about their shared dream of social reform, which is symbolized by the farewell at the Three Mountains Gate in chapter 46.

The ending seems to present no hope for the future, a picture of a lost generation. Symbolic of the literati identity crisis, the novel concludes with the story of four eccentrics, each of whom excels at only one of the four arts (zither, chess, calligraphy, and painting), all of which are supposed to be the essential accomplishments of a traditional literatus. The ideal, as represented in the character of Wang Mian at the beginning of the novel, disintegrates into the fragmented images of the four eccentrics at the end. All try to live up to the traditional literati ideal, but harsh reality often forces them into undesirable professions such as tailoring. This fragmentation of the traditional image of a literatus suggests the urgency of the need to redefine the literati identity.[21] And Wu Jingzi's autobiographical search for authentic roles is certainly complicated by this disintegration.[22]

Thus, the four sections of the novel parallel the successive stages of Wu Jingzi's *bildung* from obsessed examination candidate to detached but uneasy outsider and finally from an enthusiastic Confucian idealist to a bitter and despairing novelist. The novel becomes Wu's grand apology for his life, which was not without folly and recklessness; the writing of the novel becomes a retrospective journey through which he tries to redeem his past self by reconstructing that self in the form of a series of others. As an "autobiographical" novel, *The Scholars* is an account of the author's search for a proper identity and a proper role to play. By reading the novel autobiographically (i.e., read with the fact in mind that autobiography was often practiced in the form of biography in traditional China), the reader is able to follow the reconstruction of Wu Jingzi (albeit often symbolically) and the maturation of the examination candidate Wu Jingzi into a well-seasoned observer of social manners. Viewed from a different angle, the detached narrative rhetoric and seemingly objective biographical form enable the author to attain a sense of safe distance so that he can look back at his past self in the form of many others without having to bear the full consequences of a direct confrontation.[23]

Furthermore, the novel's quick shifting of narrative focus seems to be paralleled (or necessitated) by the frequent movements of many characters—travel is a constant occupation for many characters. Examinees travel to participate in the examinations; the few successful examination candidates, after becoming officials, travel to assume new posts; a filial son walks over half the country to seek a father who refuses to recognize him out of fear of political persecution; disgusted and bankrupt, Du Shaoqing moves from his hometown to Nanjing in self-exile; others like Kuang Chaoren run away from poverty to seek their fortunes elsewhere. Most of these journeys are not pleasant to those who have to take them. What we have here is a group of restless wanderers, who are reminiscent of the *youshi*, or wandering men of skill, in the Spring and Autumn period. The restlessness that permeates the world of the novel was an experience shared by the author, who was so frustrated in his lifelong search for personal fulfillment as a literatus. The novel itself is a restless autobiographical journey taken by the novelist in the attempt to define or give meaning to his own past and present selves. It is in this sense of defining one's self that we can perceive a general pattern shared by nearly all these seemingly endless journeys in the novel: for many journeys the two most important destinations are the imperial capital in the north, Beijing (or Jingshi, as it is called in the novel), and the "capital" in the south (Nanjing).

Although seldom directly described in the novel, the capital in the north is a mysterious and sometimes intimidating world characterized by alluring access to power, political danger, and, ultimately, moral corruption.[24] In contrast, the southern "capital" Nanjing seems to be a place where various people excluded from officialdom congregate. Early in the novel the major pattern of movement is toward Beijing. All the journeys there are related to officialdom. Zhou Jin, Fan Jin, Xun Mei, Ma Chunshang, and later Du Shenqing all go there to seek entrance into the official world via success in the examinations, and Senior Licentiate Yan travels all the way there to try to secure help from Fan Jin (then already an official) in settling a legal case. Even Zhuang Shaoguang, the recluse, is forced to take a trip to Beijing when he is invited to offer advice to the emperor. As early as chapter 8, however, the Lou brothers are complaining of feeling bored in Beijing, and their return to their hometown anticipates the movement toward Nanjing, a movement that dominates the second half of the novel. Nanjing is a place where many frustrated literati can find appreciation for their unrecognized talent. In chapter 28 a certain Mr. Xin and Mr. Jin complain that "in this vulgar place [where they are staying now] true worth is not appreciated. We mean to go to Nanking too" (*RLWS*, 28: 383; S, 307). Du Shaoqing is advised by the dying Mr. Lou to go to Nanjing to seek understanding friends.[25] When assigned to an unexpectedly low official post in Nanjing, Yu Yude congratulates himself by saying, "Nanking is a fine place. It has mountains and lakes and is close to my home" (*RLWS*, 36: 494; S, 400). Thus, Beijing and Nanjing represent two completely different choices in life for a literatus, and the change of general direction of many journeys from Beijing to Nanjing in the second half of the novel is suggestive of the constantly changing self of Wu Jingzi in his own personal journey from seeking success in the examinations to struggling hard to maintain himself as an outsider.[26] An understanding of these large structural patterns of autobiographical signification is crucial to the following discussion of various specific examples of self-re/representation in the novel.

The Burden of Memory and the Reconstruction of Self(ves)

Throughout his life Wu Jingzi seems to have been bothered by memories of the glorious achievements of his ancestors, which contrasted sharply with his own failures. The Wu family began to prosper dramatically when several members of the generation of Wu Jingzi's great-grandfather attained top honors in the civil-service examinations. His great-grandfather Wu Guodui won the third place (*tanhua*) in the palace examination in 1654 and was known as a great master of the eight-legged essay (*bagu wen*). In 1691 two of Guodui's nephews achieved *jinshi* degrees, and one of them even won second place (*bangyan*) in the palace examination. The quick rise of the Wu family was closely associated with its members' spectacular successes in the examinations. Wu Jingzi had good reason to feel pride in his family's impressive record of examination successes: "The good name of my family has always been made in the examinations."[27] The memories of the glorious past of his family constantly haunted Wu Jingzi as he repeatedly failed to pass the provincial examinations. In fact, however, the examination performance of Wu Jingzi's father's generation suffered in comparison with that of previous generations. Wu's adoptive father, Wu Linqi, did not succeed beyond the prefectural examinations and was only a *bagong* (imperial student by selection); he remained a petty official throughout his life.[28] In his "Rhapsody on Moving My Home" ("Yijia fu"), Wu expended a lot of ink describing his adoptive father in glowing superlatives, emphasizing his moral integrity and filiality.[29] Against the towering figure of his great-grandfather, who had achieved so much in the examinations and public office, his adoptive father, who failed so miserably in the same areas but was still able to act like a sage (at least in the eyes of his adopted son), must have represented for Wu Jingzi an alternative role model—a paragon of Confucian self-cultivation. Wu Jingzi thus seems to have been caught between his reverence for his ancestors' achievements in the examinations and public office and his equally reverent memories of his adoptive father as a frustrated literatus of moral integrity. His dilemma throughout most of his life was to live up to his family's glorious past by achieving success in the examinations and at the same time to maintain his moral integrity under the pressure of a series of failures. In this light, Wu's almost excessive praise of his (adoptive) father can, at least partly, be understood as an apology for himself.

Traditionally, critics have emphasized that the civil-service examinations and various efforts to seek fame are the main targets in *The Scholars*, and the reputation of this novel rests partly on this claim. Most critics believe that by the time he started writing the novel, Wu Jingzi had outgrown his earlier obsession with examination success and the bitterness caused by his various failures. Hu Shi, for example, made the following, oft-cited observation: "Before 1737 he still had the air of a frustrated *xiucai* [licentiate, the lowest examination degree], but after that year he was an awakened Wu Jingzi, the author of *The Scholars*."[30] Since the extant *Wenmushanfang ji* is a collection of Wu's works written before he was 40 and since one can still find in it many poems betraying a deep regret over his failures, especially in the examinations,[31] many scholars have concluded that Wu could not have started writing the novel before the age of 40 for the simple reason that the novel is just too "anti-examination" to allow for this fact. Here we need not involve ourselves in the controversies over when Wu started writing his novel. My main argument is that such an awakening did not happen so dramatically just after the incident of the Erudite Scholar (*boxue hongci*) examination in 1736, as suggested by Hu Shi, or earlier by others,[32] and that even if there was indeed such an awakening, it must have been a much longer and far more painful process than most scholars have argued, a process that was probably not complete even at Wu Jingzi's death in 1754.

A careful autobiographical reading of the novel demonstrates that attitudes manifested in the novel toward examination success and public fame are more ambivalent as well as more complex than usually assumed. For Wu Jingzi, the writing of the novel can be seen as an attempt to find a way out of this ambivalence and to achieve a psychological balance between a profound sense of guilt caused by failure and the conviction of his own unrecognized talents and moral superiority.

Du Shaoqing, the alter ego of the author in the novel, is the most important autobiographical character although he lacks the usual status of a novelistic protagonist. An examination of this character and his relationship with other characters in the novel should reveal much about how Wu Jingzi tried to redeem as well as criticize his past self (or selves) through the autobiographical venture of self-re/presentation in the novel.

Many scholars have called attention to the "presentness" of autobiography—how the perception of the present self (the writing autobiographer) shapes the reconstruction of the past self (a process of becoming an other). The mixed mode of self-re/presentation discussed above provides even more leeway for such a reconstruction. Bothered by the apparent satire implied in the characterization of Du Shaoqing, the commentator Tianmu shanqiao (Zhang Wenhu [1808–85]) thought that this character cannot be a strict autobiographical representation of the author himself. Rather, the character can only be a "self-metaphor" for the authorial self, largely because an author cannot mock himself in his own writing (a rather arbitrary reason).[33] My argument is that precisely because of the objectifying as well as safe distance created by the mode of self-re/presentation, the author is able to criticize and even laugh at his own past self as an other in the character of Du Shaoqing in a redeeming process of autobiographical signification.

Chapters 31 and 32 center on the "gallant deeds" (*haoju*) of Du Shaoqing—how he willfully allows himself to be cheated out of his money by many unscrupulous people. Why does he let others cheat him out of his money? C. T. Hsia offers an explanation:

With all his innate kindness, therefore, Tu's [Du Shaoqing's] militant generosity appears far more a gesture of aristocratic pride. . . . The petitioner has counted on his munificence, and he cannot therefore disappoint that expectation even though he has nothing but the greatest contempt for him. For the same reason, he disdains to look into the accounts of his steward, who regularly cheats him. It is all a matter of style, and prudential considerations for self-protection are not just Tu's style.[34]

Thus Du Shaoqing's excessive generosity is due largely to his equally excessive obsession with his self-image. Here his cousin Du Shenqing's characterization of his generosity may sound more persuasive despite his obvious intent to serve his own self-interests. When Bao Tingxi asks Du Shenqing to write a letter of recommendation to Shaoqing on his behalf, Shenqing refuses and offers the following reason: "No, no. That would never do. He likes to be the one and only patron [*da laoguan*] helping anybody—he doesn't like others to join in. If I were to write, he would think I'd already helped you, and wouldn't trouble to do anything for you" (*RLWS*, 31: 421–22; *S*, 337).

In most cases Du Shaoqing consents to help because the petitioner appeals to his unusually strong sense of filiality.[35] This is certainly in accordance with the character of Shaoqing, who would do almost anything to protect what he believes to be his public image—a bountiful as well as independent gentleman with a strong sense of filial devotion. This becomes more significant autobiographically when we know Wu Jingzi suffered much public humiliation (especially in his hometown) when he squandered most of his inheritance and failed to get a degree beyond that of *xiucai* (all this could be regarded as evidence of unfiliality). Was the author trying to justify his much-criticized dissipation in his early life by having his fictional alter ego spend a lot of money in order to be filial? Or is he trying to tell the reader that a filial act, if carried too far, will appear ridiculous?[36] "Yes" is probably the answer to both questions. Shaoqing, however, shows little regret that he frittered away most of his inherited money except once, though almost unconsciously, in chapter 44:

"What a pity, cousin," remarked Yu with a sigh, "that you gave up your fine property. You, who were once a patron, are reduced to making a living by your pen. You must find it hard to grow used to such a come-down!"

"I enjoyed the scenery here and the company of good friends," replied Tu. "I am used to it. As a matter of fact, cousin, I'm an ignorant man with simple tastes. I live quite contentedly with my wife and sons, though we can't afford meat and our clothing is all of cotton. There is no use regretting over things in the past." (*RLWS*, 44: 602; *S*, 490, trans. modified)

This is also the peace of mind Wu Jingzi wished to achieve (through writing the novel) after so many failures in his life.

In the novel, Du Shaoqing, only a *xiucai*, appears to be highly conscious of his low status in comparison with those who have already achieved *juren* (provincial graduate) or *jinshi* (palace graduate) degrees. Du Shaoqing refuses an invitation from a salt merchant to go to a party with the following remarks: " 'Tell him I have guests and cannot go,' replied Tu. 'How ridiculous the fellow is! If he wants a good party, why doesn't he invite those newly-rich scholars who have passed the provincial and metropolitan examinations [those *juren* and *jinshi*]?' " (*RLWS*, 31: 428; *S*, 343). Here those provincial and palace graduates are stigmatized as nouveaux riches and compared to salt merchants. When urged by one of his friends to call on a local magistrate, Du Shaoqing becomes upset, being extremely sensitive to that official's *jinshi* background:

"I must leave it to you, Third Brother, to call on the magistrate and pay your respects as a student," replied Tu. "Why, in father's time—to say nothing of my grandfather's and great-grandfather's—heaven knows how many magistrates came here! If he really respects me, why doesn't he call on me first? Why should I call on him? I'm sorry I passed the district examination [becoming a *xiucai*], since it means I have to address the local magistrate as my patron! As for this magistrate, who cradled out of some dust-heap to pass the metropolitan examination [becoming a *jinshi*]—I wouldn't even want him as my student." (RLWS, 31: 431; S, 345–46)

Keenly aware of his low status as a *xiucai*, Du Shaoqing is at pains to avoid giving any impression that he feels inferior before a *jinshi* degree holder by reminding (not without irony) people of his glorious family tradition (his great-grandfather, grandfather, and father are all palace graduates).[37] Here one can recall Miss Lu's complaint to her husband, who is reluctant to strive for success in the examinations: "Good sons don't live on their inheritance; good daughters don't wear clothes from their own homes after they marry. I believe a man has to earn his own success in the examinations. Those who depend on their grandfathers and fathers are actually nothing but failures" (RLWS, 11: 157; S, 124, trans. modified). Miss Lu's remarks, though specifically directed toward her husband, are certainly revealing about the psychological burden borne by Du Shaoqing (as well as the author) for being a failure who cannot live up to the achievement of his forebears.

Much to everyone's surprise, however, when Shaoqing later learns that Magistrate Wang has been deprived of his title and is soon to be driven out of his official residence, he offers him lodging in his own house: "As for Mr. Wang, it's lucky for him he knew enough to respect me. To have called on him the other day would have been making up to the local magistrate; but now that he's been removed from office and has nowhere to live, it's my duty to help him" (RLWS, 32: 442; S, 355). Behind this bit of gallantry is an unmistakable message: although he is only a licentiate, his superiority to palace graduates is beyond doubt. This is a psychological struggle Du Shaoqing (as well as Wu Jingzi) must constantly wage to keep his mind at peace under the enormous pressure of his guilt at being a failure.

This leads us to the subtle relationship between Shaoqing and Shenqing, this pair of cousins. Many critics have pointed out that Du Shenqing is based on the author's distant cousin Wu Qing. The only extant evidence testifying to a strained relationship is two poems in *Wenmushanfang ji* expressing Wu Jingzi's dissatisfaction with his cousin when Wu Qing returned from the Erudite Scholar examination bragging about its excitement (whereas Wu Jingzi, though also recommended, could not go because of illness, an issue discussed shortly).[38] Although Wu Qing did not pass the special examination, later he did attain a *jinshi* degree, a fact that probably bothered Wu Jingzi tremendously (especially read in the context of the novel, where Shaoqing repeatedly shows special resentment against examination "upstarts").

In the novel, Du Shenqing is presented as an extremely affected literatus. His homosexual romance and his sponsoring of a contest among actors or female impersonators are the two important episodes in his biography. In fact, Wu Jingzi may have pursued these "hobbies" in his life, although in the novel his alter ego, Du Shaoqing, stays clear of them.[39] Equally concerned with his self-image, but unlike his cousin in almost all other aspects, Shenqing is careful with his money and determined to become a palace graduate through the examinations. Later in the novel he indeed becomes a palace graduate, although the news is casually revealed by a friend to Du Shaoqing (*RLWS*, 46: 623). It is curious to note the two cousins are never shown together in the novel. Although Shenqing offers a fairly long negative comment on Shaoqing, the latter never expresses his opinions about the former despite the fact that several times Shenqing is the topic of the conversation (e.g., *RLWS*, 31: 425, 31: 430, 46: 621). Thus, throughout the novel, the reader never learns what Shaoqing thinks of his cousin. This curious silence is pregnant with significance. Obviously, what bothers Shaoqing most must be the painful fact of his cousin's success in the examinations, especially considering Du Shaoqing's hypersensitivity on this matter.[40]

We probably can say that, to a large degree, *The Scholars* was Wu Jingzi's endeavor to deal with his own failures in life and to put these failures in perspective. He was torn between his aspirations for success in life (recognition) and his contempt for those corrupted by success. The most explicit autobiographically redemptive effort in the novel is probably Wu Jingzi's subtle reconstruction of a key incident in his past by having Du Shaoqing feign illness in order to decline a recommendation for office. There has been much controversy among scholars whether Wu Jingzi was really so ill that he could not go to the Capital to participate in the prestigious Erudite Scholar examination or he was just feigning illness in order to avoid being forced to take it. Those who believe that Wu feigned illness usually cite the novel's detailed description of how Du Shaoqing pretends illness in order to avoid a summons to the imperial court when he is recommended by a high official as a man of talent worthy of being recruited by the government (RLWS, 33–34: 456–64).[41] They are convinced that the autobiographical (or rather biographical) nature of this character simply does not allow for the idea that the author's illness could be real. This is a typical example of using the novel as a base for reconstructing the biography of its author.

However, if we emphasize the dimension of *auto* rather than that of *bios* in the character of Du Shaoqing, as James Olney has urged us to do with regard to autobiographical writings in general,[42] we may not find it difficult to accept that Wu Jingzi failed to go to the examination because he was ill. Furthermore, we may find the discrepancy between Du Shaoqing's behavior as a character in the novel and Wu Jingzi's actions more autobiographically significant. What interested the autobiographer Wu Jingzi in this novel was what he could have done rather what he actually did. The description of Du's feigning illness is dominated by a comic tone:

"When you are invited to [the] court to become an official, why refuse on the pretext of illness?" asked Mrs. Tu with a smile.
"Don't be absurd! What! Leave an amusing place like Nanking? Don't you enjoy having me at home, to go out with you in the spring and autumn to look at the flowers and drink wine? Why do you want to pack me off to Peking? Suppose I take you along too? It's a cold place, the capital, and you're so delicate that one gust of wind there would freeze you to death! That would never do. No, no, I'd better not go."
... Ordering two servants to support him, Tu tottered out looking desperately ill to greet the magistrate. (RLWS, 34: 463; S, 372–73)

After the magistrate leaves, convinced that Du is too ill to journey to the capital to take the examination, Du Shaoqing congratulates himself:

"Good!" he exclaimed. "This is the end of my career as a licentiate. I shall not sit for the provincial examination or the yearly tests again, but take life easy and attend to my own affairs." (RLWS, 34: 464; S, 373)

The lightheartedness and the detachment with which Du Shaoqing throws away a rare opportunity for career success and fame contrasts interestingly with repeated instances elsewhere of Wu Jingzi's pride at being chosen as one of the few candidates for the prestigious Erudite Scholar examination, which was held only twice in the entire history of the Qing dynasty.[43] To be recommended as a candidate was prestigious enough, and to decline such a recommendation was even more so. In the novel, Du Shaoqing wins increased admiration in the eyes of many because of his declining of the recommendation: in chapter 34, for example, Chi Hengshan defends Du Shaoqing's moral character and achievement before others by specially referring to this "admirable" act (RLWS, 34: 467); in chapter 37, a stranger wants to meet Du Shaoqing simply because he has heard of him as a gentleman who declined a recommendation to become an official (RLWS, 37: 514). Apparently Du Shaoqing becomes more famous precisely for this honorable act. Curiously enough, however, the narrator chooses not to mention to the reader how other characters have learned of this gallant act. Apparently Wu Jingzi had Du Shaoqing do what he himself had wished but failed to do. Illness, which prevented him from taking part in that examination in actual life, is here turned into a gesture of autobiographical wish-fulfillment—a redeeming act.[44] Paradoxically, it is the apparent biographical format (in which an other is the subject) adopted in the novel that helps fulfill the task of autobiographical redemption on the author's part—the drive to become an other has helped free the author from the constraints of historical presentation otherwise demanded in a formal autobiography.

If *The Scholars* were merely Wu Jingzi's wish-fulfilling self-invention or purely an act of willful forgetting, it would have been a much less interesting novel. What makes the autobiographical redemption so complex and fascinating in the novel is that self-critique and self-negation are always involved.[45] However, this subtle aspect of the autobiographical self can be properly appreciated only with reference to the representation of other selves in the novel. Another character recommended to the imperial government is Zhuang Shaoguang. His answer to his wife's question of why he would consent to go to the capital this time when he has never shown an interest in being an official is revealing in comparison with Du Shaoqing's act: "We are different from hermits. Since a decree has been issued to summon me to the court, it is my duty as a subject to go" (*RLWS*, 34: 472; *S*, 380–81). Later Zhuang duly travels to see the emperor and offers advice although he is not given an official position.

The implications of Du Shaoqing's act are further complicated when we later learn that yet another important character, Yu Yude, is urged by a friend to seek recommendation for recruitment by the government in the following terms:

"I am thinking of asking Governor Kang to recommend you, sir."

"I am not good enough for that," replied Dr. Yu with a smile. "And if Governor Kang wishes to recommend someone, the choice is up to him. To ask such a favour is hardly a sign of high moral character!"

"If you don't want an official career, sir, wait till you receive a summons from the emperor. You may be called for an audience, or you may not; but by refusing to take office and returning home, you will demonstrate your superiority even more clearly."

"You are wrong there," retorted Yu. "You want me to ask for a recommendation, yet refuse to take office if I am summoned into the emperor's presence. That would show lack of sincerity both in requesting a recommendation and in refusing to become an official. What sort of behaviour is that?" (*RLWS*, 36: 494; *S*, 400)

Here two different reactions (Zhuang Shaoguang's and Dr. Yu's) to recommendation for governmental office are juxtaposed with Du Shaoqing's act of declining. Zhuang's emphasis on the duty of a subject to his emperor can be considered an implicit critique of Du Shaoqing's feigning illness (apparently an act in defiance of this duty); moreover, Zhuang's act—he accepts the invitation to see the emperor but avoids taking any office—seems by implication to Dr. Yu to be a bit insincere. Consequently, Du Shaoqing's slightly affected gesture of playing the hermit is subtly shown to be inadequate in retrospect. This is a good example of how the autobiographical self is (re)presented through the representation of other selves (other characters) and how autobiographical redemption and self-critique are most effectively achieved in this novel.

In fact, the autobiographical significance of Yu Yude lies precisely in his function as an alternative choice with regard to what Du

Shaoqing has done. He is an idealized version of Wu Jingzi's intended self—what he wished he could have been under the enormous pressure of personal failure and the burden of the success of his forebears.[46] The commentator of the *Woxian caotang* edition insightfully points out that Yu is the most moral character in the novel (RLWS, 36: 501). Indeed, Yu is one of the few characters shielded from satire in the novel. The nonchalant attitude with which he views success and failure are the very thing Du Shaoqing unsuccessfully tries hard to achieve. Also significant is that Yu Yude is a palace graduate but lacks the usual arrogance of a person of such status. When Zhuang Shaoguang shows reluctance to see Yu Yude because he is thought to be an official, Du Shaoqing defends him as a gentleman without the usual affectation of a palace graduate (*wu jinshi qi*; RLWS, 36: 497). To a large degree, Du Shaoqing's (and the author's) bitterness toward arrogant provincial and palace graduates is aggravated by his failure to achieve those very degrees himself. The legitimacy of his refusal to deal with these people often seems undermined by this painful fact. Only those who have proved they can have success in the examinations (if they want to) are able to fend off the accusation that feeling uncomfortable around successful people is only a result of jealousy.[47] In other words, what qualifies or authenticates Yu Yude's indifference is the fact that he has already reached the top by passing the metropolitan examinations. This is why the gesture of feigning illness to decline a recommendation for an official position becomes so psychologically important to Du Shaoqing in the novel and why the novelization of this incident becomes so meaningful autobiographically for Wu Jingzi: it serves as an effective autobiographical redeeming of his past self, an imaginative regaining of the chance he missed to vindicate himself when recommended for the Erudite Scholar examination.

In the novel Yu Yude is carefully described as someone for whom the distinction between official and commoner is truly meaningless. He seems to have transcended the traditional concern whether one should consciously play the role of a recluse or an official, a concern that bothered Wu Jingzi throughout his life and many other characters such as Du Shaoqing or even Zhuang Shaoguang in the novel. The autobiographical necessity for the author to create such an ideal other appears to stem largely from his self-redeeming desire to criticize his past self without being accused of being too forgetful about his own past. Read this way, characters such as Yu Yude function as a special other that defines certain aspects of the author's own complex autobiographical self.

Yu Huaxuan is another character with autobiographical implications.[48] Many experiences of this character are related to the author's own. The account of Wuhe county is certainly based on the author's recollections of his hometown of Quanjiao. The narrator's introductory remarks about Yu Huaxuan are quite revealing:

> Yoo Liang [Yu Huaxuan] was not an ordinary man. At seven or eight, he was a precocious boy. Later he read, studied and thoroughly digested all the Confucian canons, histories, philosophical and miscellaneous works, so that by his twenties he was an accomplished scholar. He could immediately grasp any reference to military science, husbandry, ceremony, music, engineering, hunting, water conservancy or fire-watching. His compositions and poems were excellent too. In fact, because his great-grandfather had served as a minister, his grandfather as a Hanlin, and his father as a prefect, his family has acquired true distinction. But in spite of his learning, the inhabitants of Wuho had no respect for him. (*RLWS*, 47: 633; *S*, 516)

This background is reminiscent of that of Du Shaoqing, and of the author as well. Like Du Shaoqing, Yu Huaxuan is equally proud of (as well as sensitive to) the examination successes of his ancestors, even though, like Du, he is only a *xiucai* himself: "[My family has] produced successful provincial and metropolitan graduates by the cartload—that means little to us" (*RLWS*, 46: 624; *S*, 509). Unlike Du Shaoqing, however, who willingly lets others cheat him out of his money, Yu Huaxuan is extremely careful with his. Instead of selling his property as Du does (and as the author did in his actual life), he saves money and buys land. What is most interesting about him is the way in which he metes out punishment to a snobbish broker, Old Mr. Chen, which provides probably the most comic as well as the most cruel scene in the novel (chapter 47). Here the reader is presented with a reversed version of Du Shaoqing in that Yu Huaxuan is taking revenge upon those snobs not only on his own behalf but also on that of Du, whereas the latter in the previous chapters has been too proud to settle accounts with these people. Apparently Yu Huaxuan reflects a more vengeful aspect of the author, and his saving money and buying land are the very things that the author failed to do but wished he could have done in his life. Less obsessed with self-image than Du Shaoqing, Yu Huaxuan enjoys more opportunity for taking revenge against his snobbish fellow countrymen, a concern that bothered Wu Jingzi for so long, as is attested by the bitterness implied in the description of Wuhe County in the novel.

At the end of the novel, Du Shaoqing reappears in the person of Gai Kuan. We are told that Gai Kuan used to be quite rich. Like Du Shaoqing, he behaves like a philanthropist and is soon reduced to poverty. But he shows no sign of regret, even when many turn their back on him because of his reduced situation. Obviously, Gai Kuan is a replica of Du Shaoqing, another character created by the author as a way to come to terms with his own past (his squandering of his own wealth, a fact the author seems to have found difficult to forget). Unlike Du Shaoqing, Gai Kuan has to run a teahouse in order to make a living; later he becomes a tutor. His extreme financial distress, which Du Shaoqing does not experience in the novel, is certainly telling of Wu Jingzi's own destitution in his late years. From Du Shaoqing to Yu Huaxuan and from Yu Huaxuan to Gai Kuan, the reader discerns through a series of autobiographical images a process of deterioration that shows how the literati as a whole and the author as a member of that group gradually lost their usual status and sense of identity.

The literati ideal as represented by Wang Mian at the beginning of the novel, though an image not without irony in itself, disintegrates into a fragmented "picture" in which each of the four eccentrics specializes in only one of the four arts. While, in the almost utopian-like land, Wang Mian seems to be someone who, though not rich, enjoys an immunity from the worries of daily necessity, these four eccentrics have to struggle constantly to survive economically and at the same time desperately defend their "cultivated" images. The harsh reality they face at the end of the novel, in turn, problematizes the logic of the ideal of Wang Mian presented at the beginning. The nostalgia suggested in the character of Gai Kuan only enhances this feeling of a world probably too remote to be relevant. His apparently exaggerated idealization of the golden days of Yu Yude and Du Shaoqing in turn calls attention to the inadequacies of that world, which the reader of the novel has just encountered in the preceding chapters and which is obviously far from ideal. Here Gai Kuan's comment about the ruins of the Taibo Temple (RLWS, 55: 746–47) seems to call into serious question the meaning of the ritual ideal held by people like

Chi Hengshan, Du Shaoqing, and Yu Yude and its practical relevance. More specifically, Gai Kuan can also be read as an effort on the part of the author to rethink his own past, or the ultimate meaning of his own efforts to build a similar temple. Consequently, in addition to Du Shaoqing, the author creates many different characters in the novel to alert the reader to different aspects of his self (both present and past), which are often contradictory to each other. Wu Jingzi is keenly aware of his own multiple selves and of the need of different characters or "others" to "incarnate" that multiplicity.

Masquerading and the Autobiographical Dilemma

In *The Scholars*, Wu Jingzi sometimes seems bothered by the worry that his autobiographical urge might become too strong. Many factual data about himself or others he knew in his life are meticulously altered or reorganized around different characters in the novel as a protection against appearing dishonest or self-indulgent, a "crime" many Chinese autobiographers had been accused of. For example, the question of adoption and the resultant family disputes must have been a painful experience in Wu Jingzi's personal life. He was adopted by an uncle, Wu Linqi, who had no male offspring, and this may have caused bitter disputes over Wu Linqi's estate when he died;[49] this was one reason behind his decision to move from his hometown to Nanjing in self-exile. Although the novel has a detailed description of a family dispute over property involving the problem of adoption (chapters 5 and 6), there seems to be no direct relationship between Wu's experience and this fictional incident in the novel except for the vague message that relatives and even brothers may sometimes become enemies over money. Bao Tingxi is an adopted son, and although he enjoys a good relationship with his adoptive father, he suffers a lot after the latter dies because of the hostility of other family members (chapters 26 and 27). However, the correspondences between these episodes and what Wu Jingzi experienced in his life are so tenuous (and were probably intended to be so by the author) that the reader, even if well informed, can hardly detect any significant *auto*biographical meaning between them. This leads us to the ultimate autobiographical dilemma faced by Wu Jingzi in *The Scholars*—how to keep the best balance between self-presentation and self-re/presentation. In other words, when masking becomes too dominant an autobiographical strategy it tends to hide more than it reveals, as Pei-yi Wu has complained about some autobiographical writings in traditional China. This dilemma is closely related to many cases of masquerading described with great care in the novel—a rather "meta-autobiographical" anxiety on the part of the novel.

The previous discussion of the character of Du Shaoqing and others briefly mentioned their shared obsession with their public image. The reader of *The Scholars* is likely to be impressed with the power of the "public" as represented in the novel. No aspect of a character's private life seems to escape being "publicized" and being understood according to the interpretive framework of the public. The publicity (the public outrage as well as the public admiration) surrounding Du Shaoqing's drunken stroll arm in arm with his wife in the Yao Garden is a good example. This private family outing becomes an important public event among the literati. Those romantically inclined admire its unconventionality, and the conservative condemn its dissoluteness. It is the public impact that concerns most people.

Indeed, the plot structure of the novel itself also seems specially designed to keep the reader constantly conscious of the overwhelming power of the public. The unfolding of the novel's plot is punctuated with literati gatherings in chapters 12, 18, 30, and 37—all public events. The most important one is the grand ceremony held to commemorate Taibo in chapter 37. Given the importance of the idea of ritual in the novel,[50] the public role of a literatus is certainly one of the author's most central thematic concerns.

Furthermore, the narrator seems reluctant to explore the private life of the characters. Throughout the novel, the narrator never dwells on one character long enough to allow the reader to forget that this character is merely one member of a large community of many others: his or her existence can become meaningful only when it is interpreted in the public context of the community of the whole novel. Thus, *The Scholars* can be regarded as a case study of the literati public self in eighteenth-century China, a self that lacks authenticity. The narrative power of the novel in exposing this inauthenticity seems to derive partly from this "communal" strategy.

To a certain extent, it is because of the high consciousness of this power of the public and role playing that many characters in the novel turn to ingenious manipulations of public personae for self-invention. There are many instances of *maoming* (masquerade and imposture) in *The Scholars*. To appropriate a ready-made persona is certainly the easiest way to create a desired public image for oneself. In chapter 21, the poor lad Niu Pulang conceives the ingenious ruse of assuming the identity of the dead "poet" Niu Buyi as a shortcut to inventing his own public self. The poetic reputation of this persona does bring Niu Pulang some opportunity to rub elbows with officials who would otherwise never suffer him in their presence. But they also cause him many unnecessary embarrassments; with this new identity, he is able to commit the crime of bigamy without being punished.

In chapter 49, a licentiate masquerades as a Patent Office secretary, for the simple purpose of making a living: "Because I couldn't make a living at home I started drifting from place to place. If I said I was a licentiate, I should have had to go hungry; but when I said I was in the Patent Office, the merchants and local gentry were willing to help me" (*RLWS*, 50: 676; *S*, 550). Interestingly enough, his deceit is exposed just at the moment when the impostor and his deceived friends are beginning to watch a play:

The actor in Hung Niang's role came swaying in. . . .
Hung Niang had just begun singing, when gongs were heard at the gate and guards in red and black caps marched shouting into the hall.
The guests were puzzled.
"This is a new way of performing this scene!" they thought.
Then a steward came rushing over, speechless with horror. And in came an official in gauze cap, jade-coloured gown, and black shoes with white soles. He was followed by two dozen constables. The two foremost strode up to Wan and arrested him, then fastened an iron chain round his neck and proceeded to lead him away. (*RLWS*, 49: 667; *S*, 544)

Here masquerading in real life and role playing in drama are juxtaposed, and the distinction between the two is not so easy to discern. The description of the dress of the police official (as if he were in costume) seems designed to enhance the illusion that he is also playing a role in the play. No wonder the audience would think "This is a new way of performing this scene." The whole incident is narrated as if it were an episode from some melodrama, which adds to the sense of theatricality that permeates this chapter; here everyone is shown to be playing a role (and in the following chapter the role of knight-errant is played out).

The confusion of role playing in life and in drama emphasized here is reminiscent of the grand contest of female impersonators (here the business of "impersonating" certainly gains additional significance) sponsored and conducted by Du Shenqing and Ji Weixiao in chapter 30. This is not only a contest staged to grade the looks and talents of the actors but, more important, a carefully choreographed exhibition of the fine taste of its sponsors. The sponsors' "performance" offstage symbolically parallels that of the actors on-stage. For Du Shenqing it is the success of his own performance in staging the performance contest that is important: "News of this [contest] travelled from West Water Gate to Huaiching Bridge, and the fame of the seventeenth Mr. Tu spread throughout the Yangtse Valley" (*RLWS*, 30: 447; *S*, 335). Here role playing in drama is again juxtaposed with that in real life, and everything is, in one way or another, related to "show" business.

Playing a "proper" role is, however, often no easy task because the distinctions between different roles are already so unstable. In chapter 35, when invited to offer advice to the emperor, Zhuang Shaoguang, adhering to his principles as a hermit, tries as hard as he can to resist the offer of public office. When he is later released, it seems that he has succeeded in maintaining his integrity as a hermit. However, the life-style of a hermit is so widely admired that even the emperor is anxious to show his appreciation. As if the emperor wishes to see Zhuang lead a more authentic life as a recluse, he grants Zhuang a lake as an imperial gift. The lake, we are carefully told, has a secluded island in the middle of it. Now the hermit has imperial sanction to lead the authentic life of a hermit. Eremitism thus becomes imperially sponsored;[51] its usual function as an assertion of the individual self against the normal social hierarchy is thereby co-opted by the power structure of the society. Zhuang's effort to play the role of a hermit is further jeopardized immediately after he moves to the island. He is forced to "come out of the mountain" (*chushan*) when the island is surrounded by official troops because a guest turns out be a fugitive and Zhuang has to pull strings in the official world to save him.

Facing this dilemma of role playing, Yu Yude is presented as one of the very few characters in the novel trying hard to avoid assuming any role that can be conventionally defined. When he is urged to take the examinations, he does not refuse because he has never considered himself a recluse; when he becomes an official, he maintains the detachment of a recluse. It is in his indifference (*danbo*) to role playing that the reader is able to discern a desperate effort on the part of the author to challenge the definition of any conventional literati role, a difficult but never explicitly presented autobiographical agenda Wu Jingzi tries to achieve through writing this novel.

Throughout *The Scholars* there is a tension between the desire to find a proper role to play and the determination not to play any role so as to maintain one's integrity (or authenticity). This tension is in turn paralleled by another, probably more subtle as well as more paradoxical, tension between the masking strategies Wu Jingzi adopts for his autobiographical purpose and his ultimate intention to find and present his authentic self. Overreliance on the strategy of masking is likely to result in the eventual failure of his ultimate autobiographical agenda—the overwhelming presence of too many "others" might endanger the creation of a coherent autobiographical self. The implied satire and critique of various cases of masquerading and impersonation that abound in the novel, at least indirectly, question the validity of masking as an effective autobiographical strategy. The autobiographical self sometimes runs the risk of being identified completely with various masks adopted for that self, just as the author might lose his sense of identity while trying to play all those literati roles (something the autobiographical protagonist also tries to do in *Humble Words*). Moreover, the excessive concern with the public implied in the various role-playing efforts described in the novel sometimes seems to hamper the autobiographical endeavor. An autobiographical act is, after all, a making public what is private, and the novel appears to offer little room for anything private (not even the act of withdrawal as in the case of Zhuang Shaoguang). The public form the author chooses for his private enterprise of autobiography is always a problem, a paradox probably inherent in any autobiographical act—how to publicize what is private while keeping intact the personal nature of that experience. This in turn is reminiscent of another closely related paradox of self-writing touched on at the beginning of this study—how to write about one's self, even though self-writing, because of the nature of language, has to be a process of self-othering, a process of the self being displaced by an other or others.

The sudden appearance of an explicitly autobiographical poem at the end of the novel appears to confirm Wu Jingzi's uneasiness about the invalidating of the novel's autobiographical effectiveness by the many others that he has created for the very purpose of self-presentation. As if the author feared that the reader might fail to discern the autobiographical implications of all those apparently biographical accounts of others, he steps out of his mask of a detached biographer and discourses on his self directly in the extremely lyrical poem that concludes the novel. He eventually presents himself as an autobiographer—here the narrator and the author seem to coincide with each other for the first time in the novel as in a typical autobiography.

> For love of the Chinhuai River, in the old days I left home;
> I wandered up and down behind Plum Root Forge,
> And strolled about in Apricot Blossom Village;
> Like a phoenix that rests on a plane
> Or a cricket that chirps in the yard,
> I used to compete with the scholars of the day;
> But now I have cast off my official robes
> As cicadas shed their skin;
> I wash my feet in the limpid stream,
> And in idle moments fill my cup with wine,
> And call in a few new friends to drink with me.
> A hundred years are soon gone, so why despair?
> Yet immortal fame is not easy to attain!
> Writing of men I knew in the Yangtse Valley
> Has made me sick at heart.
> In days to come,
> I shall stay by my medicine stove and Buddhist sutras.
> And practise religion alone.
>
> (*RLWS*, 56: 761; *S*, 602)

Read independently, this poem is an elusive and general autobiographical statement, but, when placed in the context of the novel, especially when placed at the end of a long prose narrative such as *The Scholars*, it becomes a desperate autobiographical voice.[52] It is interesting to note that the author still claims that his novel is an account of others (Writing of men I knew in the Yangtse Valley / Has made me sick at heart) despite the autobiographical recapping of his past that constitutes the main content of this cryptic verse, a recap that parallels the *bildung* delineated through the biographies of different others in the preceding pages of the novel. As a result, at the last moment, the reader is compelled to *re*read the prior prose narrative and to *re*interpret its apparent representation of others in terms of the self-re/presentation on the part of the author. In other words, Wu Jingzi is so worried about the excellence of the masking effect of others in the novel that he has to cast off the mask of a biographer to appeal directly to the reader to reread the novel as a discourse of self-re/presentation rather than as an innocent representation of others. However, paradoxically, once he steps out of his camouflage as a biographer, Wu Jingzi has to end his novel, largely because self-presentation or straightforward autobiography, such as the author seems to be doing by personally stepping out at the last moment, would destroy the novel's basic autobiographical rhetoric, which relies heavily on the presence of others for its overall signification. Even at the end of the novel, Wu Jingzi is still searching for that forever-elusive balance between self and others.

At a more personal level, the ultimate autobiographical predicament, as adumbrated in *The Scholars*, lies in Wu Jingzi's inability to forge an identity out of the conventional roles assigned to him as a literatus (as suggested by the title: the "forest of literati" [*rulin*]—the engulfing communal presence of too many others). He cannot be someone other than a literatus (he cannot be an outsider) even though he no longer knows with certainty what really defines someone as a literatus.

This anxiety over role playing or the reluctance to play any literati role in the conventional sense finds very different expression in *The Dream*. Its author insists on the *private* significance of the autobiographical self by presenting a protagonist who refuses to grow up in order to dodge the adult responsibility of fulfilling a definable *public* role, apparently an attempt of self-assertion by default, a tactic partly shared by Yu Yude in *The Scholars*, though without too much success.

Many readers have read *The Scholars* as a social satire directed toward many others. This is certainly a valid reading. What the preceding discussions have demonstrated is that the novel's satire is also personal and often directed toward the author himself as a member of that same social group (*rulin*). The author's stance as an outside satirist is at best only momentarily successful, whereas his status as an insider is a painful fact that his satire can never change. The novel's various auto/biographical strategies explored above are, in fact, necessitated by a dilemma faced by its author—his inescapable fate of being an insider and his simultaneous need to become an outsider in order to satirize those insiders effectively. Satirizing others in earnest makes him realize that his own self has to become a target too. It is the tension created by this dilemma—the author's split identity both as insider and outsider—that complicates the novel's social satire, making its satire autobiographical as well.

An autobiographical reading does not deny the possibilities that all the characters in the novel can be read as having an independent significance and that all the biographies can be read as biographies of different people rather than merely metaphors for the autobiographical self. In fact, one of the unique autobiographical features of the novel is that the author's personal autobiographical agenda is always carried out within the framework of a much broader picture that depicts and explores the collective fate of the literati as a social group in eighteenth-century China. The distinction between self and other(s) is never meant to be, and could never be, clear-cut. A main conclusion of this chapter, however, is that if we read *The Scholars* merely as a detached novelist's satirical account of his literati peers and if we do not take into account the author's related personal dilemma as a member of that same literati group, we are making the novel much less complex as well as much less interesting.

3

The Self Displaced: Women and Growing Up in 'The Dream of the Red Chamber'

We are both frustrated—to the sky's end.
We meet. We recognize each other. What does
  acquaintance matter?
—Bai Juyi, "The Song of the *Pipa*"

In moving from *The Scholars* to *The Dream* in our exploration of the autobiographical significance of the novel, we encounter an immediate problem: we know much less about the author of *The Dream*, Cao Xueqin, even though the rapidly growing *Hongxue* "industry" (Redology, or study of *The Dream*) has emphasized reading the novel as an autobiographical work by seeking close correspondences between what is described in the novel and what happened to the author in his personal life. Despite the tremendous efforts by *Hongxue* scholars such as Hu Shi, Yu Pingbo, and Zhou Ruchang, our knowledge about Cao Xueqin has remained at best sketchy, and almost every "fact" about his life is disputed.[1] So far all attempts to study *The Dream* as an autobiographical novel have confined themselves to examining the "biographical" aspects of the novel, that is, to finding correspondences between events in the novel and the author's life (attempts that have a merit of their own), while largely ignoring the "*auto*" dimension—how the assumption of an *autobiographical novel that the author is the subject of his own discourse has shaped the writing of *The Dream* and how we should interpret it accordingly. In the following discussion, I shall concentrate on the novel itself rather than the disputed biographical data on Cao Xueqin in order to see how Cao Xueqin's unique autobiographical strategies operate to give expression to his own anxieties as a frustrated literatus and to reconstruct his own past self.

Another common problem that complicates any discussion of *The Dream* is the novel's extremely complex textual history.[2] Since most *Dream* scholars agree that the last 40 chapters were written by someone other than Cao Xueqin or that they are the result of a substantial rewriting of an unfinished draft by Cao, I limit my discussion mainly to the first 80 chapters.[3] The basic text used here is the modern typeset edition published by the People's Publishing House in Beijing in 1982. There are two main reasons for this choice. First, it is readily available. Second, this edition is based on the *gengchen* (1760) manuscript, which, according to some critics of the text, probably comes closest among all the extant manuscript versions (*chaoben*) to the final version of Cao's repeatedly revised manuscript partly because it is the version dated nearest Cao's death. It is also the most complete version (78 chapters [*hui*]).[4] Other versions of the novel will be cited as necessary.[5]

Male Anxiety and Representation of the Female

The Dream is known for its brilliant representation of female characters and for its surprisingly "liberal" attitudes toward women, which can be considered *almost* feminist even judged by modern standards. It has been claimed, not without justification, to be a novel about women.[6] At the beginning of the novel, the author explicitly states that he is going to write a series of biographies of the many girls he has encountered in his life:

In this busy, dusty world, having accomplished nothing, I suddenly recalled all the girls I had known, considering each in turn, and it dawned on me that all of them surpassed me in behavior and understanding; that I, shameful to say, for all my masculine dignity, fell short of the gentler sex. . . .

I decided then to make known to all how I, though dressed in silks and delicately nurtured thanks to the Imperial favor and my ancestors' virtue, had nevertheless ignored the kindly guidance of my elders as well as the good advice of teachers and friends, with the result that I had wasted half my life and not acquired a single skill. But no matter how unforgivable my crimes, I must not let all the lovely girls I have known pass into oblivion through my wickedness or my desire to hide my shortcomings.

... Though I have little learning or literary talent, what does it matter if I tell a tale in rustic language to leave an accurate biography of all those lovely girls. (H, 1: 1)[7]

Here the reader is told that the novel is intended to be a collective biography or "an accurate biography of all those lovely girls" (*guige zhaozhuan*). This biography of others (females) is, however, said to be related to the "shortcomings" of the "I," the male author who, despite his "masculine dignity [*tangtang xumei*], fell short of the gentler sex." The logic is that to talk about the girls the author has to talk about his own failings. Consequently, there is embedded in the novel an implicit autobiographical agenda despite its explicit claim to be a biographical project about others. Regarding the passage "But no matter how unforgivable my crimes, I must not let all the lovely girls I have known pass into oblivion through my wickedness or my desire to hide my shortcomings," the commentator Zhiyan zhai (the Master of the Red Inkstone Studio) remarks that "a biography of others can also be used for autobiographical purpose" (*yinwei zhuanta, bingke zhuanwo*).[8] Thus, even before the novel proper begins to unfold, the reader is put on notice that in the novel the borderlines between the autobiography of the author himself and biography of others are never absolute and that the stories of members of the "gentler sex" are closely related to the "failure" of the "I"—the male author.

My main argument in this chapter is that an important aspect of the autobiographical agenda in *The Dream* is the complex relationship between the male protagonist Jia Baoyu, the apparent alter ego of the author, and other, female characters.[9] More specifically, Jia Baoyu is an autobiographical reconstruction of certain aspects of the author, whose significance, however, can fully be understood only in the context of the representation of the female characters, who are, at least in part, displacements of many other aspects of the autobiographical self. In a word, Cao Xueqin displaces his autobiographical self (selves) in more than one character in the novel (unlike the usual case in autobiographical fiction). This, to a degree, resembles what Wu Jingzi did in *The Scholars*. What makes *The Dream* unique, however, is Cao Xueqin's masterful manipulation of gender strategies to control the meaning of the intricate autobiographical relationships among these different displaced selves; it is through this manipulation that a complex, multifaceted picture of a reconstructed autobiographical self emerges.

Using female figures to project a male literati author's anxieties or autobiographical concerns is a time-honored convention in traditional Chinese literature. To appreciate how Cao Xueqin novelized this convention to fulfill his own autobiographical purpose in *The Dream*, we must make a brief digression into the history of this allegorical convention. As mentioned in the discussion of the origins of the literati in early China (prior to the Warring States period) above, the group of people known as *shi* were situated somewhere between the ruling and the ruled; that is to say, they belonged neither to the ruling class nor to the ruled. The term *wandering men of skill* (*youshi*) captures their marginal status perfectly. This marginality—of simultaneously participating in the ruling process and being controlled by it—continued to affect the literati during the following dynasties. Their sense of marginality was even further aggravated by the establishment of a united empire during the Qin-Han period; the possibility of choosing a particular lord to serve was virtually eliminated. Thus we find Yang Xiong (53 B.C.–A.D. 18) nostalgic for the golden days when "*shi* did not have to serve one lord all the time, and the state did not always have the same ministers."[10] Sima Qian bitterly complained that as a historian in the imperial court he was treated like a jester whose main job was entertaining the emperor. Beginning with the Song dynasty, practically the only avenue for getting closer to the center of power was to pass the civil-service examinations.[11]

It is largely this experience of marginality that made the analogy between deserted wives and the literati, whose political careers were so unpredictable and full of risks, so appealing to them. This sense of shared marginality was vividly captured by Bai Juyi in his "Song of the *Pipa*" (see Chapter 2): "We are both frustrated—to the sky's end. / We meet. We recognize each other. What does acquaintance matter?" Here the banished official–literati poet Bai Juyi identifies himself with the female *pipa* player, whose tragic life experiences seem to parallel the political frustrations he is suffering.

Indeed, in a patriarchal society like traditional China perhaps no other social group was more marginal than women. Polygamy seemed to have lent more rhetorical power to the correlation between

The Self Displaced   79

a male literatus in political distress and a woman rejected by her lover or husband. Just like a wife/concubine who had to vie with other wives/concubines for her husband's favor, a minister had to compete with other ministers for the emperor's favor. A minister's loss of favor was often compared to a woman's vis-à-vis her husband—both were an experience of marginality. To different degrees, many Chinese literati suffered from this "concubine complex" (*xiaolaopo qingjie*). Mainly because of this shared marginality, literati authors liked to adopt a feminine voice (to view and present themselves as women) in their lyrical discourse as a plea for appreciation of their value. In other words, in a patriarchal society, where polygamy is openly practiced and where women are marginalized because of their "femininity," a male literatus is also likely to become (or feels he is) feminized when he is marginalized. As some feminists have argued, femininity is a gender attribute, not a fixed identity associated with the female sex only.[12] What makes one feminine is the position of marginality.

Moreover, the traditional Chinese conception of the cosmos seemed to have helped to enhance this sense of shared marginality. In ancient China all phenomena (natural as well as social) were perceived according to what has been characterized as a "symbolic correlation system" in which everything was categorized through correlation.[13] The "Wenyan" commentary on the hexagram *kun* in the *Book of Changes* (*Yijing*) has the following interpretation: "Although [the subject of] this divided line has excellent qualities, he [does not display them, but] keeps them under restraint. 'If he engages with them in the service of the King, and be successful, he will not claim that success for himself:'—*this is the way of the earth, of a wife, of a minister* [my italics]."[14] Here the cosmic correlation among the three *kun* phenomena—the earth, minister, and wife—is evoked to make an ethical as well as political point. The Han Confucian Dong Zhongshu (179–104 B.C.) further elaborated on this correlation: "In all things there must be correlates. . . . The *yin* is the correlate of the *yang*, the wife of the husband, the son of the father, the subject of the ruler. . . . Thus the relationships between ruler and subject, father and son, husband and wife, are all derived from the principles of the *yin* and *yang*. The ruler is *yang*, the subject *yin*; the father is *yang*, the son *yin*; the husband is *yang*, the wife *yin*."[15] Thus this analogy between minister (*chen*) and wife (*qi*) in their respective relationship to ruler and husband was further strengthened when they were singled out together with the relationship between father and son as the essential "three bonds" (*san'gang*) by Han Confucians.

The perennial literati desire to seek recognition for one's talent and virtue resulted largely from their frustration at being misunderstood or neglected—a case of marginality.[16] In attesting to his virtue, a literati author often took pains to present himself as something desirable or an object of desire (e.g., a beautiful woman), in order to increase his visibility and to enhance his attractiveness. In this regard, the famous saying "A *shi* dies for one who appreciates his value [*zhiji zhe*], and a woman adorns herself for one who admires her [*yueji zhe*]" is illustrative.[17] Here a literatus seeking recognition is juxtaposed with a woman longing for affection. The fact that both are described as objects of desire is emphasized by the correlative relationship between *yueji zhe* and *zhiji zhe*.

Many scholars have noticed Sima Qian's crucial role in canonizing the idea that "great literature is the result of great suffering" in the literati tradition (see Chapter 1). Viewed in the light of the feminization of traditional literati, the castration he suffered as punishment for offending Emperor Wu can serve as a powerful symbol for their femininity. The emperor inflicted castration (emasculation) upon Sima Qian as a poignant reminder of his marginal position—a historian-jester should never have trespassed into the realm of centrality where he could argue against the will of the emperor. A castrated Sima Qian was supposed to act "properly" like a woman and not meddle in the emperor's affairs. Here, Sima Qian's marginalized political status as a literati official was metaphorically connected, through the punishment of castration, with the degree of masculinity he was allowed to have. The loss of political power (or favor) had to be measured in terms of the actual loss of the male sex organ. Indeed, probably no other symbol is more potent than castration in highlighting the ultimate link between political status and sexual or gender identity. Interpreting Sima Qian's theory of "great literature is the result of great suffering" in light of this poignant fact, we might say that to produce great literature the author must first be marginalized—feminized or castrated metaphorically if not literally.[18] Arguing along this line, we can almost conclude that all great literature has to be feminine in one way or another.

Given this background, one should not be surprised to find that many traditional lyrical poems are dominated by images associated with femininity or, to use a more familiar Chinese term, *yin*: flowers, the moon, a beauty pining away, melancholy. A common poetic practice was the allegorical use of the figure of a deserted courtesan or wife to poeticize the male literati poet's own frustrations in his political career—a kind of "politico-erotic" lyricism. This "beauty and flower" (*meiren xiangcao*) allegorical tradition can be traced back to Qu Yuan, a fourth century B.C. poet who first explicitly used female figures to speak about himself as well as other males caught in political entanglements. Although there has been controversy over the specific gender identities of the persons referred to by the various feminine metaphors in his poem, this *meiren xiangcao* allegorical practice became an established convention in the Chinese lyrical tradition with the rise of the cult of Qu Yuan among the literati in the Han dynasty.[19]

The allegorical mode originated by Qu Yuan had such an impact on some of the Han commentators of the earlier canonical anthology of poetry—the *Book of Songs*—that they began to read many love poems in that anthology as allegories. These poems were reinterpreted as having political implications, and the gender of the *meiren* or "the fair" presented in a poem became problematic: it could refer either to a beautiful female or to a male of great virtue.[20] This tendency to feminize the subject of a poem (often identified with the male literati poet) thus became a part of the Chinese lyrical tradition. Arthur Waley even goes so far as to assert:

Love-poetry addressed by a man to a woman ceases after the Han Dynasty; but a conventional type of love-poem, in which the poet speaks in the person of a deserted wife or concubine, continues to be popular. The theme appears to be almost an obsession with the T'ang and Sung poets. In a vague way, such poems were felt to be allegorical. Just as in the Confucian interpretation of the love-poems in the [*Odes*] the woman typifies the Minister, and the lover the Prince, so in those classical poems the poet in a veiled way laments the thwarting of his own public ambitions.[21]

Although the literati poets' allegorical use of female images for self-aggrandizement is a well-recognized tradition, strangely enough, few scholars have paid attention to the question of how this lyrical convention may have influenced the representation of women as well as its relation to the representation of men in traditional Chinese fiction, especially in those works written during the seventeenth and eighteenth centuries when literati authors were becoming more deeply involved with fiction writing and were being increasingly marginalized, as I have argued in Chapter 1 of this study.

Compared with earlier narratives, there is a drastic increase in the presence and importance of women in late Ming and early Qing fiction.[22] More significantly, concurrent with this phenomenon the male figures in some fictional works also became increasingly effeminate,[23] and there was unprecedented emphasis on female talent in "scholars and beauties" fiction.[24] This feminization of traditional Chinese fiction has been interpreted as the positive result of the more liberal cultural atmosphere of the late Ming and, particularly, the influence of the radical Taizhou school of neo-Confucianism. The iconoclast philosopher Li Zhi's unconventional remarks about female talent and women's education are often cited as evidence of the emergence of a more sensitive attitude toward women on the part of some literati during that period.[25] However, this apparent sympathy toward women in literati fiction is probably a more complicated literary phenomenon than has been suggested so far.[26] I would argue that the general feminization visible in some fictional works of that period has to be studied in relation to the anxiety experienced by male literati authors and has to be interpreted within the general historical framework of allegorical conventions in the high literati tradition discussed above. It is conceivable, even probable, that literati authors writing fiction, who were well nurtured in the poetic tradition, would resort to *meiren xiangcao* allegorical tactics to air their grievances about the frustrations in their life, just as traditional poets had always done in poetry.

"Scholars and beauties" fiction tends to have many cases of gender switching: a young female impersonates a male and achieves success in the civil-service examinations.[27] Often a daughter is raised and educated in the same fashion as a son because her parents do not have a male heir, as happens in the famous novella *The Fortunate Union* (*Haoqiu zhuan*). Here the literati authors (almost all of them probably unsuccessful in the civil-service examinations; otherwise they would not have had the motivation or leisure to turn to writing fiction) seem to have found a way to alleviate their career anxieties by producing fictional works in which they could identify with the protagonists, especially talented females, and have all their wishes fulfilled. These heroines are able either to participate successfully in the examinations (always in male disguise) or to marry a degree holder and thereby achieve the highest success, definitely something the literati authors themselves were incapable of doing.[28]

In the preface to the early Qing collection of stories *A Book of Female Talents* (*Nü caizi shu*), the anonymous literati author explicitly juxtaposes his own frustrations and the fate of his heroines: he first complains that no one has ever appreciated his virtue and talent and then declares that he wants to be "the master of romance, the caretaker of flowers, and the connoisseur of female virtue and talent," and that he has written (or collected) these stories about female geniuses so that their talents, unlike his, will be recognized and appreciated by those with true discernment.[29] In the first story in the collection, the author-narrator specifically compares one of the heroines, who is forced into concubinage, to Qu Yuan, her neglectful husband to the King of Chu, and his jealous wife to the court officials who slandered Qu Yuan.[30] Here the shared experience of marginality and the ready availability of a well-established literary convention clearly enabled this male literati author to produce a book about talented females to alleviate his own male anxiety. Female talent and virtue also figure prominently in *The Dream*, where we can find a similar example of male anxiety being released through female personae, albeit in a much more complicated manner.

Another full-length Qing novel, *The Fragrance of Forest and Orchid* (*Lin Lan Xiang*),[31] presents yet another case of male anxiety venting itself in a story of how a husband mistreats and fails to appreciate a virtuous, talented, and beautiful woman. At the very beginning of the novel, the author-narrator openly deplores the husband's neglect of the heroine Mengqing partly because of the jealousy and competition from his other wives. At the end of the novel, he asks a rhetorical question and then provides his own answer: "Does the person who has written this story consider himself as existing outside the world of theater, popular balladry, and imagination [the realm of imaginative literature]? Someone might believe that he does, but I do not think so!"[32] The commentator is quick to point out in his interlinear notes that "those who read *Lin Lan Xiang* should consider themselves inhabitants of the world of this novel."[33] Thus, the sufferings of the female protagonist, which are described in touching detail in the novel, are explicitly juxtaposed with the author's own personal experiences as a frustrated male literatus; that the novel is meant to be read as an allegory about the author himself is unmistakable.

Frustrated literati, who always considered their own talent as failing to gain proper recognition (*buyu zhi shi*), seem to have been particularly obsessed with the image of a suffering female. The more beautiful, the more talented, and the greater her suffering, the greater the appeal of that female other to those male literati. For an unappreciated male literatus, probably nothing was more appealing than a story of a beautiful, virtuous, and talented woman forced to marry a poor, illiterate peasant who cannot appreciate her. This was the fate of the poetess Shuangqing as described in Shi Zhenlin's (ca. 1693–1779) *Random Notes of Western Green* (*Xiqing sanji*). This memoir-like narrative consists of various stories about the author's as well as his literati friends' poetic encounters with various talented and beautiful women (mundane as well as supernatural); among them the story of Shuangqing stands out as the most elaborate and impressive.[34] The main story in the book is about Shuangqing's poetic talent, beauty, virtue, and, most important, suffering. It is also about the obsession of the author and his male literati peers with "female talents"—their thrill at being the discoverer of such a talent and their empathy with her misfortunes in being a wife of an unappreciative husband. In fact, discussing her sufferings becomes a much-cherished opportunity for these male literati to lament their similar fate. We are told that "one needs two kinds of 'tears,' one to weep for a man's literary talent being unrecognized and the other to weep for a beautiful woman being neglected."[35] In this literati "memoir," Shuangqing becomes the ultimate symbol for male literati marginality: one of Shi Zhenlin's literati friends declares that Heaven has made Shuangqing the universal symbol for all frustrated people suffering from jealousy or unappreciation and that to deplore Shuangqing's tragic fate was to do more than mourn the fate of one person.[36] The so-called obsession with an unappreciated talent (*liancai pi*) is an important theme in male literati writings about female talents.

Thus, by the eighteenth century, this allegorical convention was well established in various kinds of literati writings (including vernacular fiction). What may have attracted the author of *The Dream* even more to this literary convention, however, was his own unique experience of marginality. Perhaps no other literati novelist suffered more from marginality than Cao Xueqin. Cao's ancestors were Han Chinese who had lived as Manchus after being captured by the Manchus around 1621. Thus, strictly speaking, Cao Xueqin was both a Han Chinese and a creature of the Manchus, or neither.[37] His family, because of their close relationship with the Kangxi emperor, once enjoyed tremendous wealth and power, but at the same time they were Manchu banner "bondservants" (*baoyi*). In a sense, they were both masters and servants, or neither. Cao's family had long lived in Nanjing, but after they lost favor with the imperial court, they moved to Beijing. Consequently he was both a southerner and a northerner, or neither.[38] In a word, he belonged to no clearly identifiable social category and is almost a perfect case of borderline marginality. Born into such a family, with the experience of extreme riches as well as of poverty, Cao Xueqin almost seems to personify marginality: as both Han Chinese and Manchu, as both master and servant, as both southerner and northerner, and as both rich and poor, the question of identity must have been a constant source of anxiety throughout Cao's life.

As personal bondservants of the emperor, without the sanction of the normal bureaucratic institutions, the Cao family's status and fortune depended totally on the whims of the emperor and on who that emperor was. This unpredictability seems to have made irrelevant for Cao Xueqin many normal channels of social advancement open to a literatus. The drastic decline of the Cao from among the wealthiest families in the land to almost complete penury was certainly a result of such unpredictability. What bothered Cao Xueqin was not the usual literati frustrations in the civil-service examinations (it has been speculated that Cao Xueqin may have been a *bagong* [imperial student by selection], but we lack hard evidence)[39] but rather the fact that he was denied *all* opportunities, which had once seemed so easily available, merely by being born into a family that underwent a drastic decline in fortunes. The sense of being born into a family that was once powerful but now declining rapidly (*sheng yu moshi*) permeates the novel, and lamentation over this fate is one of the novel's main themes.

The myth of the goddess Nüwa repairing the heavens, which is narrated as an account of the origin of the stone (the mythical symbol of Jia Baoyu, the protagonist), at the beginning of the novel is extremely significant in this respect:

Long ago, when the goddess Nü-wa was repairing the sky, she melted down a great quantity of rock and . . . moulded the amalgam into thirty-six thousand, five hundred and one large building blocks. . . . She used thirty-six thousand five hundred of these blocks in the course of her building operations, leaving a single odd block unused. . . .

Now this block of stone, having undergone the melting and moulding of a goddess, possessed magic powers. . . . Observing that all the other blocks had been used for celestial repairs and that it was the only one to have been rejected as unworthy, it became filled with shame and resentment and passed its days in sorrow and lamentation. (*H*, 1: 2; *SS*, 1.47)

Dismay over the lack of opportunities to use one's talent is clear here. The number 36,501 is worth careful analysis: Nüwa uses only 36,500 blocks, the number of the days in a century (in the traditional Chinese calendar) and leaves one block unused (which is apparently superfluous). The symbolic implication of someone that is unwanted is obvious. Furthermore, in referring to the number of days of a calendar year, the author (or the narrator) calls attention to the powerful traditional idea of timing (*shi*) or "not being born in a right age" (*sheng bu fengshi*). Cao Xueqin apparently considered himself born out of his proper time. Traditionally, the idea of time or timing had played an important role in a literatus's rationalization of his political misfortune; this again can be traced back to Qu Yuan.[40] In relating this concept to the emotional attachment of the author toward the many female talents he creates, most of whom suffered tragic ends in the novel,[41] we will not find it difficult to perceive the intimate relationship between marginality (which a born-at-a-bad-time literatus was likely to experience) and femininity (which he tended to identify with, when frustrated). The prediction in the Registers of Beauties (*panci*) concerning Tanchun that Baoyu reads in his dream—"Blessed with a shrewd mind and a noble heart, / Yet born in time of twilight and decay" (*H*, 5: 78; *SS*, 1.134)—testifies to the shared experience of marginality by male literati author and the female characters he took pains to create (probably based on those he had seen or met in his actual life).[42] Regarding the monk's judgment that Yinglian's (later known as Xiangling [Caltrop]) is an "ill-fated creature who is destined to involve both her parents in her own misfortune" (*H*, 1: 10; *SS*, 1.55), Zhiyan zhai remarks:

How many heroes, loyal ministers, dutiful sons, virtuous men, enterprising people, and poets have been condemned by this prediction? Here the author is apparently lamenting the tragic fate of these girls. If all these womenfolk have been inflicted with such suffering, what about all the men under Heaven [how much more so is the case with them]?[43]

Read in this context, Zhen Baoyu's strange confession that whenever he is beaten by his father, he finds yelling "Girls! girls!" effective in alleviating his pain (*H*, 2: 32; *SS*, 1.81) can be interpreted as an allegorical statement about the function of discourse on the "beloved girls" as a marginalized literatus's therapeutic strategy—a roundabout way to relieve his male anxiety. Zhiyan zhai is quick to remind us: "This is the novel's allegorical game [*da tiaokan yuyi chu*]. The author has probably written this novel about the fair sex of the boudoir [*guige tingwei zhizhuan*] largely because of worries and anxiety among the men [*jiling zhi bei, tangdi zhi wei*]."[44]

At the beginning of the novel is an account of the origins of the novel (*yuanqi*). The stone takes a trip to the mundane world because it is found to be "unworthy of repairing the sky." The novel is basically an account of the stone's mundane experiences; by inference, we may say that Cao Xueqin wrote this novel because he could find no use for his talent in more conventional realms, such as public service. Metafictionally, we are told that the whole novel has to be read as a product of a frustrated literatus.

In fact, the presence of Qu Yuan and the *meiren xiangcao* tradition initiated by him are quite noticeable in the novel. Baoyu's famous rhyme-prose titled "The Spirit of the Hibiscus: An Elegy and Invocation" ("Furong nüer lei") is perhaps the most explicit reference to this tradition in the novel. Baoyu specifically mentions that he is following the example of Qu Yuan and the tradition originated by him and claims that poems in this genre must have allegorical messages (*weici*) (*H*, 78: 1130; *SS*, 3.575).[45] This piece is ostensibly composed in commemoration of his maid Qingwen (Skybright), who has just died. But his frequent references to historical male literati figures and the intended incongruity between the political nature of the discourse and the female subject (his second maid) compel the reader to read the poem from an allegorical perspective.[46] Qingwen is often compared to a male official slandered by other jealous officials. The empathy between Qingwen and Baoyu as well as the author and the presence of Cao Xueqin's own anxiety as a frustrated literatus are obvious here.[47] In this regard, Baoyu's seemingly perplexing comment on the goddess of the river Luo is revealing:

"Take this Temple of the Water Spirit. The reason it's called that is because the divinity worshipped in it is supposed to be the goddess of the river Luo. Now in point of fact no Goddess of the Luo ever existed. She was an invention of the poet Cao Zhi. . . . The only reason I feel differently about this temple today is because the *idea* of a water-goddess just happens to fit in with the thing that is at the moment uppermost in my mind; so I'm glad to make use of it *for my own purpose*." (H, 43: 599; SS, 2.357–58)

This discourse on the worship of a goddess can be read almost as a meta-commentary on the long allegorical tradition in general. Cao Zhi's (192–232) "Luoshen fu" (Rhyme-prose in praise of the Goddess of the River Luo) is famous for its success in allegorizing his political frustrations in the form of a description of an encounter with a beautiful goddess.[48] Here Baoyu's lighthearted remarks amount to a meta-poetic declaration that what is important is the poet's intent and he is justified in using any image or creating fiction to express that intent. Because Cao Zhi suffered frustrations in his political pursuits, he invented the figure of the goddess to air his grievances, which were the result of his being neglected and mistreated by his brother, Cao Pi (187–226), who later became emperor. Thus the allegorical tradition initiated by Qu Yuan flourishes in *The Dream*. In the following discussion, we shall see specifically how this allegorical convention is novelized for an autobiographical purpose.

The Engendering and Displacement of the Autobiographical Self

At the beginning of this chapter I observed that the author's claim that his novel is a collective biography of many talented girls is a clever camouflage for his autobiographical agenda. Here I attempt to answer the important questions of why and how the male autobiographical agenda is accommodated or executed in the representation of female characters.

That *The Dream* is full of praise for women's talents and beauty is a cliché that hardly needs to be repeated here. On almost all occasions in the novel, women outsmart men. The poetic world of the feminine is often sharply contrasted with the vulgar world of the masculine represented by Xue Pan, Jia Zhen, and Jia Lian. Celebration of female talent is obviously an important part of the narrative rhetoric of the novel. And the strongest advocate of female superiority is none other than Baoyu. His curious assertion that girls are made of water and men of mud has often been quoted as evidence of his feminist tendency. The narrator offers the following explanation for his unusual attitude:

> Bao-yu had from early youth grown up among girls. . . . As a result of this upbringing, he had come to the conclusion that the pure essence of humanity was all concentrated in the female of the species and that males were its mere dregs and off-scourings. To him, therefore, all members of his own sex without distinction were brutes who might just as well not have existed. (H, 20: 283; SS, 1.407–8)[49]

This feminist tilt is enhanced by the strong element of femininity in Baoyu's personality, which has captivated the imagination of generations of readers. The portrayal of Baoyu is certainly the most successful in the long gallery of effeminate male characters in late Ming and Qing fiction, a trend briefly discussed above in terms of symbolic manifestations of the anxiety of male literati authors. However, the complexities inherent in this character warrant a more careful study as well as a broader interpretive perspective.

Baoyu's femininity is emphasized throughout the novel in his liking for female company, his habit of eating rouge and lipstick, and other activities associated with women. Grandma Jia even concludes that Baoyu was born the wrong sex:

> "He's a strange boy. I don't really understand him. I've certainly never known another one like him. His other kinds of naughtiness I can understand; it's this passion for spending all his time with maids that I find so hard to make out. It used at one time to worry me; I thought it must be because he had reached puberty and was having experiences with them; but after watching him very carefully, I came to the conclusion that it wasn't that at all. It's very strange. Perhaps he was a maid himself in some past life. Perhaps he ought to have been a girl." (H, 78: 1116; SS, 3.556)[50]

Baoyu's observant page Mingyan understands his master's wishes well and prays that "Master Bao [be] reborn in his next life as a girl" (H, 43: 600; SS, 2.359). In fact, Baoyu's appearance and personality are so effeminate that he is repeatedly mistaken for a girl in the novel: "But partly because of Bao-yu's almost girlishly beautiful features, and partly because she could in any case only see about half of his face, everything above and below being hidden by flowers and foliage, she took him for a maid" (H, 30: 426; SS, 2.104). Again in chapter 50 Grandma Jia mistakes Baoyu for a girl, and both Grannie Liu and a doctor mistake his residence, because of its special decoration and arrangement, for that of a girl (chaps. 41 and 51).

Femininity as embodied in Baoyu is not, however, unproblematic. Sometimes in the novel an incident that emphasizes Baoyu's femininity is juxtaposed with another that seems designed to remind the reader of his position as a male master: right after he is mistaken for a girl by Lingguan (Charmante) in the rain, Baoyu runs back to his own residence and asserts his "masculine power" as a master: "Bao-yu was by now in a thoroughly evil temper and had fully resolved to give whoever opened the gate a few kicks. . . . 'Worthless lot!' he shouted. 'Because I always treat you decently, you think you can get away with *anything*. I'm just your laughing-stock'" (*H*, 30: 427; *SS*, 2.105–6). Of course, Baoyu would not have acted like this had he known Xiren (Aroma) would answer the door. But this interesting juxtaposition does at least caution the reader that Baoyu is not always as feminine as others believe him to be.[51]

The full significance of Baoyu's femininity and its relationship to the author's own anxiety as a male literatus, however, can be grasped only when it is interpreted in parallel with another central character, Wang Xifeng, who displays a reverse tendency toward masculinity. In the novel, Xifeng spends little time in Baoyu's presence. They seem to dwell in two different worlds: her world of daily household management is alien to the place of leisure and aesthetic pursuits that Baoyu inhabits. But many details suggest that the two characters are closely related. For instance, right after describing how Xifeng has been the busiest person in the Jia household in arranging the details of the imperial concubine's visit, a visit that leaves everyone else prostrate with exhaustion, the narrator turns immediately to Baoyu: "Of those idle and unoccupied rest, the idlest and most unoccupied was Bao-yu" (*H*, 19: 261; *SS*, 1.375).

Thus even though they are shown to be completely different, a parallel relationship is carefully set up between the two. Baoyu is often implicitly or explicitly mentioned when Xifeng is presented in the novel. Sometimes they simply go to the same place or do the same thing: in chapter 7 they go to the party in Ningguo House together; in chapter 11 Xifeng pays a visit with Baoyu to the sick Qin Keqing (Jia Rong's wife); in chapter 13 they go to Ningguo House together to pay homage to the dead Qin Keqing, and later in chapter 15 they attend her funeral together. Throughout the novel Xifeng is often the "goddess" who protects Baoyu. Xifeng and Baoyu are Grandma Jia's two favorite grandchildren, and their ups and downs are intricately connected. Both are the thorns in the side of Aunt Zhao, who employs witchcraft to call misfortune down on them. In chapter 25 they almost lose their lives when they "are subjected by witchcraft to the assaults of demons," and both recover miraculously at the same time. In a sense, their fates are politically interwoven with each other. On the other hand, structurally, as arguably the most important characters in the novel, Xifeng and Baoyu serve as the respective centers of the two worlds that constitute the main part of the narrative of the novel.[52]

Most relevant here is the implicit gender reversal between Baoyu and Xifeng suggested throughout the novel. Just as Baoyu is characterized by his femininity, Xifeng exhibits marked tendencies that associate her with masculinity:[53] "She had been brought up from earliest childhood just like a boy, and had acquired in the schoolroom the somewhat boyish-sounding name of Wang Xi-feng" (*H*, 3: 42; *SS*, 1.91–92). The word *feng* in Chinese refers to the male phoenix; we are told that her nickname is "Fengge" (Brother Phoenix; *H*, 6: 98). Questions such as "What would you be like if you were born a boy?" are often asked of her (*H*, 45: 617). Wang Xifeng consciously or unconsciously has the tendency to look at things from a male perspective. In chapter 46, she tries to please Grandma Jia by making a joke after everyone is embarrassed by Jia She's abortive attempt to take Yuanyang (Faithful) as a concubine:

"You shouldn't be so good at training young girls," said Xi-feng. "When you've brought up a beautiful young bulrush like Faithful, can you blame other people for wanting her? It's a good job I'm only your granddaughter-in-law. If I'd been your grandson, I should have asked you for her for myself a long time ago. . . ."
  . . . "In my next life, perhaps. If I'm a good girl in this life, I might be reborn as a man, and I can ask you for her then!"   (*H*, 46: 643–44; *SS*, 2.426)

No wonder in the blind woman storyteller's tale, the hero's name just happens to be "Wang Xifeng" (*H*, 54: 758).[54] Her aspirations toward masculine power (expressed in overwork) possibly cause her to lose a male fetus (*H*, 55: 769; having a son is the usual acceptably feminine way for a woman to have access to prestige and sometimes even power). Symbolically, Xifeng seems to refuse to play the assigned feminine role of producing a son (a rather unfilial act on the part of a daughter-in-law) by virtue of her efforts toward masculine power.[55] In the novel she is repeatedly praised as someone more "masculine" than most men: Leng Zixing thinks that she "has a very ready tongue and a very good head—more than a match for most men" (*H*, 2: 34; *SS*, 1.83). Qin Keqing applauds her as "such a paragon among women that even strong men find more than their match in [her]" (*H*, 13: 174; *SS*, 1.255). She is even once compared to the "Tyrant King of Chu" (*Chu bawang*) Xiang Yu (232–202 B.C.), the conventional symbol of male physical strength (*H*, 39: 534).

What is more significant, aspects of Xifeng's masculinity are often presented in careful juxtaposition with references to Baoyu's femininity. In chapter 15, while Baoyu is pursuing his friendship with Qin Zhong, which is characterized by feminine tenderness, Xifeng is shown aggressively abusing her power to seek profit and money. Immediately after the description of the leisurely poetic contest among Baoyu and his female cousins (chapter 38) comes the revelation that Xifeng had withheld many maids' monthly allowances in order to make loans to others at high interest (*H*, 39: 535–36). The most poignant gender reversal between Baoyu and Xifeng is perhaps the contrast implied in the different roles each plays in their respective sexual encounters. Xifeng's punishment of Jia Rui, who has the audacity to lust after her and who tries to treat her as a female, that is, as an object of desire (chapter 12), is memorable. In that encounter, Xifeng disrupts the passive/active gender role pattern by assuming the role of an aggressive seductress and emerges as a triumphant conqueror.[56] In contrast, in chapter 77, Baoyu is forced to assume the feminine/passive role when he is approached by Qingwen's (Skybright) aggressive sister-in-law:

> She got her backside up onto the kang and drawing him down on top of her, put up her legs and gripped him tightly between them. This was something totally outside Bao-yu's experience. His heart started pounding wildly, his face turned scarlet, and his whole body began to tremble. . . .
> She began to get to work on his clothing, while Bao-yu made frantic efforts to pull himself away. (*H*, 77: 1109–10; *SS*, 3.546–47)[57]

Here we almost have a picture of the male Baoyu being raped by a female, a complete reversal of gender roles.[58] Consequently, this kind of juxtaposition leads us to see a fascinating switch in gender as Baoyu and Xifeng move toward the opposite gender roles.

In fact, Xifeng's propensity toward masculinity is shared by many other female characters in the novel. In chapter 63, following the example of Baoyu, who changes Fangguan's (Parfumée) name to "Yelü xiongnu," many of his female cousins change their maids' names, apparently to make them sound more masculine. Xiangyun's case is worthy of special attention here. She changes her maid's name (Kuiguan) to Wei Daying: "that name pleases her a lot because it reminds her of the saying 'only great heroes can demonstrate their true qualities.' 'Why does one need make-up to become a man?' she wonders to herself" (H, 63:900).[59] This is a fairly strong feminist statement in the sense that it suggests that masculinity is not something that belongs only to the male. What makes this more significant is that Xiangyun often shows inclinations toward masculinity: "The tomboyish Shi Xiang-yun had long since shown a passion for dressing up in military uniform and was frequently to be seen wearing a cavalryman's belt and tight-sleeved riding habit" (H, 63:900; SS, 3.237).[60] Thus accompanying the apparently enthusiastic celebration of femininity, as many readers have noticed, is an urge toward masculinity in (the subtext of) the novel. All the efforts of these female characters with masculine tendencies prove futile, however. They cannot even save themselves, as in the case of Tanchun, not to mention the family. The hopelessness evoked in their futility is compounded by a despair over the deficiencies of the male members of the family.

Deficiency is implied in the characterization of many male figures in the novel. The family's fall is largely the result of many of its male members' (particularly Jia Jing, Jia Zhen, and Jia Lian) failure to do their "male" duties. The most subtle lament in this regard can be found in the description of Baoyu. In chapter 73 some maids and servants are taking advantage of the meek Yingchun; Daiyu comments:

"How on earth would she have controlled a great household like ours if she had been a man?"

"That's begging the question," said Ying-chun, smiling. "There are plenty of men who live off the fat of the land but who, in a crisis, are no better at dealing with things than I. . . ."

Before she had finished, another visitor was heard arriving in the courtyard. Who this was will be revealed in the following chapter. (*H*, 73: 1043; *SS*, 3.453)

The beginning of the following chapter reveals that the visitor is none other than Baoyu. Consequently this general criticism of the deficiency of some male members of the Jia family is subtly directed more specifically at Baoyu. This kind of implicit criticism is echoed in Zhiyan zhai's observation on another passage. In chapter 36 Baoyu is much relieved after he learns that Xiren is not going to leave him: "'I hope there'll be no more talk of leaving me now!' he said, smiling broadly at her. 'Do you remember the time when you got back from visiting your family and tried to *frighten* me with all that talk about your brother wanting to buy you out of service and how there was no future for you here.'" (*H*, 36: 492; *SS*, 2.204; my italics). Zhiyan zhai comments: "The word 'frighten' [*hu*] is superb here. If Baoyu is really a man of decisive character, why should he be afraid of a woman frightening him?"[61] Examined in this context, Baoyu's poem on the historical/legendary figure Fourth Sister Lin in chapter 78 can be seen as an ironic self-criticism, however unintentional (*H*, 78:1126–29; *SS*, 3.570–74). In this poem, Baoyu commends her for fighting more bravely than all the male generals on her prince's behalf and dying more heroically. Those men are put to shame by her heroism because they cannot do their (male) job as well as the female Fourth Sister Lin. Here Baoyu is certainly deploring the unmanliness of the generals in comparison with this heroine. It is largely a lamentation over men's inability to do a man's job, such as participating in repairing the sky (*butian*), due to either incompetence or marginalized status (such as in the case of the author himself), but the distinctions between these two kinds of male deficiency are not always clear.

As we have previously seen, the desire to celebrate female worthiness in the novel may stem from the author's willingness to identify with those female characters who share his fate of being "unworthy to repair the sky." Born into a once powerful and wealthy family, like the capable female characters in the novel who are born into a family undergoing a rapid decline, Cao Xueqin felt that these females' talents as well as his own value, due to bad timing and their marginal status, were not properly recognized. Like the judgment on Tanchun, "Blessed with a shrewd mind and a noble heart / Yet born in time of twilight and decay," that on Xifeng fits the author himself equally well: "This phoenix in a bad time came; / All praised her great ability" (*H*, 5:80; *SS*, 1.135). Here bad timing (*sheng yu moshi*) is closely associated with "born into the wrong sex" (as implied in the saying "*toucuo tai*"). Tanchun is another such female talent with whom the author seems to empathize.[62] On many occasions in the novel, she is shown to be an extremely resourceful girl, especially after she is given partial responsibility for the daily management of the garden. Apparently her female status proves detrimental to the fulfillment of her potential. Frustrated, she complains openly that she could achieve much more if she had been born as a male: "If I'd been a boy I should have left home long ago and done something worthy . . . ; but as I am a girl, I have to stay at home and never say a word out of turn" (*H*, 55: 773; *SS*, 3.52).

Perhaps Cao's own marginalized status made him feel empathetic with women and even sometimes impelled him to identify with them. He needed to identify with those talented but doomed female characters (*youming wuyun*) in order to alleviate his own sense of frustration and to enhance his own visibility. The stories of Wang Xifeng's and Jia Tanchun's managerial resourcefulness and Daiyu's and Xiangyun's poetic talent are part of this celebration of female talents. Just like the deploring of male deficiency among the men, this celebration of female talent and admiration for their inclinations toward masculinity are intricately related to the author's own sense of being emasculated. The ultimate desire is to regain or reassert the masculinity unjustifiably denied to him. What fascinates Cao is not femininity per se but the feminine appearance that a man assumes when he is marginalized and the questions of how he can regain his lost masculinity.

Thus we should not be surprised to find many instances in the novel where the author's own male anxiety interferes with his avowed purpose of celebrating female talent. While describing these female talents' poetic activities, the author sometimes presents them as if they were male literati, obviously forgetting they are maidens raised in secluded boudoirs and inadvertently betraying his own male anxiety. For example, Xiangyun's poem "Admiring the Chrysanthemums" contains the couplet: "*Bare-headed* by your wintry bed I sit / And, musing, *hug my knees* and sing to you" (*H*, 38: 524; *SS*, 2.251, my italics). A literati official or a male literatus usually wore a cap.

And the image of *ketou* (not wearing any cap or "bare-headed") was often used to express a male literatus's defiance of the bureaucratic or conventional world. A girl in a noble family, however, never wore a hat. Thus to say a girl is "bare-headed" is redundant, if not irrelevant. The same is also true of the image of *baoxi* (hug my knees). It is difficult to imagine that a girl from a family like the Shi or the Jia would sit in that manner. Both of these are conventional images used to describe male literati who choose to defy the world (*aoshi*). For instance, these images can be found in a poem by Wang Wei and are apparently employed to vindicate himself as a male literatus. Cai Yijiang has pointed out that many details, though superficially describing the activities of those maidens in the Jia family garden, are part of the picture of the cultured life of contemporary male literati.[63] We might say that the descriptions of female characters in *The Dream* contain implicit and sometimes subtle references to the male literati world that always qualify and problematize their otherwise "realistic" (re)presentation. The novel's implicit male autobiographical agenda compels the reader to read metaphorically (or allegorically) these otherwise innocent images of the feminine.

As a male literatus, the author could not (or would not) empathize or identify completely with his female characters; nor did he appreciate their femininity (even femininity as perceived in a patriarchal society) for its own sake. There are certainly differences between the marginality experienced by him as a male literatus and that suffered by a female in a patriarchal society. Cao Xueqin as a male literatus was marginalized only in comparison with male literati closer to the center of power (politically more successful). This marginalization probably brought about his empathetic treatment of women. In his actual relationship to women, however, his status as a male changed from that of marginality to that of centrality. Thus, as a male and as a sometime marginalized frustrated literatus, Cao often oscillated between the poles of marginality and centrality. It is largely this double status that problematizes the gender issue in the novel. The double reversal of gender roles as well as the puzzling bisexuality of some characters in the novel, such as Baoyu, should thus become easier to account for. The admiration for power and aspirations toward masculinity inscribed in the characterization of Wang Xifeng and, to a lesser degree, in those of Tanchun and Xiangyun reflect the anxiety of the author as a deficient male—his wishes to get himself incorporated (once again) into the power structure of the society—to be in a position to do the man's job of participating in "repairing the sky," whereas Baoyu's obvious femininity is partly a metaphor for the author's own sense of powerlessness.

A Reluctant 'Bildung': The Burden of Growing Up

Of course, Baoyu as an autobiographical protagonist in the novel is extremely complex, and his femininity (passivity) may represent another, more deliberate alternative for dealing with the autobiographical dilemma presented in the novel. The preceding discussions looked at Baoyu's admiration for females. Upon closer examination, we will find that this admiration is by no means indiscriminate. It is largely reserved for unmarried young girls. According to him, marriage contaminates: "Strange, the way they get like this when they marry! It must be something in the male that infects them. If anything they end up even worse than the men!" (*H*, 77: 1104; *SS*, 3.534). In chapter 59, a maid quotes Baoyu as saying:

"A girl before she marries is like a priceless pearl, but once she marries the pearl loses its lustre and develops all sorts of disagreeable flaws, and by the time she's an old woman, she's no longer like a pearl at all, more like a boiled fish's eye.... How can the same person, at different times in her life, seem like three completely different people?" (*H*, 59: 833; *SS*, 3.138)

Nothing is more symbolic of adulthood for a girl than marriage, and this antagonism toward marriage betrays Baoyu's own anxiety about growing up. Throughout the novel Baoyu is constantly bothered by anything that reminds him of adulthood or of the fact that he is maturing.[64]

For Baoyu the immediate consequence of growing up is the strain it places on the otherwise carefree relationship he enjoys with his endearing girls. As early as chapter 30 he is reminded of this by Daiyu when he attempts his usual intimacies with her: "Take your hands off me! We're not children any more. You really can't go on mauling me about like this all the time. Don't you understand *anything*—?" (*H*, 30: 421; *SS*, 2.96). In chapter 57 Zijuan (Nightingale) also cautions him against acting too freely:

"Look," said Nightingale sharply, "let's just *talk* to each other in future, shall we, without any of this pawing about? Now that we've all beginning to grow up, it creates such a bad impression. However much that horrible lot over there say things about you behind your back, you still carry on the same as when you were little." (*H*, 57: 798; *SS*, 3.89)

Later in this chapter Zijuan again uses "growing up" to mislead Baoyu into believing that Daiyu is returning to her hometown to get married, an act that results in one of the most touching comic scenes in the novel—Baoyu becomes literally demented over this false news.

Thus growing up is always associated with parting (*san*), an important theme in the novel. Although vaguely aware of the ineluctable doom of parting, Baoyu does all he can to stop the flow of the time or to forget or simply refuse to see the flow of the time and to live in the present forever—to remain someone who will never (need to) become an adult.

"I don't see much point in getting angry," said Crimson [Xiaohong]. "You know what they said about the mile-wide marquee: 'Even the longest party must have an end'? Well, none of us is here for ever, you know. Another four or five years from now when we've each gone our different ways it won't *matter* any longer what all the rest of us are doing."

Little Melilot [Jiahui] found this talk of parting and impermanence vaguely affecting and a slight moisture was to be observed from her eyes. . . .

"That's perfectly true. Only yesterday Bao-yu was going on about all the things he's going to do to his rooms and the clothes he's going to have made and everything, just as if he had a hundred or two years ahead of him with nothing to do but kill time in." (*H*, 26: 361; *SS*, 1.509)

Here the seemingly casual conservation between Baoyu's two maids succinctly points to what he has so persistently refused to face—the grim reality that the party will come to an end with the passage of time:

Dai-yu had a natural aversion to gatherings, which she rationalized by saying that since the inevitable consequence of getting together was parting, and since parting made people feel lonely and feeling lonely made them unhappy, *ergo* it was better for them not to get together in the first place. In the same way she argued that since the flowers, which give us so much pleasure when they open, only cause us a lot of extra sadness when they die, it would be better if they didn't come out at all.

Bao-yu was just the opposite. He always wanted the party go on for ever and flowers to be in perpetual bloom; and when at last the party did end and the flowers did wither—well, it was infinitely sad and distressing, but it couldn't be helped. (*H*, 31: 430; *SS*, 2.109–10)

Whereas Daiyu's perception of the present is always troubled by thoughts of the future, Baoyu attempts to perpetuate the present by ignoring the future.

Baoyu's profound fear of growing up and his quasi fixation on the present are probably best captured in his strange talk about death.

"Now *my* idea of a glorious death would be to die now, while you are all around me; then your tears could combine to make a great river that my corpse would float on, far, far away to some remote place that no bird has ever flown to, and gently decompose there until the wind had picked my bones clean, and after that never, never to be reborn again as a human being—that would be a really *good* death." (*H*, 36: 486; *SS*, 2.206)

Here Baoyu wishes to freeze the moment of the present through the drastic act of death while he is still among all his female companions whom he will lose when he grows up.

In terms of stopping the wheel of time, the garden (Daguan yuan) functions in the same way in the novel. It is a grand architectural space within which Baoyu can forget about the quick passage of time and thus perpetuate the presentness of his childhood. Within its walls all the inhabitants are children. The only exception is Li Wan, a widow, who, however, we learn from Baoyu's comments on her residence, is considered to be unnatural and out of place in the garden. Often a girl has to leave when she is thought to have come of her age and ready for marriage. For example, in chapter 79 Yingchun has to leave the garden because she is to be married to Sun Shaozu. Early in chapter 34 Xiren urges Lady Wang to move Baoyu out of the garden because she is worried that Baoyu is too "grown up" to live in that place:

"Master Bao and the young ladies are beginning to grow up now, and though they are all cousins, there *is* the difference of sex between them, which makes it very awkward sometimes when they are all living together, especially in the case of Miss Lin and Miss Bao, who aren't even of the same clan. One can't help feeling uneasy. Even to outsiders it looks like a very strange sort of family." (*H*, 34: 467; *SS*, 2.164)

Indeed, the garden for Baoyu is a place where the usual strict separation between the sexes is suspended and where he can pretend that he is someone not that different from a girl. For him the garden symbolizes all that is not adulthood and its accompanying male responsibilities; it is a refuge from his father's pressures to study the

Confucian classics in order to enter the adult male world of the literati.⁶⁵

This reluctance to grow up and fear of adulthood are subtly underscored by the curious fact that up to chapter 80 of the novel Baoyu is under fifteen. Baoyu's childhood is certainly the main concern of the novel. The author devotes some 35 chapters to what happens to Baoyu during the year he is thirteen (chapters 18–52).⁶⁶ Although the reader is constantly reminded in the novel of an impending catastrophe, the pace of the novel slows conspicuously after chapter 18 (approximately the time the reader is introduced to the garden; a few chapters later Baoyu and his female cousins move into the garden) as if the author were also reluctant to move beyond that year and shared Baoyu's wish that the party never end. In other words, the year Baoyu is thirteen is extremely significant.⁶⁷ It is a year characterized by Baoyu's carefree life in a garden that is an architectural space where the passage of time can be temporarily ignored or even believed to be stoppable.

Some scholars have expressed doubts about the chronology of the novel implied in the changing age of Baoyu, as suggested in the reading above. For example, Dai Bufan theorizes that the present version of *The Dream* (as found in various manuscripts commented on by Zhiyan zhai) is the result of Cao Xueqin's substantial rewriting of an earlier work by someone else; one of the important arguments Dai presents to support this theory is that the confusion about the ages of some of the characters is due to Cao's careless rewriting.⁶⁸ Although many people have found Dai's theory unconvincing, some cases of anachronism Dai finds in *The Dream* are important and may in fact help us see more clearly the omnipresence of the anxiety over adulthood in the novel. One of Dai's arguments is that much of Baoyu's behavior in the novel demonstrates that he is older than he is said to be (or not as young as scholars such as Zhou Ruchang argue). In chapters 5 and 6, for example, Baoyu is said to have learned the lesson of "clouds and rain" in his dream and later has sex with Xiren. But apparently Baoyu is only eight at this point (according to the chronology worked out by Zhou and others), and it is rather inconceivable that he has become sexually active at such an early age. Later in chapter 25, Baoyu, at the age of thirteen, is entertained by prostitutes. Indeed, there are only too many examples in *The Dream* showing that Baoyu, despite his tender age, is sometimes capable of doing many things only a mature adult could do. Dai further argues that the character of Baoyu is composed of two personalities, one *xiao Baoyu* (the young Baoyu) and one *da Baoyu* (the old Baoyu).[69] This splitting of Baoyu's personality into two personae, I believe, may attest to greater subtlety vis-à-vis the anxiety over growing up that permeates the novel. It is as if the author is trying to keep Baoyu forever young while allowing him to experience various aspects of adult life at the same time. Being young, Baoyu avoids adult responsibilities (as a male member of the family or an adult literatus supposed to make choices, as many characters do in *The Scholars*); but simultaneously, Baoyu's sometimes almost uncanny precocity enables him to offer many perceptive comments on the adult world, thus addressing the concerns of the author, an adult who has already experienced so many radical changes in his life.

More specifically, this anachronism may reflect the author's own autobiographical dilemma; we know that the age of thirteen meant a lot to Cao Xueqin, and he seems reluctant to allow his autobiographical protagonist to grow beyond that age. There is evidence that in 1728 the Cao family's estates were confiscated and Cao Fu, whom some scholars believe to be Cao Xueqin's father or adoptive father, was deprived of the position of textile commissioner by imperial decree.[70] It is highly probable that Cao Xueqin was born in 1715, making him thirteen when this calamity struck his family.[71] The significance of the age of thirteen is also indirectly emphasized in chapter 78, where Jia Lan is said to be thirteen (*H*, 78: 1125). We know this is the year when the garden is searched by the servants sent by Lady Wang, an incident apparently designed to foreshadow the imminent search of the family house ordered by the imperial court and the resultant confiscation of the family estates, two tragic incidents to be described after the first 80 chapters.[72] It is reluctance to move beyond the age of thirteen on the author's part that results in the splitting of Baoyu's personality into two persons, the young and the old.

This discussion of the possible correspondences between events in the novel and the author's personal experiences is not intended as an exercise in looking for biographical facts behind the novel. Instead, it is presented to help illustrate an important facet of the autobiographical rhetoric of the novel—its persistent dwelling on the age of thirteen is something more than a mere psychological fixation on the part of the author. Rather, it is a deliberate attempt to search for an imaginary escape from harsh reality; it is as if the author were imagining what he, or anyone for that matter, could have done in the face of such an irreversible tragedy if he were allowed to relive that experience. Writing a novel about his past certainly creates an opportunity for reliving. What is of special interest here is that, unlike the reluctance of a typical child who just wants to have fun as a non-adult, Baoyu's refusal to grow up is not innocent. Baoyu's view on death (he would not hesitate to die if the tears of his female cousins and maids floated him to "nowhere," never to be reborn again as a human being), as we have previously examined, has such a cynical tone that it could probably have come only from a disappointed adult, such as the author, who had already experienced a tragedy. There are many places in the novel where Baoyu is shown to be almost deliberately indifferent to the decline in the family fortunes, as in this revealing conversation between Daiyu and Baoyu:

"We are all *much* too extravagant. Although the management of the household is not my business, I have frequently, just out of curiosity, made a few calculations, and I can see that our expenditure is vastly in excess of our income. If we go on in this way without economizing, the time will surely come when our credit is exhausted."

"Even it does," said Bao-yu gaily, "I don't suppose you and I will have to go short." (*H*, 62: 878; *SS*, 3.206–7)

A conversation in chapter 71 is even more telling of Baoyu's cynical indifference toward responsibility. Baoyu is advising Tanchun not to be too serious about her job of managing the household:

"You're much too thin-skinned, Tan," said Bao-yu. "I'm always telling you: you should pay no attention to what vulgar people say or do but concentrate on *enjoying the luxuries and opportunities that wealth and position make available to us.* Others who lack these things have some reason to complain. Why make yourself miserable when you have got them?"

"We can't all be as happy-go-lucky as you are," said You-shi. "All you think about is amusing yourself with the girls, eating when you are hungry and sleeping when you are tired. Each year to you is like the last. You haven't a thought in your head about the future."

"It's the time I spend with the girls here that really matters," said Bao-yu. "If I die, I die. What do I care about the future?"

. . . "Man's life is uncertain," said Bao-yu. "Which of us knows when his time will come? Even if I die today or tomorrow or this year or next year, at least I shall have lived my life as I wanted to." (*H*, 71: 1014; *SS*, 3.413; my italics)

Here the pessimistic and cynical undertone of Baoyu's remarks alerts us to another, more complicated aspect of Baoyu (the older Baoyu), whom many readers have long considered to be only a pampered but innocent child. Indeed, considering the imminent and unavoidable tragedy, we might appreciate a bit more the possible wisdom implied in Baoyu's philosophy of *anfu zunrong* (enjoying luxuries and wealth when they are available). Baoyu seems to possess the foreknowledge that calamity is to happen, although he is seldom shown as taking a conscientious interest in preparing for such an eventuality. This also explains partly why Baoyu appears to be so young and at the same time so adult-like. This complex character represents the author's ambivalent effort to come to terms with his own past self or selves.

That is to say, Baoyu is by no means a product of a simple reconstruction of the author based on his memory of what happened when he was a child. Autobiographically, as a character, Baoyu represents, to a large degree, a deliberate choice of life-style Cao Xueqin probably wished he could have made, just as Wang Xifeng and also Tanchun represent another alternative, a more "responsible" attitude toward the fate of a member of a rapidly declining family. And the choice itself is ambivalent, as demonstrated in the split personalities of Baoyu. In writing the novel, Cao Xueqin seems to have presented himself with at least two possible alternatives in dealing with reality, both of which aim to prolong the good days: Baoyu tries to perpetuate them by refusing to grow up and face the future, whereas Wang Xifeng attempts to prolong them by manipulating the management of the household. Both prove equally futile. Each alternative functions as a critique of the other: Baoyu as an alternative is a critique of the path pursued by Wang Xifeng and vice versa, and neither is a choice taken for granted.

Viewed in the light of this desire to delay the calamity, the fact that only the first 80 chapters of the novel survived reasonably intact may be partly explainable (albeit hypothetically) as the result of the author's reluctance to work out in full the tragic conclusion he originally planned for his novel—he could not bring himself to relive those painful moments in his life once more. *The Dream* is a "reluctant" *Bildung* in the sense that throughout the novel the autobiographical protagonist Baoyu remains basically the same. What changes is his surroundings rather than himself.[73] And furthermore, there seems to be a deliberate attempt to avoid change on the part of both Baoyu and Cao Xueqin: Baoyu tries to avoid change by refusing to grow up to assume the responsibilities a adult literatus is supposed to assume for himself as well as for his family; the novelist Cao Xueqin seems reluctant to move beyond his cherished memories of childhood and tries to delay the onset of calamity as long as he can by reliving his past through writing the novel.

The Dream seems to try to solve the dilemma of a literatus mainly through the expedient of presenting Baoyu as refusing to accept any of the traditional literati roles. In addition, it illustrates the frustrations one will suffer if one takes any of these roles through the slightly allegorical representation of a series of female characters who almost invariably suffer a tragic end despite their enormous talents. The novel is an apology for the author in the sense that no matter what one does one cannot reverse the irreversible. Thus, Baoyu's callous indifference and refusal to take any responsibility (or Cao Xueqin's own sense of hopelessness) are at least excusable if not admirable.

To look at this issue from the broader perspective of the literati identity crisis, we can say Baoyu represents an alternative, a choice not to make a choice—not to be anything. This is a much more radical choice than Yu Yude's in *The Scholars*, although both represent an alternative by default. In the novel, Baoyu rejects almost all the traditional roles available to a literatus. He detests the civil-service examinations as well as the company of *shidafu* (scholar-officials) (H, 36: 486; SS, 2.194) and mocks the long-honored literati tradition of *wen sijian* (H, 36: 493; a civil official who sacrifices his life to remonstrate his superior or the emperor). Although Baoyu is occasionally linked with the image of a *wenren* (for example, his liking for poetry), the association is never comfortable. Early in the novel, Jia Yucun groups Baoyu with some well-known historical figures famous for their artistic achievements and for their bohemian behavior such as Ruan Ji (210–63), Tao Qian, and Tang Yin (1470–1524) (H, 1: 20). Jia Yucun's characterization of Baoyu becomes problematic, however, as we gradually find out that not all of his words can be trusted; indeed, his name itself is a homophone with *jiayu cun* (false words remain). Cao Xueqin's quondam attraction to this *wenren* image is beyond doubt. In fact, one of Cao's courtesy names was Mengruan (dreaming of Ruan [Ji]), and a friend, Dun Cheng, compared him specifically to Ruan Ji in a poem addressed to him.[74] According to Dun, when bankrupt, Cao Xueqin had once pursued the bohemian lifestyle of a *wenren* for a while (drinking, being involved in theater, and the like).[75] What makes Baoyu so different from a typical *wenren*, however, is his obvious indifference toward his self-image; in contrast, figures such as Ruan Ji are known for their high degree of self-consciousness as *mingshi* (romantic scholars—there are many such examples in *The Scholars*). The traditional choices for a literatus such as "involvement" and "withdrawal" (*shiyin*) are simply not relevant in Baoyu's case until the Jia family goes bankrupt, a tragedy that was to take place in the part of Cao's novel which we do not have now.

As noted above, due to his unique background, Cao Xueqin's experience as a literatus may have been different from those of the other two literati authors examined in this study. As Manchu Banner bondservants, many of his male relatives did not have to follow the normal channels (the civil-service examinations) to enter the official world and earn a living. In other words, the literatus's traditional choice of service (*shi*) had very different implications for Cao Xueqin. This remained so until his family experienced a drastic decline. Pressures probably began to build on Xueqin to make a career or earn a living by assuming a serious literati role (that is, as an examination candidate) only after that decline. By then, learning, such as the ability to compose fine verse (which Baoyu has in the novel) or to paint well, was no longer a symbol of cultivation but a practical skill for making a living.[76] Cao's unique experience must have made his self-image as a literatus more problematic, an important factor to bear in mind when discussing Baoyu as a character embodying the author's literati anxiety. Through creating this character, Cao may even have mildly mocked his own past self—his infatuation with the *wenren* life-style when he was in distress. As a character, Jia Baoyu may be an ambivalent as well as tentative autobiographical attempt on Cao's part to transcend the stereotyped image of a *wenren* (though such an attempt is ultimately futile).

This ambivalence of Baoyu as an autobiographical character (that is, his inconsistent behavior patterns as demonstrated by the "old" Baoyu, the "young" Baoyu, and the "feminine" Baoyu) and the reverse tendencies exhibited by many female characters toward masculinity may also reflect a more general eighteenth-century literati anxiety caused by an increasingly painful awareness of the ambiguous self. Consequently, the long-standing allegorical convention of using female figures as projections of a literati author's male anxieties gained new significance during an age when various boundaries (including gender boundaries) were so frequently being crossed.

A Digression: The Problem of Confession

A discussion of the autobiographical dimension of *The Dream* would be incomplete without touching on the question of whether the novel is confessional. Many readers have found confessional elements in *The Dream*, and some even consider it a confessional novel. For example, C. T. Hsia finds that one of the main differences between *The Dream* and *The Scholars* in terms of their autobiographical propensity is the lack of the "confessional element" in the latter: "What is missing in Wu [Jingzi]'s self-portrait, therefore, is the confessional element, and it's precisely this autobiographical compulsion to tell the private truth, to recapture a more intimate reality that makes Ts'ao Hsüeh-ch'in so much more of a revolutionary against the impersonal tradition of Chinese fiction."[77] Thus being confessional is an important feature distinguishing *The Dream* from the other two novels examined in this study. The most confessional passage in *The Dream* is certainly the opening of the novel, a passage discussed above in the context of the strategy of self-re/presentation and the implied relationship between the implicit autobiography of the male author and the explicit biographies of the female characters. What also dominates this highly autobiographical passage is a sense of shame and remorse. His purpose in telling the stories of the girls, the author seems to be trying to convince us, is to alleviate his own sense of guilt about a life without achievement. In relating this confessional opening to various descriptions of Baoyu's indulgence and irresponsibility later in the novel, we might indeed conclude that *The Dream* is, at least partly, a confession of the author's past wrongdoings (the commentator Zhiyan zhai's repeated mention of *hui* [regret or remorse] on the part of the author seems to also confirm this reading).

However, the novel is much more complex than that. As is well known, there is no well-defined genre that can be called "confession" in traditional China.[78] Some scholars have tried to relate the sense of guilt and shame that permeates the writings of certain Ming loyalist authors after the fall of the Ming to this confessional aspect of *The Dream*. For example, Zhang Dai's "Self-Written Preface to *Tao'an's*

Dream Memories" ("*Tao'an mengyi zixu*") has been considered confessional, and it certainly has reminded people of the opening autobiographical passage of *The Dream*.[79] However, after reading Zhang Dai's "Preface" carefully, one feels that this is hardly a confession, because the author's present destitution is not the result of any personal wrongdoing, as he halfheartedly tries to convince us. His misfortunes, were, rather, related more to the collapse of the Ming, something totally beyond his control. In other words, Zhang cannot be held responsible for the tragedy that happened to him. Thus, the remorse he expressed is not personal and therefore hardly confessional.[80] The case of *The Dream* is somewhat similar. Despite all the obvious ironies implied in the presentation of Baoyu and his various idiosyncratic actions (all made much easier for Cao Xueqin by his stance as an autobiographical novelist because of the distance created between his present writing self and his past self), most references to "regret" or "shame" are at best superficial. Baoyu is seldom shown to be genuinely remorseful although he often expresses regret for what he is: a male born into a rich family, a fact beyond his control. The novel, in fact, eloquently demonstrates that no matter how Baoyu behaved, he could never change his own fate or that of his family. As I have tried to show, Baoyu's refusal to grow up and face reality and his almost blind insistence on staying within the protective garden are the only ways he can deal with what is totally beyond his control. There is obviously a sense of regret (*hui*) suggested about this self reconstructed through hindsight by the author. But this feeling of regret or even shame is different from that of true guilt because there simply never was a better choice he could have made (the alternative represented by Wang Xifeng is certainly no better). In a typical confession, the confessant usually wishes he or she could have made a right choice (otherwise there would be no feeling of guilt), but this is apparently not true of Baoyu. The prevailing sense of doom in the novel seems to have drastically weakened any feeling of personal guilt (if there is any) in the novel.

Another element typical of confessions absent in the novel is "conversion," or a sense of new spiritual discovery.[81] On the surface the novel's conclusion (either in Gao E's version or inferred from various clues provided in the first 80 chapters) seems to conform to the conversion pattern. But Baoyu's taking of Buddhist vows, as I argued earlier, can hardly be regarded as a genuine religious conversion. His motive for this action is his disappointment at his present situation rather than a positive faith in religion. Some students of Western confession have emphasized the close association between the need to confess and a sense of personal crisis.[82] In *The Dream*, strictly speaking, Baoyu does not experience a personal crisis. If indeed there is any crisis, it is rather a crisis of the whole Jia family or, more symbolically, the crisis of the literati class that Baoyu as a character seems to symbolize. Although we may be able to say that the novel is permeated by a sense of impending crisis, we cannot pin down any particular moment of crisis that would change Baoyu dramatically (even the drastic decline of his family fortunes fails to change him in any real sense). Furthermore, the novel's strategy of self-re/presentation and masking makes any true confessional expression (which always relies on direct presentation) difficult.

In brief, *confession* is a term that has to be used with great caution in discussing *The Dream*, a novel that is hardly autobiographical in the sense of being a narrative of radical self-transformation. Traces of the confessional can be found in this novel only if we understand confession as frank disclosure of one's private self rather than a publicizing of one's sinful self (Shen Fu's *Six Records of a Floating Life* is similar in not emphasizing personal guilt).[83] For a true confessional novel, we have to wait until the twentieth century when Chinese fiction underwent dramatic changes under influence from the West.

4

The Self Reinvented: Memory and Forgetfulness in 'The Humble Words of an Old Rustic'

If one cannot fulfill one's desire in real life, one can produce
an imaginary realm in which to do exactly as one wishes.
—Li Yu

If one judged the three novels examined in this study by their titles, Xia Jingqu's *Humble Words* (*Yesou puyan*) would probably appear to be the most autobiographical (the case of *The Dream* is a bit more complicated because it has more than one title).[1] The full title, *The Humble Words of an Old Rustic*, seems to imply that the novel contains important advice from an old man of great modesty, who considers himself to be of humble origins or a hermit. The title sounds like a formal petition (or a memorandum) addressed to someone of superior status.[2] The title *Yesou puyan* is closely associated with such expressions as *yeren xianri* or *yeren xianpu* (the rustic recommends to the king the method of sitting in the sun to get warm), which originated in the *Liezi*. In the "Yang Zhu" chapter of that book, a farmer who has never enjoyed fine clothing and housing discovers that he can get warm by sitting in the sun and he tells his wife that he will recommend this "warming" method to the ruler in order to be rewarded.[3] As a result, *xianpu* (sometimes also written as *xianqin*) came to be used as a polite term (*qianci*) to mean that one considers one's advice or gift to someone else humble but sincere.[4] On the other hand, the word *pu* also means "exposure," and the title may imply a confessional aspect to this novel (understood in the sense that it is a revelation of the author's inner thoughts). Thus I translate the novel's title as "The Humble Words of an Old Rustic."[5] The old rustic obviously refers to the author himself because at the end of the novel he is identified as the "unofficial historian" (*waishishi*, or fiction writer). Consequently, the most likely intended receiver of the author's humble words is a superior or at least someone in a position to reward the author's worthiness with recognition. The title compels one to infer that the novel centers on the author himself.

At first glance, the title may appear to have little to do with the novel's content—the story of its protagonist, Wen Suchen.[6] When we learn that the protagonist is meant to be identified with the author (the old rustic), the autobiographical dimension of the novel becomes obvious. One of the clever autobiographical devices the author uses is the manipulation of wordplay between the names of the characters in the novel and his own name or the names of some historical figures. For example, some readers have pointed out that "Wen Bai," one of the protagonist's names, is apparently a play on the radicals that make up the author's own last name, Xia; the last name of the protagonist's mother is Shui (water), and the water radical constitutes part of the surname of the author's own mother, Tang.[7] When this allegorical connection is made, the novel can be seen as an eloquent argument for the author's worth, a proof to be presented to someone who can truly appreciate him (*zhiyin*) or a demand for full recognition; the detailed account of the autobiographical protagonist's glorious career that makes up this lengthy novel is the author's ultimate self-vindication.

There is a direct reference to the concept of *yeren xianpu* (presenting one's humble gifts) in the novel proper. In chapter 144 two old men come to see the emperor. One of them, Ji En, claims to be an uncle of the emperor (the brother of the emperor's late mother). The other is the brother of Madame Shui and uncle of Wen Suchen. Their claims are later validated. In explaining to the emperor why he has decided to abandon his eremetic life to claim kinship, Ji En lists many reasons. The most important is that the knowledge that his mother's brother is alive will probably be a source of consolation for the emperor. By revealing to the emperor that he is his uncle, he is sincerely presenting to the latter a "humble gift" (*yeren qinpu*; W, 144: 1402). This implicit reference to the novel's title might suggest that the author is trying to underscore the fact that his autobiographical protagonist's claim to be a worthy literatus is as valid as Ji En's claim as the emperor's uncle. Consequently, the old rustic or the author is anything but a man of low social origins. He is, rather, a hermit (implied by the term *yesou*), whose great talents have not been properly recognized even though in the novel the protagonist achieves all the recognition he sets out to attain.

In fact, Xia Jingqu did try to present one of his works to the Qianlong emperor and complained about the difficulties in gaining access in exactly the same phrase, *xianqin wulu* (having no access to present his "humble gifts").[8] Apparently Xia was very confident about the value of that work. Scholars have been able to determine that the work Xia planned to present was his *Corrections of Mistakes in the "Outline and Digest of the General Mirror"* (*"Gangmu" juzheng*), rather than this novel as argued in some references.[9] The writing of the novel might have been, to some extent, an imaginary self-presentation (*xianpu*) to compensate for Xia's various failed attempts (actual or symbolic) to solicit recognition from an insightful superior. Thus, the modesty suggested in the title underscores the significance of the protagonist's marvelous deeds in the novel. Modesty and humility are nowhere to be found in the author's compulsive recitations of the glories of his autobiographical protagonist.

Consisting of 154 chapters, *Humble Words* is probably the longest known traditional Chinese novel. To summarize the plot briefly, after a series of adventures, the protagonist Wen Suchen achieves the greatest success imaginable for a literatus in traditional China: he rises to the top of the bureaucratic hierarchy—becoming the most powerful minister under the emperor—at the same time heading a huge and harmonious family of numerous wives, concubines, and offspring. The novel concludes with Wen Suchen achieving the ultimate ideal of a literatus as envisioned in the Confucian classic *The Great Learning* (*Daxue*)—attaining simultaneous successes in "cultivating personal self, regulating the family, putting the state in good order, and pacifying the world" (*xiushen, qijia, zhiguo, ping tianxia*). Here the profound sense of frustration and doom associated with a literatus we frequently encounter in *The Scholars* and, more indirectly, in *The Dream* completely disappear. Instead, what dominates this novel is, at least on the surface, an overwhelming sense of self-confidence in one's role as a literatus. Obviously, *Humble Words* has a completely different approach to the literati identity crisis examined in Chapter 1. To a large extent, this novel incidentally provides answers to the very questions posed in the other two novels about the meaning of being a literatus in eighteenth-century China. However, the ultimate implications of the protagonist's phenomenal successes in the novel have to be explored autobiographically in terms of the miserable failure the author's life seems to have been. It is this enormous disparity between the protagonist's successes in the novel and the author's failures in his actual life that alerts the reader to the possibilities that the novel's exaggerations might be calculated and ultimately meant to be read ironically.

Indeed, the contrast between Xia Jingqu's own life and that of his alter ego, Wen Suchen, is striking as well as pregnant with significance. By traditional standards, Xia Jingqu, like his contemporaries Wu Jingzi and Cao Xueqin, was a failure (if not a more miserable one). Among literati authors who turned to writing fiction to vent their personal frustrations, Xia's life was perhaps the most pathetic. He failed even to get the lowest degree (*xiucai*; licentiate) in the civil-service examinations.[10] He is said to have been recommended for the Erudite Scholar examination but failed (here we may recall Wu Jingzi's similar frustrating experience with that examination).[11] During his relatively long life (1705–87) he was dogged by poverty and illness. At the age of 47, he suffered an almost fatal illness. His sister took care of him and nursed him back to health, an experience that probably inspired the strange episode of Wen Suchen's getting sick and being nursed by Ren Luanchui and her maid Su'e in the novel.[12] Xia Jingqu must have felt particularly frustrated by the fact that throughout his life he served as a private secretary to various officials. He also befriended quite a few influential scholar-officials such as Yang Mingshi (1661–1736) and Sun Jiagan (1683–1753). He was close to the center of power and personally witnessed its effects, yet he had to be content to stay in the shadowy domain behind that power as a private secretary with almost no official status and recognition. This marginality Xia Jingqu experienced must have played a central role in shaping the autobiographical dimensions of the novel. The gaps between the glorious career of Wen Suchen and the pathetic life of the author should tell us most about the novel's autobiographical significance—how the author took enormous pains to create an autobiographical fictional other who is presented as having achieved virtually everything he wished for but never achieved. Here the autobiographical act is largely a self-healing process through willful forgetting and misremembering.[13]

Quite aware of the cathartic nature of his autobiographical endeavor, Xia Jingqu concludes the novel with dream scenes in which the protagonist and his mother find themselves showered with honors and praises by the Confucian sages of previous dynasties and their mothers; it is as if he is reminding the reader that the whole novel is a wish-fulfilling fantasy that should not be taken too literally. This kind of self-conscious playful touch is certainly not unique in the novel. In chapter 146, "Events in [Suchen's] Life Are Re-enacted One by One in a Play That Contains One Hundred Scenes / The Life-Experiences of the Spectators Are Dramatized Right Before Their Own Eyes by One Hundred Actors on the Stage," all important events in Suchen's life are dramatized in a play. We are told that this is a recap (almost at the end of the novel) of what the reader has read so far about the protagonist. The chapter is a detailed account of the interactions between the dramatic scenes of the play and the members of the audience, who are participants in the events being re-enacted on stage at that moment. The boundaries between real-life experiences and theatrical performances become even more blurred when Suchen's mother offers the following comments on one particular act that has no basis in the past: "The whole drama is based on actual events; only this act is based on pure fiction, and, therefore, it must be a real drama for that very reason!" (W, 146: 1425). Is the reader to conclude that a real novel, such as *Humble Words*, should be based on nothing but pure fabrication? On another occasion in the novel (chaps. 48 and 49), a Daoist priest compares Suchen to the well-known daydreamer Scholar Lu. According to the legend, a Daoist immortal gives a frustrated young student, Scholar Lu, a magic pillow. Falling asleep on this pillow, he begins to dream that he has achieved all the glories he has hoped for. Upon awakening, he is disappointed to find out it was only a dream.[14] Although Suchen laughs at this comparison, declaring that the story is nothing more than Daoist propaganda, he immediately falls asleep and dreams that he has been condemned to death by the emperor. At one point in the novel, the narrator refers to Suchen by the name of Scholar Lu, a synonym for a daydreamer who can fulfill his wishes only through dreaming (W, 48: 472).[15]

The suggestion that the reader should not take the author to task too harshly if he is found guilty of exaggeration in willfully forgetting and misremembering his past self(ves) in his autobiographical adventure is always there in the novel. *Humble Words*, in other words, can be read as the author's playing with his memories and imagination rather than an earnest autobiographical enterprise in the usual sense, a gesture related to the eighteenth-century cynicism we have discussed. This is a factor to keep in mind as we examine the specific autobiographical implications of this novel.

Reality and Fantasy: The Dilemma of Being a Super-literatus

A convenient point of departure for discussing autobiographical signification in *Humble Words* is the identity crisis experienced by many literati in eighteenth-century China. The preceding chapters have shown how two other literati novelists, Wu Jingzi and Cao Xueqin, tried to cope with this problem in their respective autobiographical agendas, a problem that seems to loom especially large in *The Scholars*. The seriousness and urgency of this crisis are symbolically captured at the end of this novel in the allegorical description of the four eccentrics, each of whom can master only *one* of the four arts (zither, chess, calligraphy, and painting) considered the necessary accomplishments of a cultivated literatus. The ideal of Wang Mian carefully presented at the beginning of the novel disintegrates into the fragmented picture of these four figures. Recall Chi Hengshan's bitter remarks in the novel: "Scholars should stick to scholarship without trying to become officials, and officials should stick to officialdom without trying to be scholars too. A man who wants to be both will succeed in neither!" (*RLWS*, 49: 662; *S*, 540). Here Chi Hengshan is dismayed at the increasingly obvious fact that the ideal of being both a learned scholar and a successful official is no longer attainable. In the novel, almost all the traditional literati roles are paraded forth one by one, only to be found inadequate. Furthermore, the large number of literati characters presented in *The Scholars* as well as the novel's overall episodic structure (the fact that the novel is made of various seemingly independent biographies of different characters) contribute to the effect of fragmentation and disintegration, an effect that has apparently enhanced the sense of an identity crisis.

Like most autobiographical novels in the West, *Humble Words* is structured around the life-story of a single character, Wen Suchen. This is rather unusual in the history of the traditional Chinese novel, which consists mostly of works characterized by a "decentered" structure with a long gallery of characters, none of whom is a protagonist in a strict sense (not even Baoyu in *The Dream*). This becomes even more significant given the novel's enormous length—154 chapters. This unique structure is partly a result of the author's concentrated endeavor to create an unforgettable autobiographical other—a superhero of magnificent proportions.

Contrary to many frustrated literati in *The Scholars*, Wen Suchen seems to be not only comfortable but also extremely successful in all the traditional literati roles he chooses to play, a learned scholar, an able official, and a great military strategist. Numerous events in the novel showcase him as a paragon of a Confucian literatus. The novel is in fact an elaborate account of how Wen Suchen fulfills his potential as a traditional literatus. What receives special emphasis in the novel is the intimate relationship between Wen Suchen's enormous success in public service (though he does not enter the service through the normal channel of the examinations) and his deep attachment to the neo-Confucian idea of self-cultivation. He is repeatedly praised by the crown prince as a perfect example of "sage within and king without" (*neisheng waiwang*; W, 87: 814, 88: 825), a perennial ideal that many Confucians strove hard to fulfill but found unreachable and even irrelevant, as we have seen in the other two novels discussed here.

On many occasions in the novel, the reader is indirectly urged to compare Wen Suchen and the ultimate sage, Confucius, whose ideas and life played a central role in forming the literati tradition. In chapter 66, despite Suchen's repeated displays of modesty, his friend and follower Feixiong insists on calling him "loyal Minister Wen" (a title the crown prince grants to Suchen when he risks his life to remonstrate with the emperor Xianzong) and argues that "even Confucius claimed to be inferior to an old farmer. You will naturally refuse to accept the title of a loyal minister" (W, 66: 625). Later in the novel when Suchen apologizes for appearing in disguise, the crown prince comforts him by saying, "This is like what Confucius had in mind when he passed through the state of Song disguised. There is nothing to apologize for" (W, 87: 812). In his dream at the end of the novel,

Suchen finds himself in the Heritage Temple (Xinchuan dian). In that temple, he sees his own spirit tablet (*shenwei*) standing right next to those of Zhu Xi and other famous Confucian sages. According to his friend Jingting, who has ushered him there, because of his glorious achievement of successfully eradicating Buddhism and Daoism throughout the country, his tablet should proceed even those of Cheng Yi (1033–1107) and Zhu Xi on the rostrum of Confucian sages. A further link to Confucius is the name "Suchen" (literally meaning the "unappointed minister"), which would immediately remind the traditional reader of Confucius, who has often been called the *suwang* (the uncrowned king).[16] Thus, Suchen, the unappointed minister, is following the cause of the uncrowned king, Confucius. Furthermore, the concept of Confucius as an uncrowned king is closely associated with a particular tradition in Confucianism that tends to portray Confucius as a messiah-like giant, a king without the formal title of a king, as implied by the title of *suwang*.[17]

Suchen is often presented as a messianic crusader on a mission to save the country and to eradicate heresies. His meticulous attention to the proper ritual between an emperor and a minister notwithstanding,[18] Suchen is a powerful political figure who tends to replace the emperor and become the country's de facto ruler. In the last third of the novel, Suchen often acts in the capacity of an "uncrowned king." We are told that the emperor grants him the title "Sufu" (literally "a father figure without the actual title of father"). Thus, his role is changed almost from unappointed minister to "father of the nation" (W, 119: 1129). Read in this context, the old emperor Xianzong may be justified in worrying that Wen Suchen's unprecedented popularity among the people will pose a serious threat to the rule of the imperial family (W, 116: 1092). In fact, to minimize the potential of possible conflicts between the father of the nation and the emperor, the author has many of Suchen's offspring marry members of the royal family (the emperor suggests these marriages; W, 141: 1366). This large-scale intermarriage seems to help diminish the sacred distinction between the royal and the nonroyal and that between a crowned king and an uncrowned king. Despite his obviously conservative ideological background, Xia Jingqu's autobiographical self in the novel does carry some unexpectedly subversive implications. The loyal minister might not be so loyal after all. In his endeavor to apotheosize his alter ego, the author may have inadvertently undermined many conservative values he set out to promote, among which was probably the idea of loyalty, an important part of the orthodox Confucian ideology the Qing monarchy tried to promote.

Equally problematic is the author's effort to present the protagonist as a man of superior talent. Wen Suchen's unprecedented achievements in his public career are largely a result of his enormous talent, which, however, is not confined only to those areas conventionally reserved for a literatus. He is a skilled fighter, an accomplished mathematician, and a superb medical doctor. In chapter 1 of the novel we are told the protagonist is a *tongcai* (a man of all-around talents):

Wen Suchen is a "tough" man with a rare talent; he has traveled all over the country, and his mind is as broad as the sky; not seeking glory and fame in public office, he is capable of political insight just like Qidiao; not appearing to be romantic, he can be a great lover like Song Yu; he can compose verse like Xiangru; his knowledge of military strategies can be compared to that of Zhuge; with a gentle appearance, he possesses enormous physical strength; he is brave enough to slay a dragon, and his commanding presence often awes people; his knowledge of mathematics and astronomy is even greater than Yixing; his expertise in medicine is as good as that of Zhongjing; willing to give up his life for his friends, he strictly follows the Confucian idea of ritual propriety; he is a genuine Confucian with great courage and a man of repute with no regard for snobbery. (W, 1: 2)

This introduction of Wen Suchen in glowing superlatives at the beginning of the novel should prepare the reader for the achievements of this superhero in the following pages. What is most relevant to our discussion of the issue of literati identity here is that some of the talents listed might not be considered essential to the makeup of a model literatus, such as Wen Suchen's rare physical prowess and his superb skill as a doctor. In fact these two special "talents" are instrumental in helping him in his crusade to save the country from being destroyed by crooked officials, plotting eunuchs, and rebellious princes and from being corrupted by the nefarious influences of the two "heterodox" religions, Buddhism and Daoism, despite the novel's more ostensible emphasis on Wen Suchen's orthodox Confucian virtues. The battleground is the main arena in which Wen Suchen proves his worth to others and carries out his various missions of knight-errantry. The first two-thirds of the novel is full of descriptions of physical feats in which Wen overpowers his otherwise formidable enemies. It is largely because of his willingness and, more important, his incredible ability (mainly martial as well as medical) to save people from various threats (often death) that he is able to win over so many friends and followers, who later help him to crush all the rebels and defend the crown prince, who later becomes the emperor Xiaozong.

In the first half of the novel, Wen Suchen is presented as a great knight-errant rather than a sagely Confucian literatus who makes claims by virtue of his moral cultivation and book learning, although the reader is repeatedly reminded that Wen Suchen is extremely learned in the Confucian classics and other kinds of knowledge. Whenever someone (often a girl) is in danger, it is always Wen Suchen who comes to the rescue. Actually, his first adventure in the novel (his study-tour to Hangzhou) is only an excuse for knight-errantry. He saves Luanchui from the hands of the evil monks and thus initiates a strange "Confucian" romance that ends with the two becoming sworn brother and sister. And later Liu Dalang urges his sister, Xuangu, to offer herself to Wen Suchen as a concubine in order to show his gratitude to the latter for saving his life. The pattern of rewarding chivalrous deeds (particularly saving another's life) with the devotion of a beauty or with the friendship and loyalty of an able friend is repeated again and again in Wen Suchen's adventures throughout the first half of the novel.

This emphasis on knight-errantry and physical prowess may reflect a desire on the author's part to redefine or rectify certain aspects of the conventional image of a literatus. In trying to create a perfect literatus of superheroic dimensions, the author, in fact, presents an uneasy image of a *wenxia* (a literati knight-errant).[19] This attempt might belie an anxiety at a deeper level. Xia Jingqu must have felt a lack in the conventional image of a literatus—an effeminate scholar who takes pride in his book learning rather than in martial arts.[20] This is reminiscent of Lynn A. Struve's finding that in some writings of the mid-Kangxi period there was a marked preference "for a more martial brand of heroism similar to that of the traditional Chinese 'knight-errant' (*yu-hsia*), and for subjects who, though they may not have died in the [dynastic] changeover, took vigorous, necessary, practical, and physically demanding action to save their dynasty and their people."[21]

Looked at from a different, but related, angle, this emphasis on practical and physical ability may be understood as a reaction to the author's feelings of emasculation (powerlessness) as a frustrated literatus. In the previous discussion of *The Dream*, we examined how the experience of marginality tended to feminize literati and how this feminization found expression in literati fiction (the phenomenon of male characters becoming increasingly effeminate in Ming and Qing fictional works). Although we can surmise that Xia Jingqu similarly suffered from marginality and feelings of emasculation, he, rather than identify with the marginal female as Cao Xueqin apparently did in his novel, tried instead to reassert his masculinity in his alter ego by underscoring, among other things, Wen Suchen's physical prowess and male sexual potency. Nothing looks more masculine than being an invincible knight-errant who always comes to the rescue of defenseless women. Wen Suchen's sexual potency is also repeatedly emphasized in the novel.[22] The tendency to emphasize the masculinity of a literati protagonist is certainly not unique to *Humble Words*. A novel produced in the previous century, *The Fortunate Union*, exhibits a similar tendency. In that novel, the male protagonist Tie Zhongyu is presented as a literati knight-errant with a strong sense of Confucian morality; he, too, is known for his physical (though not necessarily sexual) prowess.[23]

Knight-errantry as an unofficial means for achieving success in the public arena is probably also necessitated by the fact that until late in the novel Wen Suchen is not an official—not all his actions have governmental sanction (as mentioned above, his name carries suggestions that he is an unappointed or self-appointed minister). As we are also told fairly early in the novel, he is excluded from officialdom because he fails to pass the examinations, a painful fact that must be the main reason for the author's own frustrations in life. Consequently, the novel can be read as an autobiographical act of self-apology on the part of Xia Jingqu: he is trying to convince his readers that his own failures in the examinations must not be taken as a sign of his lack of talent and desire to serve in the public office. In the novel Wen Suchen's impressive achievements are shown to have little to do with success in the examinations; rather, they are the result of his unconventional and chivalrous efforts.

However, knight-errantry sometimes proves to be a problematic issue in the novel. In chapter 56, Suchen's boast about his chivalry provokes the following warning from his mother, Madame Shui:

"What you have done is just the deeds of those knights-errant in ancient times, nothing more than blind valor, and it departs far from the teachings of the Sage. If you continue to behave like this, you will degenerate into a pugnacious seeker after the fame of bravery while endangering your family and your own life. What kind of books have you read that made you so hot-headed? Is there any trace of the Confucian scholar left in you?" (W, 56: 533)

When Suchen's elder brother, Guxin, tries to defend him by citing Confucius's saying "failure to uphold justice is a sign of lack of courage," Madame Shui cautions them by pointing out the importance of discrimination between different cases (e.g., between helping one's own family and one's neighbors) and proclaims that indiscriminate response to all calls for help is Mohist rather than Confucian (W, 56: 533).[24]

Wen Suchen is often caught in the dilemma of trying to be a Confucian paragon and a romantic knight-errant at the same time. Aware of this dilemma, Xia Jingqu introduces into the novel the idea of "expediency" (*quan*) to justify the unorthodox behavior of his protagonist.[25] The word *quan* is often paired with *jing* (norm or standard). For example, when Xuangu insists on sharing a bed with him, Suchen consents to her request by appealing to the concept of *quan* (W, 7: 63).[26] Expediency allows Suchen to act "properly" under various circumstances without being accused of compromising his strong sense of Confucian morality.[27] It is also this rationale that justifies Xia Jingqu's venture into accounts of bizarre sexual scenes in a novel supposed to be a book about the exemplary life of an orthodox Confucian.[28] The same is probably also true of the strange combination of Confucian orthodoxy with an obvious admiration for knight-errantry displayed in the novel. In other words, being a knight-errant is a strategy of expediency.

Despite his ostensible claim to be a wise Confucian sage, Wen Suchen is far from a perfect literatus. He is often shown to be short-tempered as well as wanting in wisdom, attributes often associated with a fearless but rash knight-errant. Because of his lack of vigilance, several times he almost loses his life when he is coaxed into drinking drugged wine. For example, he is drugged by Li Youquan, a harem master who drinks other men's semen in order to enhance his sexual potency, and would have died if his friends had not miraculously turned up to save him (chapter 70). Hearing that the government will send troops to crush the rebellion in Jiangxi and overwhelmed by regret for causing trouble for his friends and for endangering his family, Suchen decides that he will return to Jiangxi to surrender to the officials, an act described by the Prince of Chu as "seeking his own doom," or more literally "a moth darting into flame" (*fei'e touhuo*; W, 99: 928).[29] Suchen's megalomania or arrogance is also criticized by Madame Shui (W, 59: 563–64). As a "great Confucian sage among the women" (*nüzhong daru*; W, 1: 3), Madame Shui is perhaps the only character in the novel who tends to openly undermine the "sageliness" of her son. Obviously, in his enthusiastic adoration for knight-errantry to reassert his own masculinity, Xia Jingqu sometimes tends to neglect other aspects of his protagonist crucial to his Confucian integrity. In his efforts to present his autobiographical self as a perfect Confucian, Xia Jingqu was troubled by different claims on being a literati paragon. He was often bothered by the impossibilities of creating a coherent Confucian superhero.

It is probably no coincidence that the only person who tends to undercut the image of Suchen as a super-literatus in the novel is Madame Shui. Throughout the novel, she seems to possess the final moral authority.[30] She also happens to be the staunchest believer in Cheng-Zhu neo-Confucianism and often gives lectures on this school. She is certainly the most "philosophical" person in the novel, never failing to provide explanations for various phenomena according to the relevant neo-Confucian doctrines. Whereas Madame Shui appears to personify a neo-Confucian sage who symbolizes the best results of self-cultivation (*neisheng*; of course, her gender status as a woman denies her opportunities for achievement in public office), her son Suchen is most impressive for his public career (*waiwang*) even though he is also presented as a strong believer in neo-Confucianism and in the idea of self-cultivation. No matter how wise Madame Shui is, she is confined within the realm of self-cultivation, whereas Suchen's achievement lies almost exclusively in the public arena of imperial politics. Thus, the repeated claim that Suchen is a "sage within and king without" (*neisheng waiwang*) is implicitly questioned. Despite a tremendous effort on the author's part, the general disparity between self-cultivation and political activism suggested in the representation of these two important characters in the novel betrays a deep sense of frustration at the inability to envision the ideal of a perfect *shi*, probably an inaccessible ideal for eighteenth-century literati.

What is important for this exploration of the autobiographical dimension of *Humble Words* is that the author's effort at autobiographical self-reconstruction is always accompanied by this even more ambitious but also desperate attempt to infuse new life into the image of the traditional literati, a complex response to the identity crisis among many literati at the time. Xia's personal frustrations are always related to this much larger sense of crisis shared by other literati. The uneasy image of a super-literatus that Xia Jingqu takes so many pains to create is full of contradictions that belie the predicament many frustrated literati had to face in eighteenth-century China—the nagging questions about what roles a literatus should and could play. All these are crucial aspects of the specific autobiographical strategies the author adopts in the novel, as the following discussion should make clear.

Autobiographical Vindication:
The Self and Its Extensions

A careful reader of *Humble Words* should not find it difficult to detect traces of deep frustrations lurking behind the grand facade of the protagonist's almost uncanny successes. The traditionally dominant motif of recognition (recognition and appreciation of one's talent) and the perennial obsession with finding a *zhiji* (a person who truly understands oneself) often encountered in literati literature appear regularly in the novel. For example, the most emphasized quality in Suchen's best friend, Hong Changqing, is his ability to recognize another's talent (he is able to recognize talent and virtue only by listening to a person's voice; W, 11: 105);[31] for the same reason, Suchen's sadness over the death of Luanchui's father is largely caused by his memories of the latter's appreciation of his talent (W, 20: 197–98). The idea of recognition also plays an important role in Suchen's romances with various talented beauties, most of whom end up becoming his concubines. While revealing to Xuangu his ambition to marry four concubines—each of whom he will train to master one of the four skills, poetry, military strategy, medicine, and mathematics—Suchen emphasizes the concept of *zhiji* (W, 8: 73). He discovers a *zhiji* in Xiangling, another future concubine, after reading her poems (W, 21: 211). When two other beauties, Luanchui and Su'e, learn that Suchen has been sentenced to death because he has angered the emperor Xianzong, they vow to commit suicide in order to repay his kindness of "appreciating them" (*yibao zhiji*). Xiangling's mother tries to dissuade her daughter from the same action by arguing that Xiangling should not die in the name of the maxim that "a gentleman dies for the one who appreciates his talent" because Suchen has never explicitly indicated that he is willing to marry her (W, 40: 391–92).[32]

Suchen's frustrations over his unrecognized talent and virtue find their most explicit expression in a long poem he composes when he learns of the death of his patron, Shigong, who recommended him to the court for governmental office (W, 10: 89–90).[33] Interestingly enough, in the poem, Suchen openly deplores the fact that in his twenties he is still a low degree holder while his friends have achieved success in the examinations and that he has failed to bring glory to the name of his ancestors (W, 11: 104–5). This is probably the only place in the novel where Suchen openly laments his failures in the examinations, a rare moment when the author allows his masked "other" in the novel to come close to expressing his own feelings of failure. In this poem, Suchen also refers to the Goddess Nüwa's repairing of the sky and complains that she failed to do her job. This is reminiscent of the important reference to this same mythical figure at the beginning of *The Dream*, discussed in the preceding chapter in terms of its relationship to Cao Xueqin's personal disappointment at his own unrecognized talent and his fate of being left "unused" for the job of "repairing the sky." It is not easy to pin down the exact meaning of the reference to Nüwa here. But this image of the broken sky and the associated sense of frustration certainly accord with the general tone of the whole poem. Curiously enough, on another occasion in the novel, in the course of criticizing various Daoist legends, Suchen dismisses this legend of Nüwa as ridiculous (W, 62: 588). This interesting self-contradiction on Suchen's part may parallel a more subtle conflict within the author himself, a conflict between his wish for examination success and his simultaneous bitterness toward and contempt for this examination system. After all, the whole novel shows how an "unappointed minister" achieves much more than a successful examination candidate ever could.

In fact, the reader is often told that Suchen is interested neither in examination success nor in the advantages and fame that might bring him. In chapter 9, apparently unenthusiastic about the examinations but following his mother's instructions Suchen takes the preliminary test for the provincial examination (*suikao*) and fails; two friends who succeed both admit that their essays are much inferior to his. A bit later in the novel, however, the reader is specifically told that Madame Shui's anger at Suchen's failure dissipates quickly after she reads her son's examination essay:

"Is this the very essay you wrote in the Examination Hall?" Madame Shui asked.

"Your son has never cheated. How does he dare to deceive you, his mother?" Suchen said.

Madame Shui's long face turned quickly into a smile, and she said: "I should not have wronged you. You have written such an excellent essay, but they chose not to place you on the top. This must have been the examiners' fault. You have nothing to be blamed for." (W, 9: 87)

The message is clear: Suchen failed to pass the examinations because of the examiners' blindness rather than his own incompetence. Loathing the examinations by nature, Suchen seems to lose interest in them after this experience. Moreover, while taking the examination he dreamed that a god delivered to him the following message:

"You have such great learning about Heaven and man and about the rules of everything; many heroic and capable men will be only too willing to devote themselves to your cause; all people, from the noblest to the humblest, will be under your leadership; your glory and success will be tied together with the fate of the country; your virtue will be remembered by people as long as Heaven exists. Why should you bother yourself with this hardship?"

From that time on he completely gave up preparing for the examinations and devoted himself wholeheartedly to the study of the Confucian classics and statecraft. (W, 13: 129–30)

Not only would Suchen do well in the examinations if given a fair chance, but also his great public career does not have to depend on this normal ladder of success. We know that the author had much worse luck in the examinations (he did not even get a *xiucai* degree). In carefully describing how the examiners unfairly dismissed Suchen's superb examination essays and at the same time how Suchen never takes the examinations seriously, the author, burdened by the memories of his own failures, is apparently trying to vindicate himself. He wants to demonstrate that, in the first place, he, Xia Jingqu (like Suchen in the novel), does not care if he succeeds in the examinations, and, second, his ability can never be properly evaluated by those examinations because of the incompetence of the examiners. However, the memories of failure are so persistent that Xia has to misremember very ingeniously in order to effect a more gratifying vindication.

We are further told that later almost all Suchen's sons receive top honors in the examinations at an extremely young age (often the first or the second place in the palace examinations). Among them the most amazing is, of course, his oldest son, Wen Long. The emperor is so impressed with Wen Long's knowledge and virtue that this eight-year-old boy is unprecedentedly granted the *juren* title and then allowed to take the metropolitan examination in secret (even without the knowledge of his family). Much to everyone's surprise, Wen Long not only passes the metropolitan examination but also takes the first place in the palace examination (thus becoming a *zhuangyuan*). We are immediately informed, however, that Wen Long's impressive examination essays were copied from those originally written by his father, Suchen, during his failed attempt to pass the provincial examinations!

"Lin," said Lady Tian [Suchen's first wife], "look at the glory your elder brother [Wen Long] has achieved today. From now on, you must study very hard!"

"The goal of study is not the fame of examination success [*keming*]. But it should not be too difficult to achieve if I really aim at it," answered Wen Lin.

"Don't be so pompous, little boy," said Suchen. "Given the present social status and reputation of our family, it will naturally be easy for you to succeed in the examinations. However, I have before suffered so many setbacks in the examination hall despite my excellent essays, and Rijing had even worse luck in the examinations. How dare a young boy like you claim to have mastered the secrets of essay composition?"

"I would not dare to hide this from you, father," said Wen Long. "In fact, my first essay is a result of my copying your earlier essay draft. Deeply impressed by it, His Majesty said that the essay could win me the honor of *huiyuan* [this should be *zhuangyuan*, the first place in the palace examination]. But after reading the other two essays written by myself, His Majesty said that it was a pity that they appeared a bit weaker and that I could only win the title of *huikui* [the first place in the metropolitan examination]."[34]

"The first topic Wen Long had for the metropolitan examination this time happened to be exactly the same as the topic for my provincial examination many years ago. This essay of mine was ranked among the third class. Your grandmother at first suspected that this disappointing result was due to my having neglected my studies and wanted to punish me. Only after reading that essay did she conclude that it must be due to mistakes on the part of the examiners. This shows that there is no absolute standard by which you can judge an essay. Timing is also very important."

After listening to Suchen, Wen Long and Wen Lin would never think again that examination success was something to be taken for granted. (*W*, 123: 1166–67)

It is further revealed that the essays that later enable Wen Long to win the honor of first place in the palace examination are also based on an essay written by Suchen. But Suchen's essay, which wins Wen Long the highest honor of *zhuangyuan*, earlier failed to impress even the examiners for the prefectural examinations (*xiankao*). These facts induce the following bitter complaint from the always insightful Madame Shui:

"A third-class provincial examination essay could win one the title of *huiyuan* [first place in the metropolitan examination], and an essay that even failed to pass the prefectural examination could bring one the title of *zhuangyuan* [first place in the palace examination]! Ancient people said that an essay could not be considered to be a good essay until its author passed the examination. During the more than one hundred years of this dynasty, how many excellent essays have been condemned to be buried among those failed attempts. What a pity!" (*W*, 123: 1173)

Thus far we have been presented with a carefully choreographed self-vindication on the part of the author, or, to use a more accurate Chinese term, a well-calculated effort of *fan'an* (reverse a "verdict" [on oneself]). It tells us: first, Suchen is not interested in the examinations; second, his ability to pass all the examinations is absolutely beyond doubt; third, his examination failures result from the incompetence of the examiners. In order to convince the reader of these important facts, Suchen's son Wen Long is shown as acquiring the honor of *zhuangyuan* simply because he is wise enough to copy the essays written by his father, who, despite his superb talent, earlier failed at much lower levels of examination because of the blindness of the examiners. Apparently, Xia Jingqu was worried that the validity of the image of his fictional alter ego might appear questionable if he shows only how Suchen manages to achieve so much through unconventional routes. He must also demonstrate that Suchen is equally capable of achieving the highest rank in the examinations if not denied the chance (presumably like Xia himself). Madame Shui's sigh over the fate of those denied this chance is certainly very telling of the degree to which a heartbroken literatus, such as the author, suffered for failures in the examinations.

Of course, there is another implication of Suchen's achieving the highest success in the examination in the person of his eight-year-old son. Eager to remind the reader that the ultimate significance of Wen Long as a character in the novel lies in his function as an extension of his father or a surrogate for demonstrating his father's worthiness, the author even risks having him commit the "crime" of plagiarism. This is partly because sometimes Wen Long does threaten to outshine his father in terms of personal achievements. A *zhuangyuan* at the age of eight, he is appointed regional inspector of Zhejiang province by the emperor at the tender age of nine. Later when he is about to be transferred to Fujian, thousands of locals gather in front of his office, crying and desperately asking him to stay because of his remarkable governing record. Afraid that the reader might forget the function of this son in the novel—merely an additional vindication of his father's (or the author's) talents, which have not been properly recognized before the son reveals to us that his own essays can win him only the title of *huiyuan* while it is his father's essays that bring him the highest honor of *zhuangyuan*—the author is assuring the reader that there should be no question of the father's superiority to his son. Wen Long, like Suchen's other sons, is presented only as an extension of his father. As the commentator on the 1881 edition of the novel pointed out in his chapter-end commentary, "the story of Wen Long is presented to enhance the image of Suchen" (Y, 130: 10b). The same is also true of Suchen's four marvelous concubines. Each is a specialist in one of the four arts (poetry, military strategy, medicine, and mathematics), whereas Suchen is a master of all four. In this sense, they are Suchen's extensions too. As his concubines, their talents are mentioned only to emphasize Suchen's even greater talents.

By virtue of this strategy to enhance the image of Suchen as a super-literatus through extension, Xia Jingqu is able to have his alter ego in the novel help him to fulfill, at least in imagination, a lifelong obsession—to achieve the highest examination success without invalidating the legitimacy of his claim as an unappointed minister. This is a result of a complex psychology of ambivalence: despite the repeated assertions in the novel that examination success proves nothing about one's true value, the author, nevertheless, seems to be unable to bear the fact that his autobiographical protagonist, like himself, should be considered an examination failure.[35]

The burden of examination failure was so heavy on the author that he could not avoid referring to it even in the otherwise lurid orgy (*jiaogou hui*) scene in chapter 67 of the 1881 edition (corresponding to chapter 69 in the 1882 edition; this scene is expurgated in many modern typeset editions). In order to drink as much semen as possible from Suchen, the harem master Li Youquan orders his concubines to hold a contest of "sexual acrobatics" to arouse Suchen. The winner of that contest will be awarded the title of *zhuangyuan* and rewarded with the opportunity to have sex with Suchen. Li's fifth concubine is chosen to be the examiner (*kaoguan*). Her evaluation of the other concubines' performances is deliberately coached in the vocabulary of an examiner:

"With the authority of a decree, I will act in the capacity of chief examiner. The purpose of this examination is to select a *zhuangyuan*. The examination topic is designed to focus on the function of vagina. The six 'examination papers' by Sister Ten, Sister Eleven, Sister Twelve, Sister Thirteen, Sister Sixteen, and me all fail to demonstrate the magic of the vagina. Although written in elaborate vocabularies, they did not answer the question. The decision that all should fail is beyond doubt."   (Y, 67: 9b–10a)

Finally, Concubine Nine is selected to be the *zhuangyuan* and given the chance to have sexual intercourse with Suchen. Thus, in this game of palace examination the *zhuangyuan*'s ultimate prize is the opportunity to sleep with Suchen, who, in fact, failed to pass the preliminary tests in the provincial examinations. Despite the apparent parodic tone of this incident, the author's own bruised ego is healed somewhat by this ingenious presentation of the autobiographical protagonist as someone whose sexual potency is, albeit symbolically, the highest prize an examinee can hope to enjoy. Consequently, Suchen's proven sexual potency, an ultimate symbol of his worth, is somehow (consciously or subconsciously) juxtaposed with his unrecognized ability in the examinations.[36]

Here the novel's rhetoric of exaggeration is pushed to the extreme with a clear sense of its own absurdity. The apparently fantastic nature of this incident compels the reader to see the possible self-conscious irony implied in the novel's willful exaggeration and self-glorification. This sense of irony is reinforced in the concluding chapters of the novel where Wen Suchen's glory reaches an apex, but the illusionary images of dream and theatrical performance begin to dominate.

Autobiographical Invention and the
Memories of Historical Others

In the novel Xia Jingqu adopted another, even bolder, though subtler, strategy of misremembering—appropriation of "many historical others": the author attributes many great deeds of various others (famous historical figures as well as his own well-known contemporaries) to his protagonist to enhance the persuasiveness of his autobiographical self-reconstruction. Many readers have pointed out the surprising resemblance between the protagonist's glorious career as described in the novel and that of Wang Yangming, the famous Confucian scholar and statesman of the Ming dynasty. This resemblance is surprising largely because throughout the novel Wen Suchen is always presented as a Confucian believing deeply in what is called the Cheng-Zhu school of neo-Confucianism (*lixue*, or the School of Principle), the kind of neo-Confucianism sanctified as the only orthodox ideology by the Qing court. Wang Yangming represents the other major competing school of neo-Confucianism, the Lu-Wang school (*xinxue* or the School of the Mind). As a reaction to Cheng-Zhu neo-Confucianism, which came to dominate the intellectual arena during the Yuan dynasty, the Lu-Wang school began to flourish around the mid-Ming but began losing popularity after the fall of the Ming and the establishment of the Qing. Many early Qing thinkers blamed the radicalism of Lu-Wang neo-Confucianism for the downfall of the Ming; Cheng-Zhu neo-Confucianism enjoyed a strong resurgence in the early Qing, culminating in the elevation of Zhu Xi to the Confucian pantheon by the Kangxi emperor in 1712. The specific ideological differences between these two schools of neo-Confucianism need not concern us here. What is of interest is Suchen's attitudes toward Wang Yangming and the Lu-Wang school the latter represents.[37]

Although the novel's main targets of ideological criticism are Buddhism and Daoism, Lu-Wang neo-Confucianism is also ridiculed whenever there is an opportunity. In chapter 62, through the mouth of the maids, Xia Jingqu underscores the superiority of Zhu Xi over Lu Xiangshan (1139–93) as a thinker:

"Master Zhu relies on solid facts, doing one thing and accomplishing one thing," said Bingxian. "Master Lu relies on empty speculation, wishing to achieve everything but ending up with nothing accomplished; Master Zhu's teaching is just like Sister Zihan's needlework, practical and solid, one piece of work for one day; Master Lu is just like Sister Qiuxiang, who would like to study and become a woman scholar more learned than Third Aunt. But she is never persistent and finally does not finish a single book."

"Don't you say that I haven't finished reading any book! Do you dare to compete with me by reciting the *Book of Songs*?" answered Qiuxiang.

"You already wanted to read the *Book of Songs* when you even haven't learned the *Four Books* by heart," said Bingxian. "Your mumbling of '*Guan, Guan,* go the ospreys' would make another perfect Lu Zijing [Lu Xiangshan]. One's study has to start from the *Four Books*. Her Ladyship has told us that the first sentence from the *Analects* 'Learn something and then try it out at due intervals' is an instruction we will have to follow all our life. Having carefully read the *Four Books*, Master Zhu emphasized study, whereas Master Lu, not knowing how to read the *Four Books* properly, neglected study. Not interested in reading the *Four Books* carefully, you would jump into the *Book of Songs*. This is where your fault lies." (W, 62: 592)

Later Suchen formally memorializes the emperor that the study of the teachings of Lu Xiangshan be outlawed and that Lu's tablet be removed from the Confucian pantheon (W, 124: 1179). Furthermore, in the last chapter of the novel, in Madame Shui's dream of the gathering of all the mothers of Confucian sages, the attempt by Lu Xiangshan's mother to defend her son is thwarted, and his teachings are severely criticized for wrongly emphasizing "sudden enlightenment" and for neglecting "hard study." Here Lu's teachings are treated almost as "heterodox," just like Buddhism and Daoism (W, 154: 1504–6).

All these feverish attacks on Lu-Wang neo-Confucianism, though rather far-fetched, are understandable given the unique intellectual environment of the author Xia Jingqu's education. During the Qing, Jiangyin county, Xia's birthplace, was known for its long tradition of Cheng-Zhu neo-Confucian scholars; among them Yang Mingshi was probably the best known (he appears briefly in the novel as Shigong in chapter 9).³⁸ However, curiously enough, the novel never mentions Wang Yangming, who was such a pivotal figure in the development of "heterodox" Lu-Wang neo-Confucianism (in fact, Lu's teaching rebounded in popularity largely due to Wang's effort). This reticence becomes all the more remarkable given that the historical time frame of the novel covers the period of Wang Yangming's life and Suchen's glorious public career in the novel neatly parallels that of the historical Wang. This silence about (or failure to criticize) Wang Yangming is, I would agree, made necessary by a more important autobiographical agenda on the author's part: to appropriate "others" for self-reconstruction—the need to model the life of his autobiographical protagonist on that of Wang Yangming.³⁹ Regarded by many literati as an extremely successful statesman as well as a great Confucian sage, Wang Yangming must have appealed to Xia Jingqu so much that he ignored the embarrassing ideological antagonism between Wang's *xinxue* and the *lixue* in which he fervently believed in order to reconstruct his autobiographical self by using the career of this "reluctant" example as a model. Indeed, probably no other figure in Chinese history personifies so perfectly the literati ideal of "sage within and king without" as Wang Yangming.

Like all legendary figures, Suchen's birth is marked with a good omen. A jade swallow flies into the arms of the mother when the son is born (W, 1: 3). This is probably based on the legend associated with Wang Yangming's birth: Yangming's grandmother dreamed that a god wearing a dress made of jade flew down from the sky to deliver a baby to her. When she woke up, she heard a baby crying.⁴⁰

In the novel, the four-year-old Suchen is asked by his father about his future aspirations:

"Do you want to grow up to be rich?" asked the father.
"I want to study," answered the son.
"Do you want to grow up to be a *zhuangyuan*?" asked the father.
"I want to be a sage," said the son.
The father was greatly surprised.   (W, 1: 3)

The biography of Wang Yangming contains a similarly remarkable display of precocity by a child destined to become a great sage and statesman. At the youthful age of eleven (much older than the four-year-old Suchen in the novel), Wang Yangming was promised by a fortuneteller that he would grow up to become a sage and immortal.

Later he asked his teacher what was the most important thing in life. The teacher said that it was to study hard and pass the examinations. Wang Yangming disagreed: the most important thing for him was to study to become a sage ("Nianpu," 32.2a).

The repeated demonstrations of Suchen's ability to convert others to his "purified" version of Confucianism (for example, saving a monk or a nun from the delusion of Buddhist beliefs) mirror an anecdote recorded in Wang's biography about his abilities to convert others:

> There was a Buddhist priest who shut himself in a cell for three years without speaking or looking at anything. In a loud voice, Yang-ming said: "This priest mutters the whole day long, but what does he say? He stares the whole day long, but what does he see?" The priest was quite startled and, opening his eyes, began to converse with him. Yang-ming inquired about his family when the priest replied that he had a mother living. Yang-ming asked: "Do you think about her?" The priest replied: "I cannot help thinking about her." Yang-ming then gave him a discourse on the human nature of loving one's parents. The priest wept and thanked him. When Yang-ming called on him the next day, the priest had already gone.[41]

An important turning point in Suchen's political career is his remonstration of the emperor Xianzong in which he openly calls on the emperor to outlaw Buddhism and Daoism and accuses the powerful eunuch Jin Zhi of plotting rebellion. As might be expected, the emperor is upset, and Suchen is sentenced to death. The sentence is later changed to exile (chapters 34 and 35). Jin Zhi tries every means to have him killed. In order to hide from Jin Zhi's people, Suchen fakes a death by drowning in a river (chapter 46). Suchen's courageous act of open remonstration wins him the reputation of "Number One Loyal Minister" and gains the attention of the crown prince (this serves to authenticate his mission as an unappointed minister). This important episode in Suchen's political life is partly inspired by a similar incident in Wang Yangming's life. In 1506, Liu Jin, a eunuch, was the emperor's favorite and became extremely powerful.[42] Dai Xian and other officials who remonstrated with the emperor for his dereliction of duty were imprisoned. Hearing of this, Wang Yangming memorialized the throne to pardon them and thus angered the emperor. He was given 40 blows with the light bamboo and exiled to Guizhou. Liu Jin sent people to murder Wang on the road. To evade them, Wang Yangming also faked evidence to show that he drowned himself in a river ("Nianpu," 32.6a–b). The parallel between the two incidents here is almost perfect.

Many of Wang Yangming's important political achievements, such as his successful suppression of the rebellion by the Prince of Ning, the suppression of the bandits in Jiangxi, and his pacification of the Miao aborigines, are repeated one by one by Suchen in the novel with some fictional modification. Suchen's achievements are, however, even more glorious and more dramatic. For example, his defeat of the coup d'état plotted by the Prince of Jing is accomplished during his attempts to save the besieged crown prince in the palace while the emperor is out of the capital, a heroic deed on the part of Suchen much more crucial to the survival of the Ming monarchy than the corresponding achievement by Wang.[43]

The novel ends with Suchen dreaming that he is inducted into the Confucian pantheon with his tablet set right next to that of Zhu Xi. It is interesting to note that Wang Yangming was not officially honored by elevation to the Confucian pantheon until 1581, more than half a century after his death.[44] Here Xia Jingqu had his autobiographical self achieve something Wang Yangming failed to achieve when he was alive. On the other hand, modeling the protagonist's life on that of Wang Yangming undermines the authority of Cheng-Zhu neo-Confucianism the novel obviously tries to uphold. Suchen's physical prowess and medical skills, which prove so crucial to his impressive successes in the public arena, sometimes do make those teachings on self-cultivation look irrelevant. The novel's frequent juxtaposition of lectures on various neo-Confucian doctrines with various shows of Daoist magic (such as Suchen's ability to kill fox-spirits or demons) also makes the otherwise straight-faced preaching of neo-Confucian orthodoxy sound ironic.

Another important historical person whose life story may have inspired Xia's autobiographical self-reconstruction is his own contemporary, Sun Jiagan, a well-known Confucian scholar of the Cheng-Zhu School as well as an accomplished civil official (Xia Jingqu knew Sun personally).[45] Sun was known for his daring remonstrations with the emperor and was even considered a *kuangshi* (a man of audacity) by the emperor himself. Like Suchen in the novel, Sun Jiagan was once sentenced to death for upsetting the emperor, and that sentence was reversed only at the last moment. Sun later also served as a tutor to the Qianlong emperor's sons, just as Suchen often did to the crown prince in the novel (although he is never formally appointed as a tutor). Besides being a learned Confucian scholar and official, another interesting aspect of Sun's personality is his propensity toward knight-errantry in his early youth (his father was known as *yixia*, or knight-errant of justice). It is said that he even once took the law into his own hands to avenge a relative and killed someone.[46] This unique aspect of Sun Jiagan must have appealed to Xia Jingqu tremendously and helped him to conceive his own reconstructed autobiographical self in the novel. Suchen is presented as extremely audacious and sometimes impulsive. His audacity finds its strongest expression in his remonstration of the emperor Xianzong. Suchen is well aware of the fact that what he is going to say will not please the emperor and probably will result in his own death.[47]

In the process of appropriating the memories of these two historical others to reconstruct his own autobiographical self, Xia Jingqu resorted frequently to "alternation" and "improvement." For example, the tension between filiality toward one's parents and loyalty toward one's sovereign was a problem that figured significantly in both Wang Yangming's and Sun Jiagan's lives. Throughout his public career, Wang Yangming repeatedly asked for leave or for permission to resign in order to attend to his aged grandmother and later to his father and in order to remain home during the mourning periods after they died. His requests were often denied, however, and this must have been a constant source of regret to him.[48] Sun Jiagan is said to have left his post to return home when his mother died without even waiting for his superior's approval.[49] In *Humble Words*, although Madame Shui takes every opportunity to emphasize that "complete loyalty" is "complete filiality" (W, 64: 610), the idea of filiality sometimes does make Suchen hesitate before devoting himself wholeheartedly to the cause of the crown prince. However, Suchen's elder brother, Guxin, is a recluse, and by staying home he is able to assume the responsibility of taking care of the mother, thus relieving his younger brother of any obligation to avoid involvement in dangerous political activities. This is one example showing how Xia Jingqu tries to maintain the balance between loyalty and filiality for his autobiographical protagonist in the novel.

Despite the fact that they lived almost two hundred years apart and that they represented two competing schools of neo-

Confucianism as it developed in late imperial China, Wang Yangming and Sun Jiagan did share an attribute that appealed strongly to Xia Jingqu: in his eyes both of them must have represented the personification of the ideal of a perfect literatus with high achievements in both the inner (self-cultivation and the attaining of sagehood) and the outer (success in public office) realms. In other words, both of them, for Xia, came close (especially Wang) to the complete fulfillment of the literati ideal of "sage within and king without."

Xia Jingqu's acts of autobiographical appropriation are by no means confined to these two. Many splendid achievements by Suchen and his sons are based on those of other historical figures, for example, Qi Jiguang's (1528–87) defeat of the invasion by Japanese pirates.[50] In a word, through various strategies of unabashed appropriation and deliberate misremembering, Xia Jingqu's vision of his autobiographical self is expanded to include many well-known historical personalities of great achievements. His reconstructed autobiographical self is an epitome of the greatest Confucian literatus, a rectification of the collective image of the literati. That is to say, the magnitude of Xia's self-invention determines the large number of others to be appropriated; all of them are necessary for his transformation of his past self through careful misremembering and forgetting. This is precisely the opposite of what we witness in *The Dream* and *The Scholars*, where the autobiographical self is *re*presented by dispersing that self into different other selves (through the collective image of those different textual selves created in the novel). *Humble Words*' autobiographical strategy is, rather, to incorporate many different historical others into a single autobiographical self in order to create a superhero whose dominance in the novel should never be in doubt. This reverse strategy is necessitated by Xia's overall autobiographical agenda of self-celebration and self-invention.

Finally, the potentially embarrassing but ironic fact that the author has to look for inspiration for his self-invention in the life of Wang Yangming, who may represent one of his worst ideological enemies, sheds light on the problematic nature of his autobiographical effort at reconstructing his "self" as a model literatus—the remoteness of the long-cherished literati ideal of sage within and king without as well as the frustrations Xia suffered in his endeavor to define himself as a literatus. Furthermore, judging from the novel's relatively close attention to the historical background of that particular period of the Ming and from the apparent affinities between the political career of the protagonist and that of Wang Yangming, the author is trying his best to make sure that his modeling of his autobiographical hero's life on that of Wang is not overlooked. It is this deliberate effort to draw the reader's attention to the obvious incongruities between the novel's explicit anti–Lu Xiangshan rhetoric and Wang Yangming's appeal as model literatus that compels the reader to see another side to this otherwise hilarious self-celebration on the part of the author—the possible self-conscious irony implied in the novel's autobiographical endeavor and the presence of a profound awareness of the inauthenticity of any vision of the literati self. Xia's autobiographical reconstruction of his self is predicated on his memories of a series of historical others without whom that self would make no sense.

The Historical and the Topical: Beyond the Autobiographical

The novel's effort to incorporate the deeds of many historical figures into the creation of the autobiographical protagonist is related to the author's meticulous design in setting the novel's story in a particular historical period in the Ming dynasty. By claiming that the novel is about events in the Ming, a strategy employed by many Qing novelists, the author could protect his various autobiographical projects, some of which might have direct contemporary political relevance, from possible censorship. Xia Jingqu was quite serious about the novel's historical accuracy. Throughout he was careful about periodically providing information about the day, month, and year of the events described, apparently to enhance the historicity of the novel. The novel's story starts in 1465, the first year of the Chenghua reign of the emperor Xianzong (W, 1: 2) and ends in 1521, the thirty-fourth year of the Hongzhi reign of the emperor Xiaozong.[51] The Hongzhi reign actually lasted only eighteen years, and it started in 1488 after the emperor Xianzong died in 1487 in the twenty-third year of the Chenghua reign period (the death is faithfully noted in the novel; W, 135: 1291). In order to enable Suchen to enjoy the favor of this "enlightened" emperor for a much longer period, the author twisted a few historical "facts." As a result, the emperor Xiaozong's period of rule (the Hongzhi reign period) is expanded to at least 47 years (when the novel ends in 1521, the Emperor Xiaozong is still alive). In chapter 117 the emperor Xianzong is frightened by the hallucination that the crown prince's (the future Xiaozong) mother, Lady Ji (Ji Shufei), is flogging Lady An (An Gueifei) and staring at himself.[52] Xianzong interprets this as a sign that the dead Lady Ji does not want him to continue to rule. Consequently, he asks the crown prince to ascend the throne. Due to his filiality, the crown prince, though acceding to this request from his father, declines to change the reign title. As a result, Xiaozong's (or Zhu Youtang in history) ascension of the throne is moved forward to 1475 (twelve years earlier than in history), even though the Chenghua reign continues until 1487 when the Emperor Xianzong dies in the novel (W, 135: 1291; thus compatible with history). According to the historical record, the Hongzhi reign ended in 1505, but when the novel ends in 1521 it is said to be the Hongzhi reign period and the emperor Xiaozong is still alive, an apparent "alteration" of historical fact. This alteration is achieved by subsuming the sixteen-year-long Zhengde reign of the emperor Wuzong into the Hongzhi reign in the novel.

Anticipating possible outrage from a highly history-conscious reader about this "inaccuracy," Xia Jingqu inserts into the novel an interesting episode to show how his sense of poetic license accommodates historicity. In chapter 141, the emperor Xiaozong suddenly becomes sick and begins to think about having his crown prince (the future Wuzong in history) ascend the throne. However, the emperor recovers and changes his mind after listening to a lecture by Suchen (W, 141: 1366–68). This incident takes place in the eighteenth year of the Hongzhi reign (1505), the same year the emperor Xiaozong actually died according to the standard histories. Hence, this emphasizes by implication that the protagonist is the kind of person capable of changing the course of history—Suchen changed the mind of the emperor Xiaozong by virtue of his lecture. It is through this kind of tortuous twists that the novelist prolongs the reign period of the emperor Xiaozong in his novel while insisting on its general historicity. The author is thus indirectly making fun of those trying to read a novel as a strict "history" as well as those who would insist on reading it as a "true" autobiography following the usual historiographical conventions.

But why did Xia Jingqu take so much trouble to alter history in order to set events in the novel mostly within the Hongzhi reign? Another compelling reason can be found in the reputation of Xiaozong among the literati of later ages and in Xia's own frustrated aspiration to find a worthy lord who might appreciate his unrecognized talent. Historians have generally considered Xiaozong one of the few enlightened Confucian rulers in the long history of the Ming dynasty:

> No other emperor of the Ming, and perhaps no other emperor in history, accepted that tradition's teachings about the heavy responsibilities of emperorship as sincerely as he did. None strove so hard to live up to those demanding obligations. He was punctilious about meeting his court, about performing all the prescribed ritual acts, about having the classics mat lectures (*ching-yen*) reinstated and faithfully conducted, and especially about appointing worthy exemplars of Confucian conduct to his court and heeding their advice. He was deeply concerned about the welfare of the people.[53]

This picture certainly fits the image of Xiaozong in the novel. The longer he rules, the more likely literati talents, such as Suchen, will find opportunities for a grand political career. It is in this "appreciative" emperor that Wen Suchen finds his ultimate appreciator. Suchen is often compared to Zhuge Liang (181–234) (W, 1:2, 141:1367), and Xiaozong is described as playing the role of Liu Bei (161–223) (W, 141:1367); this can only serve to remind the reader of the celebrated case of a talented literatus being appreciated by a wise lord as described in various historical or semi-historical sources.

There is more at stake in setting the novel in this particular period of the Ming. Indeed, despite their despotic nature, most emperors in the Ming were relatively weak in character. Protesting an emperor's wrongdoings or remonstrating became almost a fashion among scholar-officials during that time. "The Ming dynasty, as a matter of fact, had a disproportionately large number of China's most famous remonstrators, perhaps because Ming remonstrators were so likely to be martyred."[54] That dynasty produced many "heroic" Confucian martyrs, such as Fang Xiaoru (1357–1402), Hai Rui (1514–87), and Zuo Guangdou (1575–1625), famous for their adherence to their beliefs. However, in the early and middle Qing, especially in the reigns of those strong-willed and capable emperors, such as the Qianlong emperor, heroic acts of defiant remonstration were increasingly impossible. Despite their enthusiastic promotion of orthodox neo-Confucian teachings, these Manchu emperors were extremely sensitive to any threat to their power and appeared to have been particularly annoyed by the traditional Confucian emphasis on the importance of literati ministers in the management of the government. The Song Confucian Cheng Yi claimed in a memorandum to the throne:

Generally speaking, if in the course of a day the emperor is in the company of worthy men much of the time and is in the company of monks and concubines only a small part of the time, his character will automatically be transformed and his virtue will become perfect. . . . Since ancient times, no ruler has attained perfect sagehood who has not honored virtuous men and respected his ministers.[55]

And he further observes that "the most important responsibilities in the empire are those of prime minister and imperial tutor in the classics. Order and disorder in the world depend on the prime minister; and the perfecting of the ruler's virtue is the responsibility of the imperial tutor."[56] The Qianlong emperor, however, found Cheng Yi's views—otherwise part of the imperially sanctioned neo-Confucian ideology—extremely dangerous: "Who after all employs a prime minister if it is not the sovereign? . . . If a chief minister habitually thinks of the world's welfare as his own sole responsibility, for all the world as if he had no sovereign, his conduct is surely intolerable."[57] Having learned lessons from Ming history, these Qing monarchs would tolerate no expression of even "loyal" dissent.

Thus, the novel's historical setting may reflect nostalgia on the part of Xia Jingqu, a frustrated and depoliticized literatus living in an age that offered no chance for literati heroism, for a glorious past when Confucian ministers could distinguish themselves by acts of heroism. In the novel one of the most important reasons that the emperor Xianzong changes Suchen's sentence from death to exile is that he is convinced that an execution will help Suchen achieve the fame of an "upright minister who dies in remonstrating" (*wen sijian*, a traditional literati ideal of heroism that is, as we have discussed in Chapter 3, ridiculed by Baoyu in *The Dream*) and pass that reputation down to future generations (W, 35: 353). Indeed, the picture in which the emperor sits "humbly" listening carefully to the lecture by a minister (such as Xiaozong often does during lectures by Suchen in the novel) was an ideal that many literati such as Xia Jingqu longed for during an age when literati heroism was only a dream or remote memory.

Furthermore, the chaotic Ming empire described in the novel may reflect Xia's own careful observation of contemporary Qing society and his prophetic vision about what was soon to happen to the Qing monarchy. During the late eighteenth century the Qianlong emperor's favorite, Heshen (1750–99), who reminded many of the notorious and powerful eunuch Wei Zhongxian (1568–1627) of the late Ming, took advantage of the aging emperor, usurped great power, and began the so-called Heshen era (ca. 1776–99), which many historians consider the point at which the Qing dynasty began to decline.[58] In his recent study of the origins of Qing New Text Confucianism, Benjamin Elman detects a re-emergence of literati activism during that period and relates the rise of the New Text movement to this re-emergence.[59] The kind of political corruption and literati political activism discussed by Elman certainly resembles events in *Humble Words*. As we have observed before, the messiah-like image of Confucius (*suwang*) advocated by New Text Confucianism must have been in Xia's mind when he named his autobiographical protagonist "Suchen" (the unappointed minister) and set him on a heroic crusade to save the Ming monarchy. Suchen is a literati hero the author Xia Jingqu envisioned himself to be in his act of novelistic autobiographical redemption during an age when the immediate possibility of becoming such a hero was nonexistent.

Despite the obvious despair revealed, this careful autobiographical fantasy does point to a prophetic vision of the possible arrival of such a heroic age in the near future—the revival of literati political activism by the end of the eighteenth century. *Humble Words* was very likely completed by Xia Jingqu in his seventies, about the time China was entering a stage of political instability with the rapid rise of Heshen's influence in imperial politics.[60]

Likewise, the literati activism exemplified in Suchen's political career anticipates in a way the revival of political activism in the late eighteenth century and early nineteenth century, as discussed by some historians.[61] The full subversive implications of the idea of Confucius as a visionary messiah revived by New Text Confucianism in the late eighteenth century did not make themselves fully felt until 1898 when Kang Youwei (1858–1927) and others launched their abortive Hundred Day Reform.[62] The autobiographical epic of Suchen's political adventure in *Humble Words*, a novel completed in the 1770's but probably not published until 1881 (the earliest extant printed edition is dated that year), may parallel, to a degree, this unexpected twist in the fortunes of New Text Confucianism in the Qing.[63] The ideal of a literati messiah in imperial politics advocated by the New Text Confucianism finds its fullest expression in the grand career of Wen Suchen in the novel, and it was certainly fervently shared by Xia Jingqu as an ambitious but disenfranchised literatus. Xia Jingqu's autobiographical endeavor to reclaim the status of the literati as the "few enlightened" (*xianjue*), as pointed out earlier, exposes the "radical" side of this otherwise rather conservative New Text Confucianism. "In place of the emperor to whom the official owed complete loyalty, the New Text scholar-officials felt that they were ultimately answerable to God on high or heaven."[64] It is this strong sense of divine mission and the self-imposed responsibility for being a messiah that prompt Xia Jingqu to claim his autobiographical self, Suchen, as the "unappointed minister" engaged in a crusade to save China from heterodoxy and corruption in the novel.

All these almost uncanny achievements and successes attributed to the autobiographical protagonist in the novel, when read against the background of the author's life of failures and disappointments, seem to bring forth an image of a megalomaniac-like author, the kind of self-celebrant Pei-yi Wu has found in some seventeenth-century autobiographers who "carried the range and intensity of self-celebration to new limits."[65] For example, Wu's following characterization of the audacious autobiographer Wang Jie (1603?–82?) fits Xia Jingqu almost perfectly:

> Wang Chieh's [Wang Jie's] almost compulsive recitation of his feats should be viewed against the background of a frustrated and uncompleted life, a life of setbacks and adversities.... For Wang Chieh the humiliation of failure was hardly softened by time, for he spend the rest of his working life as *mu-yu*, a private secretary to magistrates or governors, a position with no official status and little recognition, so close to the seat of power but forever barred from a share of the fame or glory. His disappointments were all the greater because his hopes were higher.[66]

However, what makes Xia Jingqu's *Humble Words* so unique is that it is a curious product of audacious self-celebration carefully framed in the straitjacket of the rigid orthodoxy of Cheng-Zhu neo-Confucianism. The unabashed self-aggrandizement is occasionally reminiscent of the kind of egocentric self-invention found in some autobiographical writings of the late Ming, an age, in the words of

Pei-yi Wu, when the ego was allowed more leeway than at any time in Chinese history since the Wei-Jin period.[67] However, in this novel, no matter how self-indulgent, the opportunities of uplift granted Xia Jingqu's own deeply bruised ego always remain within the limits of what he perceives to be the parameters of neo-Confucian orthodoxy, a repressive ideology that seems antagonistic to the individual ego. The novel is a strange combination of a heightened consciousness of the individual self typical of the late Ming and the repressive ideology of orthodox neo-Confucianism officially sanctioned in the eighteenth century. It is as if Xia Jingqu, a late Ming egotist by disposition, had been born by mistake into the relatively more repressive eighteenth century. This problem of "wrong timing" might help to explain, at least partly, the reason why the novel was not published until 1881, almost a century after the death of the author, when the long-forgotten image of a messiah-like Confucius advocated by the otherwise conservative New Text Confucians (an image of superman clearly shared by the novel's autobiographical protagonist) was being appropriated by radical literati in order to justify political reform.[68] Here the boundaries dividing past, present, and future or those dividing the historical, the topical, and the prophetic are blurred by an intent to create something "timeless," an ideal of the literati self able to transcend the limits of time and to attain immortality (an absolute act of *liyan*), no matter how inauthentic the result may turn out to be.[69]

Of course, *Humble Words* is a fantasized version of the literati self with implications beyond those its author may have intended; the novel's many ostensible claims in the name of neo-Confucian orthodoxy belie a more profound fear of the possibility of losing control of an even stronger desire for self-celebration repressed for too long and capable of exploding at any moment. Examined in this way, *Humble Words* might be read as an author's therapeutic adventure in its grandest form, a strange but unique literati auto-hagiography written at a time when the literati as a social group were finding themselves in a precarious position and trying desperately to (re)assert their identity as cultural elite.

Conclusion

In the preceding readings I have attempted to demonstrate how all three novelists rely heavily on the representation of "others" for self-presentation. However, unlike *The Scholars* and *The Dream*, where different aspects of an ambiguous autobiographical self are carefully dispersed into different fictive others (characters), *Humble Words* adopts by and large the reverse strategy of incorporating representations of many "historical" others into the presentation of its autobiographical self. In other words, Wen Suchen is largely Xia's autobiographical self-reconstruction assembled from the memories of his own personal experiences as well as those of many historical figures through willful forgetting and imaginative misremembering. The conscientious mixing of memories (of himself and other people) is an important tactic.

No matter how different their specific autobiographical strategies, however, all three novels meticulously explore the advantages of a "mask," and all three novelists try their best to avoid a direct confrontation with their selves in their autobiographical ventures. The advantages of a mask are obvious and sometimes even absolutely essential for certain discourses of autobiographical signification. Here an observation made by a scholar of nineteenth-century English fiction about what she calls the "mask confession" mode may be pertinent:

> [Mask confession] allows for simultaneous involvement and detachment of both author and reader from the first-person narrator. Writers like Charlotte Brontë, D. G. Rossetti, Tennyson and Dickens are thus able to explore sexual dilemmas, a topic normally forbidden to the Victorian author, by putting

the subject matter in an objective, fictional form and by employing a narrative strategy which eases the reader into a comfortable state of sympathy with the confessor-narrator. At the same time, each writer overcomes his/her culturally inherited personal reticence about sexuality by speaking, not through his or her own voice, but through the author's, which nevertheless retains the spontaneity and intuition needed to adequately probe a problem so deeply rooted in their instinctive and emotional natures.[1]

That is to say, the mode of mask confession enabled these writers to discuss publicly many aspects of their private selves that were otherwise forbidden territory in a cultural atmosphere such as that of Victorian England. Although the Chinese novels under discussion here were written in the third-person narrative mode, this characterization of mask confession in some Victorian novels illuminates the similar masking function of the self-re/presentation strategies adopted in their eighteenth-century Chinese counterparts. Without the masking pretense of self-re/presentation, it would be difficult to imagine that Cao Xueqin could have described many aspects of his life experience so intimately. By the same token, without the safe and objectifying distance created by the biographical format (or the biographical mask of others), Wu Jingzi would have been unable to criticize his past self or selves with such subtlety. The following observation about Dickens by another critic seems particularly helpful for understanding the significance of masking in relieving autobiographical anxiety on the part of many Chinese literati authors: "There appears to be an almost inverse relation in Dickens's writing between overt autobiography and the most powerful rendering of emotional experience. The thinner the mask of fiction, the less Dickens reveals. The thicker it is, the more he can tell. That the lies of art are to reveal deeper truths is not, even in a personal and psychological application, a startling discovery."[2] It is the "mask" of writing about an explicit other that makes self-revelation even more effective.[3]

Given the function of masking in self-writing, we should not be surprised to see the kind of autobiographical sensibilities typical of the late Ming in novels of the eighteenth century, when explicit self-celebration and fervent self-examination were out of fashion. For example, the open and almost defiant self-celebration Pei-yi Wu finds so fascinating in the autobiographical writings by seventeenth-century writers such as Wang Jie and Mao Qiling was no longer condoned in eighteenth-century China.[4] Yet the same kind of self-celebration reappears in Xia Jingqu's *Humble Words*, this time hidden behind the elaborate mask of a fictional other and presented with an almost self-conscious irony.

Of course, excessive reliance on masking and others may also sometimes pose serious problems for a writer's ultimate autobiographical purpose, as Pei-yi Wu has complained (a point discussed in relation to *The Scholars* in Chapter 2). This conscientious autobiographical "recoil" and reluctance to confront one's self directly, while necessary or even inevitable in a culturally conservative environment such as that of eighteenth-century China, can be detrimental to the overall development of the autobiographical novel. Although the choice of masking sometimes allows an author to explore more deeply into his own personal psyche with less inhibition, it can, at the same time, also furnish the same author with excuses for avoiding embarrassing or painful experiences. Masking is a double-edged device that can be employed for purposes of self-revelation as well as of self-concealment. As I mentioned in discussing *The Scholars*, in a novel that explicitly claims to be about others, the autobiographical self runs the risk of being completely eclipsed by the overwhelming presence of too many others. In fact, all three novelists had to struggle hard to negotiate a fine balance between revelation and concealment in the process of autobiographical masking.

Furthermore, there are more profound reasons for this fascination with masks (others). One reason is the increasing awareness among some eighteenth-century literati of the ambiguity of the self. In the case of *The Dream*, its two main autobiographical features—the metaphorical representation of female characters (the frequent crossing of gender boundaries) and the anxiety over growing up—reflect Cao Xueqin's painful appreciation of his own ambivalent self as a disenfranchised literatus. Throughout the novel, the reader is repeatedly reminded of the problematic relationship between "real" and "unreal," "dreaming" and "waking," and "reality" and "fiction." This emphasis on "liminality" and "thresholdness" adds to the ambiguities of the autobiographical self as presented in the novel.[5] What problematizes the author's autobiographical agenda in *The Dream* is not the issue of inauthenticity (as suggested by many cases of impersonation and masquerading in *The Scholars*). Instead, the meaningfulness of the very distinction between authenticity and inauthenticity itself is questioned. Indeed, as one of its titles (*The Dream*) suggests, the novel can be read as a desperate but futile effort to achieve self-knowledge. In the novel, what one encounters in a dream is often truer than what one experiences while awake.[6] Moreover, the supernatural framework of the novel enhances the impression that its characters' fates are completely beyond their control. The poems they write, the riddle games they play, and even the words they speak always carry some "truth" about themselves that is often beyond their own comprehension (suggesting that self-knowledge is for them necessarily incomplete if not entirely impossible). Paradoxically, the novel is also successful in showing how each individual is responsible for his or her behavior by virtue of its unprecedentedly convincing exploration of the psychology of many characters.[7]

This paradox is certainly related to the author's deep appreciation of his own ambiguous self as well as of the difficulties in conveying such ambiguities. Examined within this context, the manipulation of gender strategies and the emphases on the anxiety over growing up to be an adult (an adult presumably should have a more stable self-identity) can also be interpreted as an attempt to come to grips with the blurring of the distinction between self and other (the unstable boundaries of the self) experienced by many literati in the eighteenth century. If Wu Jingzi in *The Scholars* is still bothered by the worry that his autobiographical self might be overwhelmed by the excess of others he creates, Cao Xueqin in *The Dream* is frankly acknowledging the futility of any effective autobiographical attempt to present a coherent self. What is presentable are only a few moments or glimpses of the self—a self that is only presentable through metaphors. To an extent, the ultimate autobiographical significance of *The Dream* lies precisely in its acknowledgment of such a radical fact. The profound skepticism expressed in this novel is indicative of the degree to which many contemporary literati experienced a crisis of identity.

Somewhat less sincere, Xia Jingqu chose to avoid confronting such issues by means of willful forgetting or misremembering, trying instead to reinvent his self by appropriating the memories of various historical others (such as Wang Yangming). Thus, we can read *Humble Words* as an illustration by default of this eighteenth-century skepticism of self-knowledge: the author tries to avoid struggling with questions of the authenticity of his "true" self by turning to others (mainly in the past) for inspiration to reconstruct or to fantasize a coherent self. A possible message is that one's vision of one's own self is always contaminated by the perceptions of others—a definition of the self without the intervention of others is virtually impossible. The final dream scene of the novel forces the reader to rethink the ostensibly exuberant self-confidence exhibited by many characters and reminds the reader of the more subversive implications of dreaming in Cao Xueqin's work.

Although forgetfulness is an important autobiographical feature that characterizes *Humble Words*, the other two novels share this feature. Forgetting is as important as remembering to any autobiographical act, and *Humble Words* demonstrates this in its typically exaggerated manner. All three novelists are fascinated with the autobiographical opportunity for self-invention provided by the novel as a narrative genre. To be autobiographical, for them, is not to record or recall a past self as it was but to *re*construct or *re*invent that past self according to the perceptions of the present self. These novels are not memoirs but elaborate acts of self-(re)invention. At the same time, they demonstrate the perils and dilemmas involved in such an act. This is especially true in the case of *Humble Words*.

Another important factor complicating the autobiographical nature of these novels is their authors' simultaneous interest in rethinking and re-examining (or celebrating) the whole literati culture, an interest not unrelated to the eighteenth-century consciousness of the unstable boundaries of the self.[8] The fate of the autobiographical self is always explored within the broader context of the fate of the literati as a social group, an endeavor to contextualize the self in a large community of many others and to present a collective picture of the whole literati class. This relational view of the literati self predetermines that the autobiographical agenda of these novels cannot be confined to a single self and that they address many other issues in addition to those normally considered "autobiographical."[9] This certainly accounts in part for the popularity of the strategy of self-re/presentation with these novelists: its relatively higher capacity to accommodate concerns for both self and other(s) and to dramatize the ambiguities of the self. Obviously, *The Scholars* is more than an autobiographical novel; it is also a novel about the collective fate of the literati in the eighteenth century, and it is certainly a social satire taking the whole literati class as its target. But it is also a satire directed toward the author himself, who was definitely one of those literati being critiqued. It is this double focus on both the self and the other (individual and collective) that has made these autobiographical efforts so unique.

I emphasize that the readings of these novels proposed in this study do not exclude the possibilities of reading various characters in these works as having an independent (or non-metaphoric) significance. For example, Wang Xifeng in *The Dream*, despite her metaphorical function in the author's autobiographical agenda, can certainly be read as an "independent" character with her own representational value in the novel. In other words, my readings of these novels are not meant to deny the possibilities of other readings that concern themselves with issues other than the autobiographical dimension. This is why in this study I have been hesitant to classify any of these three works as an "autobiographical novel" (a loaded generic term). In fact, all three novels demonstrate, to different degrees, how complicated and sometimes even paradoxical an autobiographical act can be.

An important conclusion of this study is that the rise of autobiographical sensibility in the traditional Chinese novel did not parallel neatly the development of various "individualistic ideologies" in late imperial China, although Pei-yi Wu has shown how late Ming individualism contributed to the flourishing of formal autobiographical writings during that same period. In explaining the ascendancy of the autobiographical in the novel during the eighteenth century when individualist fervor had significantly subsided, simple citation of this late Ming obsession with the individual *alone* is not enough.

What characterizes these novels' autobiographical tendencies is a complicated and revisionist desire to rethink this late Ming obsession with the individual self in a much larger social and cultural context—namely, how concern for the individual can be accommodated in the exploration of the much broader issue of a rapidly changing literati culture during a relatively more conservative age when the whole late Ming heritage was often viewed with suspicion. This task was certainly made easier by the encyclopedic nature of the Chinese novel and by its historical development as a fictional narrative genre during that particular period (that is, the movement from the "literati novel" to the "novel of the literati" and the "privatizing process" this genre was undergoing). Due largely to its open claim of fictionality, the novel was able to accommodate the exploration of the individual self, which had found more explicit forms in the late Ming, while recontextualizing such concerns in a more problematic eighteenth-century matrix.

Many readers of *The Dream* have found in Jia Baoyu traces of the so-called late Ming temperament: his indulgence in *qing* (emotion), his unconventional behavior, his disrespect for orthodox Confucianism, and even his adoration for the feminine.[10] However, Baoyu as a character can also be read as a rethinking of various late Ming ideologies (such as the cult of *qing*) he seems to embody, and the apparent irony implied in his characterization can be regarded as a subtle critique of the same legacy. One remarkable thing about Jia Baoyu is his nonchalance about his self-image, something few late Ming "individualists" could afford. Some critics have pointed out the strong desire exhibited in *The Scholars* to return to "original" Confucianism; this may also be interpreted as an attempt to come to terms with some of the radical aspects of the late Ming heritage. The novel's conscientious effort to frame its autobiographical agenda within the re-examination of the larger question of literati self-representation is itself a questioning of the adequacy of the radical individualism prevalent among certain literati during the late Ming.[11] More specifically, Wu Jingzi's scathing critique of various practices of the *mingshi* and their inauthenticity (the compulsion to startle and to be eccentric) is certainly relevant to the same phenomena that were once so common in the late Ming.[12] *Humble Words*' uneasy juxtaposition of a carefully exaggerated celebration of the self with various obviously rigid Confucian orthodox ideologies, which were politically dominant in the eighteenth century, also problematizes the kind of unabashed self-invention Pei-yi Wu finds in some late Ming autobiographers. These eighteenth-century literati novelists' complex and sometimes even revisionist responses (via various strategies of mask manipulation, self-re/presentation, and conscious mixing of memories of one's own self and those of others) to aspects of the late Ming legacy produced some of the most authentic as well as compelling examples of literati self-culture in late imperial China, at a time when that legacy was being interrogated and criticized despite its persistent appeal to many sensitive minds of the mid-Qing.

Having examined the unique autobiographical features of these novels and the relevant cultural background of this period, particularly the severe constraints placed on the writing of formal autobiography, we should no longer consider it a mere coincidence that the novel became the most important medium through which some eighteenth-century literati authors attempted to explore and reconstruct their self-images. In brief, the rise of autobiographical sensibility in the eighteenth-century novel was occasioned first of all by this narrative genre's "evolution"—its becoming increasingly "privatized" and "literati-ized." The relatively more repressive intellectual atmosphere of the mid-Qing also added to the appeal of the novel for many literati authors as an "autobiographical" outlet for continued exploration of their increasingly complex self-identity and for an re-examination of the new relationship between their individual selves and their collective fate as literati that was emerging in eighteenth-century China.

Within the history of the traditional Chinese novel, although the explicit autobiographical concerns found in these three works marked an important and significantly new trend in the Chinese novel, this trend was by no means a dominant one (at least in terms of quantity). Outside these three works, we can find hardly any other novels of the period that exhibit a similar persistent autobiographical concern.[13]

However, literati self-representation continued to be a main thematic concern of some nineteenth-century novels. Li Ruzhen's *Destinies of the Flowers in the Mirror* (*Jinghua yuan*) and Wen Kang's (d. ca. 1865) *Tale of Heroic Lovers* (*Ernü yingxiong zhuan*) are two novels shaped by a fairly consistent autobiographical agenda. Like Cao Xueqin, Li Ruzhen invests a lot of male anxiety (over a frustrated literati career) in the representation of a series of talented women, albeit in a less subtle manner. Wen Kang uses the same gender strategy, but another of his particular autobiographical strategies—willful misremembering—resembles that of Xia Jingqu. In that novel, the author's autobiographical self(ves) achieves all those goals he failed but wished to achieve in his actual life.[14] However, these authors' autobiographical endeavors are much less complex than those examined in this study. We might also mention Shen Fu's well-known *Six Records of a Floating Life* as another autobiographical fiction. As many critics have claimed, Shen Fu was probably the first Chinese writer who, without the aid of a mask, wrote directly about the intimate details of his private life, especially his love for his wife.

But this unique piece of self-writing can hardly be considered a fiction in the sense that the three novels studied here have always been. They belong to different narrative genres: formal autobiography (for lack of a better word) and the novel. The manuscript of *Six Records of a Floating Life* had to wait more than half a century until the late nineteenth century, when Chinese culture was being seriously challenged by Western influences, to be discovered and published (it was published long after the author had died, a fate shared by Xia Jingqu's *Humble Words*). Its belated publication tells us that publication during Shen Fu's own times would probably have scandalized the reading public. Eighteenth-century China was probably not ready for such direct self-presentation without the camouflage of self-re/presentation (biographical form as a cover).[15]

For another novel that demonstrates a persistent autobiographical agenda, we have to wait until early in the twentieth century when Liu E (1857–1909) published his *Travels of Lao Can* (*Lao Can youji*). Like the three eighteenth-century novels discussed here, this novel takes up the theme of a literatus's search for a proper social role to play. It explores the dilemma a literatus faced at a time when traditional Chinese society was undergoing drastic changes under the encroachment of Western culture. The strategy of self-re/presentation is also an important part of the novel's autobiographical rhetoric. Mainly re/presented in the person of Lao Can, the novel's protagonist, the author also invests other aspects of his self in other characters, such as Yellow Dragon (Huang Longzi).[16] In fact, Lao Can and Yellow Dragon represent two aspects of the author's own ambivalent attitude toward the perennial literati dilemma—the choice between involvement and withdrawal.

The role of literati or "men of letters" (a more proper term given the changing social environment) in society continued to be a major theme of autobiographical fiction in twentieth-century China,[17] although the forms it takes become more varied and sometimes much more confessional (for example, in works by writers such as Yu Dafu [1896–1945] or Guo Moruo [1892–1978]). With the influx of Western culture, with serious challenges to the long dominant Confucian ideology (including its strong sense of propriety), and with the rise of a new consciousness of individuality, autobiographical fiction became a much more common phenomenon. A comparison of the autobiographical sensibility in traditional fiction with that of the twentieth-century is beyond the scope of this study, but one thing seems quite certain: reliance on self-re/presentation or other masking strategies is not as crucial for twentieth-century Chinese autobiographical fiction as it was for its predecessors in the eighteenth century, largely because of the changed cultural milieu.

REFERENCE MATTER

Notes

For complete author names, titles, and publication data for the works cited here in short form, see the Selected Bibliography, pp. 203–21. For the abbreviations used here, see pp. xi–xii.

INTRODUCTION

1. de Bary, "Introduction," in idem, *Self and Society*, p. 3.
2. For a study of the rise of "individualism" during that period and its association with the so-called Taizhou school—the "left wing" of the neo-Confucian *xinxue* (the study of the mind)—see de Bary, "Individualism and Humanitarianism"; see also Ray Huang's discussion of Li Zhi in his *1587*, pp. 189–221.
3. Pei-yi Wu, p. xii.
4. Ibid., p. 235.
5. Pei Huang (*Autocracy at Work*, pp. 187–204) has an interesting discussion of why the Yongzheng emperor (r. 1823–35) found Confucian orthodoxy so appealing or useful.
6. Nivison, *Chang Hsüeh-ch'eng*, p. 18; Nivison (p. 19) further observes that the Qianlong emperor often cautioned his ministers to be careful with their criticisms: "For to do otherwise is to behave like Ming officials, who attacked each other with 'empty words' and criticized the court merely to seek fame! The ideological atmosphere built up by the Manchu establishment must surely have had as pervasive an effect intellectually as any single thinker or school of thought."
7. *Da Qing huidian* (Kangxi ed.), 51.20a; quoted and translated in Guy, pp. 18–19.
8. Guy, p. 21.
9. See Goodrich; and Jin Xingyao; see Guy for a revisionist interpretation demonstrating how the community of Chinese scholars, out of personal or ideological interests, actively participated in the literary inquisitions carried out in the Qianlong period (1736–96), which have previously been viewed mainly as the campaigns conducted in the interests of the Manchu monarch.

The notorious case against Dai Mingshi (1653–1713) in 1711 is implicitly referred to in *The Scholars* (see chap. 8). Jin He (fl. 1867), in his preface to an edition of the novel (*RLYZ*, p. 129), was the first to point this out. Considering the increasingly tightening governmental censorship in the Qianlong period, this act of the author Wu Jingzi (1701–54) was rather daring. For a general discussion of various expressions of dissent in late imperial China, see Ropp, "Vehicles of Dissent."

10. Paul Ropp (*Dissent in Early Modern China*, p. 40) observes that "in the search for scapegoats, a most logical target was the T'ai-chou school with its iconoclasm toward Ch'eng-Chu neo-Confucianism, its egalitarianism, and its tolerance for non-Confucian heterodoxy. . . . The Ming collapse and Manchu conquest stimulated the growth of philosophical conservatism. Both Manchus and Chinese scholars emerged from the seventeenth-century political and social upheaval with a firm belief in the validity of and need for the Ch'eng-Chu emphasis on hierarchy, order, loyalty to superiors, and obedience of authority."

Here Gu Yanwu's (1613–82) writings may be representative. In an essay on Li Zhi (*Rizhilu jishi*, 18.28b–30a), Gu accused Li of being disrespectful to Confucius, admiring the "notorious" First Emperor of the Qin, and demoralizing the common people by praising a woman for choosing her own lover (in this case, Zhuo Wenjun of the Former Han dynasty [206 B.C.–8 A.D.]), etc. In short Li Zhi was a public enemy of the whole society, someone who "disrupted the Dao and deluded the common people [*luandao huoshi*]"; Gu also criticized another late Ming figure, Zhong Xing (1574–1624; see ibid., 18.29b–30b).

11. Chow; see also de Bary's (*Message of the Mind*, pp. 124–229) relevant discussion of "Confucianism" during the early and high Qing periods, especially the phenomena of what he has called "mandarin Confucianism" as well as its differences from other kinds of more "private" Confucianism, and Wing-tsit Chan's ("*Hsing-li Ching-i*") discussion of the early Qing Confucian minister Li Guangdi.

12. In her review of Wu's study, Cynthia Brokaw (pp. 181–83) speculates that other intellectual trends and social changes in the late Ming may also have contributed to the flourishing of autobiography.

13. The nineteenth century may not be so much a part of the "envoi" of formal autobiographical writings as Pei-yi Wu argues. Besides Shen Fu's (b. 1763) *Six Records of a Floating Life* (*Fusheng liuji*), which Wu considers to be a rare exception in that period, there were other autobiographical writings produced in the nineteenth century that were intensely "self-revealing," such as some of Zeng Guofan's (1811–72) diaries and Luo Siju's (1764–1840) *Annalistic (Auto)Biography of Luo Siju* (*Luo Zhuangyong gong nianpu*). More research is needed before Wu's characterization of the nine-

teenth century as an envoi of autobiographical writings can be fully substantiated; see also J. Handlin Smith's review of Wu's book.

14. Curiously, Pei-yi Wu (p. 232*n*22) only briefly mentions Zhang Dai's autobiographical writings in a note.

15. "Ziwei muzhiming," in Zhang Dai, pp. 294–97; see also *LZW*, pp. 349–50.

16. For a discussion of the conventional self-humbling rhetoric in traditional Chinese autobiographical writings and how the Confucian sense of decorum and the historiographical conventions of being "exemplary" or "cautionary" resulted in the underdevelopment of autobiography in early China, see Pei-yi Wu, pp. 3–67.

17. In an earlier autobiography, "Self-Written Preface to *Tao'an's Dream Memories*" ("*Tao'an mengyi* zixu," in Zhang Dai, pp. 110–11; *LZW*, pp. 199–201), Zhang Dai castigates himself even more for his past wrongdoings and explains his present sufferings as retribution for his past "sins." However, despite this exaggerated pose of self-critique, the autobiographer never apologizes for his writing on his "sinful" past self by justifying it as a warning or as a cautionary tale to his readers, and the recalling of past transgressions is always tinged with a nostalgia that ultimately negates any serious sense of guilt. Stephen Owen (*Remembrances*, pp. 131–41) has translated this piece into English and has an interesting discussion of what he calls the "doubleness" of Zhang Dai as an autobiographer (the desire to assert his own uniqueness as an alienated self and the equally strong longing to be recognized and be reintegrated into the society).

18. "Yuwei zizhiming," in *LZW*, pp. 357–60.

19. Of course, the reasons behind the differences between these two autobiographical tomb inscriptions are necessarily more complex than I suggest here. The different personal experiences of each autobiographer, for example, might well be another contributing factor.

20. Without offering further explanation, Pei-yi Wu (p. 236*n*2) acknowledges that the "autobiographical sensibility, no longer welcome in self-written biography, found its fullest expression in the great eighteenth-century novel, *The Dream of the Red Chamber*."

21. For discussions of the possible resemblances between Zhang Dai and *The Dream*, see Hou Hui; and Zhou Ruchang, "*Honglou meng*" *yu Zhonghua wenhua*, pp. 137–38; and idem, "*Honglou meng*" *xinzheng*, pp. 829–31.

22. Průšek.

23. It is perplexing in that in the West the rise of autobiographical sensibility in the novel was generally paralleled by the development of autobiography (see Stewart; and Spacks). However, in the case of traditional China, the novel became significantly autobiographical only after the golden

age of autobiography is supposedly over (if we accept Pei-yi Wu's observations on the history of Chinese autobiography).

24. Here Pei-yi Wu's deploring of the end of an age of "individualist thinking" and "bold self-expression" is shared by James Cahill (pp. 222–25), who finds a similar cessation of "creative activity" in Chinese painting during the same period: "In painting—as in the rest of Chinese culture—through the two centuries that remained to the empire, tradition continued to assert itself, ever weaker and more compromised but still ultimately in control. Even the survivals of individualism and unorthodoxy were absorbed into it, and tamed. . . . It is enough to say that virtually no painting of originality and power comparable to what we have seen was to follow. The Chinese paintings that stand with the finest achievements of world art, the truly compelling images, end with the early eighteenth century."

25. Spengemann (pp. 187–88) has noted a shift in emphasis in recent scholarly study of autobiography from its origin in biography to the examination of it as an "imaginary" form: "Increasing number of critics came to associate autobiography with fiction rather than with biography."

26. According to Pei-yi Wu (p. 8), one of the most important obstacles to the development of formal autobiography in traditional China was the dominant biographical tradition in historiography. He further observes that "the development of autobiography both in China and in the West lies precisely in its movement away from *shih* (history) in the direction of *wen* (belles lettres)." For a discussion of a somewhat similar "dehistoricization process" the traditional Chinese novel underwent, see my "Dehistoricization and Intertextualization," esp. pp. 49–59.

27. Pei-yi Wu, pp. 163–64. For discussions of the attribution of Li Zhi as the possible author of the commentaries on some of the Ming novels, see Plaks, *Four Masterworks*, pp. 513–17; and Rolston, *How to Read the Chinese Novel*, pp. 356–63.

28. For discussions of these increasingly fictionalized autobiographies, see Pei-yi Wu, pp. 163–86. The autobiographer Mao Qiling was also quite active in the field of "fictional" literature. He wrote commentaries on the well-known drama *The Romance of the Western Chamber (Xi Xiangji)* and authored several plays himself.

29. Of course, due to the powerful influence of historiographic conventions (particularly the emphasis on "historicity"), "fictionality" was not something *always* openly claimed or advocated by traditional Chinese fiction (*xiaoshuo*), which was often considered a handmaid to history. But it is probably safe to say that by the late seventeenth century, when fiction seemed to have achieved the status of independent narrative genre, fictionality had become a feature some novelists and commentators would not hesitate to emphasize in their writings and that it indeed became an avowed quality of

Notes to Pages 10–15   159

many novels. For relevant discussions, see my "Dehistoricization and Intertextualization"; and Fang Zhengyao, pp. 105–19, 148–54.

30. Kant, pp. 165–69; see also Johnstone, pp. 103–5; and Organ, pp. 114–15.

31. Compare Roland Barthes's observation: "When a narrator recounts what has happened to him, the I who recounts is no longer the one that is recounted" ("To Write: An Intransitive Verb?" p. 162; quoted in Renza, p. 276). Renza (p. 279) further points out that autobiographical writing "entails a split intentionality: the 'I' becoming a 'he.'" Here I use the much broader term *self-writing* instead of *autobiography* in order to refer to all those writings that contain self-references and to avoid the narrower generic implications of the latter.

32. "Zixu," "Buyi," in Wang Zhong, 23a–24a; reprinted in *LZW*, pp. 75–77.

33. *LZW*, pp. 81–83.

34. Olney, *Metaphors of Self*, pp. 30, 31, 40. Olney's concept of the metaphor of the self is all-embracing, and it refers to all "the order-produced and order-producing, emotion-satisfying theories and equations." For a discussion of Olney's theory, see Eakin, pp. 187–91.

35. Needless to say, the autobiographical or authorial self as discussed here, because of the textual nature of any self-writing, has to be an "other" or "metaphor" in the final analysis.

CHAPTER I

1. In this section I try to outline a general development in the history of the Chinese novel from a concern with "public/past" to "individual/present," arguing that this trend ultimately led to the ascendancy of autobiographical sensibility in this genre during the eighteenth century. A full account of this complex process would require much more space than I can take here. The following discussion is heavily indebted to several important studies on the traditional Chinese novel, and the reader is referred to them whenever appropriate.

2. See Plaks, "Full-length *Hsiao-shuo*," p. 165.

3. See, e.g., Lu Xun, "Zhongguo xiaoshuo de lishi"; and Zheng Zhenduo, "Zhongguo gudian wenxue."

4. Here the Chinese term *wenren* (translated as "literati" in English) is used in a broad sense to refer to the cultural elite in traditional China. Later in this chapter I discuss its meaning in a narrower sense (translated as "men of culture" in English, understood as referring merely to a group within the elite). Among those scholars of the Chinese novel who have made use of the concept of "literati novel" or its equivalent are W. L. Idema (Idema uses the term "literary novel"); Plaks, "Full-length *Hsiao-shuo*" and *Four Master-*

works; Hegel, *Novel in Seventeenth-Century China*, esp. pp. 51–65; and C. T. Hsia ("Scholar-Novelist," p. 269), who employs the term *scholar-novelists* to refer to the authors of the Qing literati novel: "I would propose the term 'scholar-novelist' to designate a special class of literary men who utilized the form of a long narrative not merely to tell a story but to satisfy their needs for all other kinds of intellectual and literary self-expression." However, Hsia (pp. 267–69nn5–6) disagrees with Idema regarding the specific standards for defining the "literary novel."

5. For a recent study of the development of "literati drama" in Ming-Qing China, see Guo Yingde.

6. Hegel, *Novel in Seventeenth-Century China*, pp. 228–29. For a discussion of the involvement in reading and commenting on novels of many well-known late Ming literati, see Chen Dakang, *Tongsu xiaoshuo*, pp. 145–57 (this important study did not become available to me until after the initial editing of this volume had been completed).

7. Quoted and trans. in Widmer, p. 47.

8. D. C. Lau, p. 114. See also Yang Bojun, p. 115.

9. Li Yu (1611–79?), in the guise of a commentator, defended his novel *Rou putuan* (The carnal prayer mat) with the same rhetoric, although not without a tongue-in-cheek touch: "Let me spring to the sage's defense with another quotation from the *Four Books*: 'Those who understand me will do so through *The Carnal Prayer Mat*; those who condemn me will also do so because of *The Carnal Prayer Mat*' " (quoted and trans. in Hanan, *Invention of Li Yu*, p. 136). Another of Chen's contemporaries, Pu Songling (1640–1715; "*Liaozhai zhiyi*" *huijiao huizhu huipingben*, p. 3), also alluded to this saying by Confucius in the preface to his *Strange Stories from the Studio of Leisure* (*Liaozhai zhiyi*). However, the earliest case in which this Confucian rhetoric was used to elevate the status of a vernacular fiction, as far as I know, was Yang Dingjian's preface (*Shuihu zhuan huipingben*, p. 30) to the 120-chapter version of *The Water Margin* (*Zhongyi Shuihu quanzhuan*) published by Yuan Wuya in 1614. Yeshi zhuren (the Master of Unofficial History) also referred to this Confucian saying in his preface (dated 1631) to the novel *The Romantic Tale of the Emperor Yang of the Sui* (*Sui Yangdi yanshi*; see *Ming Qing xiaoshuo xuba xuan*, p. 137).

10. For discussions of the development of traditional Chinese criticism of the novel, see Wang Xianpei and Zhou Weiming; and Rolston, *How to Read the Chinese Novel*, pp. 3–41.

11. See Widmer, pp. 100–102; Widmer (p. 100) also characterizes Jin's reconstruction of the "authorial personality" as a way of "personalization"; cf. my "Author(ity) and Reader" for a discussion of the question of the author in fiction commentary.

12. See Zhang Zhupo's remarks in the essay "Kuxiao shuo" attached to his commentary on the *Jin Ping Mei*, in Huang Lin, pp. 63–65.
13. Translated in Watson, pp. 65–66.
14. "*Jing Tan changhe shi* xu," in Han Yu, 20.9b.
15. "*Mei Shengyu shiji* xu," in Ouyang Xiu, 42.7a–8a. For discussions of the historical development of this canonical idea, see Zhongshu Qian; and Wang Yingzhi.
16. See Owen, "Self's Perfect Mirror."
17. ZXLX, p. 142. For a discussion of Li Zhi's *fafen* theory, see Wang Xianpei and Zhou Weimin, pp. 145–49.
18. Of course, my argument does not deny the possibility that some fiction writers and commentators might have used the *fafen* theory to lend moral weight to their writing or even did so in a tongue-in-cheek manner.
19. See Chen Lang's "Zixu" in *Xue Yue Mei*, reprinted in *Ming Qing yanqing xiaoshuo daguan*, p. 588.
20. See Plaks, "After the Fall," pp. 554–56; and Yenna Wu, chap. 1. See also Hegel's (*Novel in Seventeenth-Century China*, pp. 141–42) relevant discussions of the authorship of several other seventeenth-century novels.
21. See Li Baichuan, *Lüye xianzong* (100-chap. version), pp. 15–16. According to this modern typeset edition, Li Baichuan's preface is titled "zixu" (self-written or authorial preface). But in the Qianlong version of the manuscript copy (see the facsimile reprint edition published by Beijing University), this piece is simply titled "xu" (preface, 43a). However, the emphasis and care with which Li Baichuan details the connections between his personal life experiences and the writing of the novel must have been very impressive and quite unconventional, because immediately following the "Preface" is a suggestion by a commentator demanding that this "authorial preface" (*zixu*) be expunged, given the few precedents for an "authorial preface" to a work of fiction; this suggestion was apparently accepted by the editor of the (presumably) later woodblock edition of the novel (for brief information on the different editions of this novel, see ZMTY, p. 525). Indeed, prior to *The Footsteps of an Immortal in the Mundane World*, few novels contained a preface by the author himself (although editor's prefaces were quite common) and even fewer had prefaces explicitly titled *zixu*.

Pu Songling attached an "authorial preface" to his *Strange Stories from the Studio of Leisure*, although he called it a *zizhi* (self-record). Of course, this collection of short stories is written in the literary language and, strictly speaking, belongs to a different narrative genre. For a discussion, see Zeitlin, pp. 43–58. Lü Xiong (ca. 1640–1722), another seventeenth-century novelist, attached a *zixu* and a *ziba* (authorial postscript) to his novel, *An Unofficial History of a Female Immortal* (*Nüxian waishi*), although they say little about the author himself (see the facsimile reprint of the Kangxi edition of *Nüxian waishi*, pp. 5–8, 13–14). Here the term *zixu* is more accurately translated as "self-account" because the character *xu*, although pronounced the same, is written differently and literally means "narrative," even though the two *xu* are often used interchangeably in titling autobiographical writings (*zixu*, self-written preface, versus *zixu*, self-account).

Li Baichuan's contemporary, Li Lüyuan (1707–90) also attached a *zixu* to his novel *The Warning Light at the Crossroad* (*Qilu deng*). See Luan Xing, "*Qilu deng" yanjiu ziliao*, pp. 94–95. The attachment of *zixu* by an author to his fiction (especially vernacular fiction) was a significant development in the history of the Chinese novel because it points to the increasingly close relationship between the personal concerns of the author and his work, a necessary step toward the "autobiographical."

Zixu, according to Pei-yi Wu (p. 166), is "the most flexible of all subgenres" of Chinese autobiography. Wu (pp. 42–67) translates *zixu* as "self-written preface" and discusses it at length as an important subgenre of Chinese autobiographical writing.

22. For example, some readers have called attention to the autobiographical links between the author and the tragic character Wen Ruyu; see, e.g., Zheng Zhenduo, "Qingchu dao zhongye de changpian xiaoshuo," p. 467; and Qing Sanxiang.

23. Full discussion of the autobiographical dimension of the novel must be based on more knowledge about the author.

24. See my "Dehistoricization and Intertextualization," p. 57. In that article I argue that the development of the Chinese novel, to a large degree, is a "dehistoricizing" process (in terms of both moving away from the "bondage" of historiography and focusing increasingly on the private and the contemporary).

25. At the same time, this shift of focus onto the private and the contemporary was also taking place in many short stories produced in the sixteenth and seventeenth centuries. See Patrick Hanan, *Chinese Vernacular Story*; McMahon, *Causality and Containment*; and Chen Dakang, *Tongsu xiaoshuo*, pp. 115–26.

26. Y. W. Ma (pp. 40–41) notes that "before the popularity of *ts'ai-tzu chia-jen* novels in the late Ming period, a setting in the past with at least token reference to some well-known historical personages and events seems to have been the norm. From the time of the *ts'ai-tzu chia-jen* novels to the eve of the late Ch'ing boom, possibly one-third of all novels used contemporary settings." According to Chen Dakang ("Lun Ming Qing zhiji de shishi xiaoshuo"; and *Tongsu xiaoshuo*, pp. 126–34), there was a sudden boom in "the novel of the contemporary events" or "the topical novel" (*shishi xiaoshuo*) during the Ming-Qing transition; these works dealt largely with

contemporary political events. In fact, among what are usually classified as "historical novels" produced before the Republican period, he believes, one-fifth should be considered *shishi xiaoshuo*. Most such works are concerned with newsworthy public events and more susceptible to the constraints of historiographical conventions because of their public nature; see also Qi Yu-kun.

27. Plaks, "After the Fall," pp. 553–54; see also Frederick Brandauer's (*Tung Yüeh*) discussions of *The Supplement to the Journey to the West* (*Xiyou bu*) and Hegel's (*Novel in Seventeenth-Century China*, pp. 105–39, 141–66) discussions of this novel and *The Romance of Sui and Tang*. Pei-yi Wu (p. 207) has detected a parallel phenomenon in literati autobiographical writings of that period: "a deep awareness of the human proclivity to evil, an urgent need to counter this proclivity, a readiness for self-disclosure, and a deep anguish over one's own wrong doings, all to an extent and with an intensity never known in Chinese history."

28. See Plaks's (*Four Masterworks*, p. 501) observation about the differences between the late Ming novel and the Qing novel: "Obviously, these four narratives [of the late Ming] are not literally about the Confucian lifestyle: the world of the examination system, official service, classical scholarship, and the gentlemanly arts, such as came to dominate a large segment of the fiction of the Ch'ing period." See also C. T. Hsia's discussions in "Scholar-Novelist."

29. Stephen Roddy (p. 9) has also noted that "during this period [the middle years of the Qing] fiction came not only to be written by the literati (as is often meant by the term 'literati novel'), but also to show a certain preoccupation with literati experiences and concerns, so that we might be justified in calling some examples of it 'fiction of the literati.'"

30. Of course, early in the development of the *chuanqi* fiction of the Tang dynasty we have a somewhat similar phenomenon, albeit on a much smaller scale and only confined to fiction written in the literary language.

31. For a discussion of Pu Songling's examination failures and how they shaped his fiction writing, see Barr. Surveying the history of the reception of Pu's *Strange Stories from the Studio of Leisure* in traditional China, Zeitlin (pp. 25–34, esp. pp. 29–30) finds that one interpretive strategy popular in the eighteenth century was reading the work as "a vehicle for the author's self-expression." However, Zeitlin is reluctant to attribute the reason for this shift in focus to "self-expression" to the "historical differences between the intellectual climate of the seventeenth century and that of the eighteenth century." Although Zeitlin's cautious interpretation here is understandable, we are justified in saying that with the tremendous efforts by such writers as Li Zhi and Jin Shengtan in the sixteenth and seventeenth centuries, the "expressive theory" that had dominated the Chinese poetic tradition had, by the

eighteenth century, become almost equally influential in the field of literati fiction (as I have argued earlier) and that this new emphasis on the expressive is well reflected in the three novels discussed in this study. It is probably more persuasive to attribute this particular shift in the reception of this work in the eighteenth century to the ascendancy of the expressive theory in the field of literati fiction during that period. For a discussion of how various important values in the literati poetic tradition are incorporated into *The Scholars* and *The Dream*, see Yu-kung Kao; and my "Dilemma of Chinese Lyricism," pp. 41–55.

32. The particular stories I have in mind are "Sanyu lou" and "Wenguo lou" (the third and twelfth stories in *Shi'er lou*). See also Sun Kaidi, "Li Liweng yu *Shi'er lou*," pp. 194–95, 201–5; and Shen Xinlin. Hanan (*Invention of Li Yu*, p. 33) observes that Li Yu, in his stories as well as his novel, "made over the traditional narrator's persona almost into his own image, so that his personal opinions and comments intrude upon, and even dominate, the narrative. . . . The characters in some stories represent one persona of Li Yu's while the narrator represents another. . . . To the extent that a novelist can be an essayist who offers us his personal opinions, Li Yu is such a novelist."

33. See Liao Yan's four plays *Zui huatu*, *Su pipa*, *Xu Su pipa*, and *Jinghua ting* (collected in his *Chaizhou bieji sizhong*).

34. Arguing that "irony" is the most essential generic feature of the novel and pointing out how important the rhetorical stance of irony is in autobiographical fiction in the West, Plaks ("Full-length *Hsiao-shuo*," p. 172) observes that "the turning of novelists toward themselves as central subjects for mimetic presentation is simply the logical conclusion of the fundamental tendencies of the genre, and interestingly enough the history of the Chinese novel also evinces an overwhelming shift to the autobiographical focus in the Ch'ing period." As I demonstrate later in this study, irony is certainly an "autobiographical" feature discernible in the three novels discussed here. Especially in *Humble Words*, irony enables its author to celebrate his autobiographical self without being bothered by the question of credibility. The sense of irony in these autobiographical ventures was also related to the increasing awareness of the ambiguous self experienced by many literati in the eighteenth century, a topic explored in detail later in this chapter.

35. For example, Li Yu, the best-selling author of his time, complained bitterly about publishers' pirating his books (Hanan, *Invention of Li Yu*, pp. 12–13). It was probably for this reason that Li Yu became involved himself in publishing (Hegel, *Novel in Seventeenth-Century China*, p. 185; and Chun-shu Chang and Shelley Hsueh-lun Chang, p. 71).

36. Li Baichuan's "Preface" to *Lüye xianzong* (100-chap. version), p. 15. See also Wu Jingzi's poem, "Ti Wang Shushan zuomaoyoujiang tu," in idem,

2.8b. According to Chen Meilin (*Wu Jingzi pingzhuan*, pp. 439–40), the words *zhushu* (writing a book) and *ziyu* (self-amusement) in this poem refer to Wu's writing of *The Scholars*. Many students of the Chinese novel have mentioned the eighteenth-century phenomenon of the "novel of erudition," a novel that displays the literati author's learning. *Humble Words* falls into this category. This emphasis on learning certainly limits the novel's readership. See also C. T. Hsia, "Scholar-Novelist," pp. 269–71.

37. "Yuqiu xiaosi," *Xianqing ouji*, collected in Li Yu, 3: 47; quoted and translated by Hanan, *Invention of Li Yu*, p. 36.

38. *Pingshan lengyan*, p. 233.

39. For more general discussions of the social and intellectual backgrounds of the Ming-Qing novel, see Plaks, *Four Masterworks*, pp. 3–52 (concentrating on the sixteenth century); Hegel, *Novel in Seventeenth-Century China*, pp. 1–65 (the seventeenth century); Chun-shu Chang and Shelley Chang, pp. 146–62, 267–304 (the seventeenth century; full of information but sometimes not persuasively argued); and Ropp, *Dissent in Early Modern China*, pp. 11–55 (the seventeenth and eighteenth centuries); Susan Naquin and Evelyn S. Rawski provide an overview of various aspects of eighteenth-century China in their *Chinese Society in the Eighteenth Century*. In the rest of this chapter, I limit my discussion to what I perceive to be the urgent issue of identity crisis confronting the literati during the eighteenth century and try to trace how the general anxiety produced by this profound sense of crisis gave rise to some of the special autobiographical features of the novels examined in detail later in this study.

40. See Schwartz, pp. 57–59. For a more detailed discussion of the rise of *shi* class in early China, see Yu Yingshi, "Gudai zhishi jieceng."

41. In a recent study of the intellectual transitions in Tang and Song China, Peter Bol (pp. 6–14, 32–36, 44–48) traces the transformation of *shi* identity during that period. He observes that the *shi* class was composed mainly of aristocratic great clans of illustrious pedigree (*shizu*) in the seventh century, civil bureaucrats in the tenth and eleventh centuries, and in the Southern Song more numerous but rarely illustrious local elite families. According to Bol (p. 33), "Between 600 and 1200, the three most important categories for defining qualities that made men shih were culture, birth, and office holding. . . . By 1200 the quality of birth had been redefined, and an illustrious pedigree was no longer important. . . . 'Culture' outweighed birth . . . and education was the normative ground for gaining high office." As we shall see, culture continued to be a decisive factor in determining one's status as a *shi* during the seventeenth and eighteenth centuries, although the specific content of that culture had become much more problematic.

42. Ibid., p. 342.

43. The ideal of "sage within and king without" is said to have been revived and fulfilled in the person of Wen Suchen, the protagonist of the novel *Humble Words* (see Chapter 4).

44. See Metzger's (pp. 75–76) pertinent observation: "After the failure of Wang An-shih's reforms, Neo-Confucians came generally to perceive this 'outer' realm as unmalleable, as drained of any inherent power to 'renew' itself without prior progress in the 'inner' realm of the mind." Cf. Peterson's (p. 3) related remarks: "In the Sung dynasty, there was a tendency among a relatively small segment of the educated elite away from *wanting* to assume administrative responsibilities and toward choosing instead to concentrate on improving one's moral self and teaching others about the Way. An important justification for the decision not to accept a government appointment was found in the claim that one could better serve the commonweal by promoting morality."

45. de Bary, "Neo-Confucian Cultivation," p. 204; many Qing literati liked to quote Zou Shan's (fl. 1556) criticism of Li Zhi to show how disgusted they were with the idea of sagehood in the late Ming: "Who does not want to be a sage or to be called virtuous, but it was always so inconvenient to become one. Now [according to Li Chih] nothing seems to obstruct the path to enlightenment—not even wine, women, wealth, and lack of self-control. This is quite a bargain, and who does not like a bargain?" (quoted and trans. in Nelson Wu, "Tung Ch'i-ch'ang," p. 280).

46. Elman, *From Philosophy to Philology*, p. 55.

47. In discussing the changing image of the literati in mid-Qing writings, Roddy (pp. 4, 7) relates the rising *kaozheng* movement of that period to this loss of moral authority of the literati: "For with the growth of an empirically oriented scholarship only tenuously tied to the realm of ethical value, Neo-Confucian thought seems to have lost its relevance as a guiding 'ideology' for the literati. This development inevitably affected how the literati defined their own tasks and even the justification for their position within society" because "the grand synthesis of Cheng-Zhu doctrines seems to have served to define the literati as a vocation, an 'identity' as the moral leaders of their communities." Roddy's discussions in his first chapter, "The Image of the Literati in Qing Discourse," are relevant to my argument here about the literati identity crisis in the eighteenth century, although he emphasizes more the intellectual factors behind this crisis, while I have so far approached this issue from a more sociological perspective. Ropp (*Dissent in Early Modern China*, p. 44) also notes that "intellectually, socially, and politically, Chinese scholars found themselves in a rather precarious position by the eighteenth century; while Ch'eng-Chu neo-Confucianism was being discredited through textual research, the exclusive study and mastery of Ch'eng-Chu the-

ories alone could guarantee the attainment and perpetuation of elite status through examination success."

48. "Fanxian shu zhong ji shedi Mo disishu," in Zheng Xie, pp. 12–13; trans. Lin Yutang, pp. 1076–77.

49. See Ping-ti Ho, *Ladder of Success*, pp. 188–92.

50. Probably because of this deteriorating situation there was a sudden surge in the Qing of fictional works dealing with many literati's frustrations in the civil service examinations (see Lien-hsiang Lin).

51. Yoshikawa, pp. 84–85. Although expressing reservations about Yoshikawa's emphasis on the "newness" of this *wenren* phenomenon in the Yuan, Peterson (pp. 32–33) agrees that it was on the rise in late imperial China.

52. In the late Ming, *wenren* was often associated with other catchy terms such as *shanren* (mountain man), *jushi* (recluse), and *buyi* (commoner). For example, *shanren* implied a person outside the official world (*wuweizhe*, or one who does not have official position). All these terms appear frequently in *The Scholars*. Another aspect of *wenren* is antagonism toward neo-Confucianism: the late Ming writer Gu Dashao commented that "to be a *wenren* one has to spend fifteen years in study, but one needs only three months to become a neo-Confucian scholar [*daoxue xiansheng*]"; quoted in Chen Wanyi, p. 51; see also Chen's general discussion of the *wenren* phenomenon in the late Ming, pp. 44–83. Thus, in a sense, to become a *wenren* was a conscientious choice made by those literati who could not be (or did not want be) either a *shidafu* or a neo-Confucian sage.

53. Withdrawal became a widespread social practice among the literati during the Wei-Jin period (220–420). One major difference between withdrawal during this period and that in the Ming and Qing periods is the overtly political nature of the former and the lack of political undertone in the latter (with some exceptions soon after the fall of the Ming). For a discussion of the kind of withdrawal that received Confucian sanction, see Mote, "Confucian Eremitism," pp. 202–40. In the novel *Humble Words* the idea of withdrawal in general receives severe criticism (see, e.g., chap. 140).

54. "Zaida Tao Guancha shu," *XWJ*, 16.7a.

55. Gu Yanwu ("Wenren zhiduo," *Rizhilu jishi*, 19.7b–8b) criticized the late Ming *wenren* by observing that in their various dilettantish pursuits they neglected the Classics, statecraft, and other practical learning that might otherwise have contributed to social well-being. Elsewhere in *Rizhilu* (19.11b–12b, 19.14b–16a and 26.34b–35a), Gu also attacked various "bad" habits of *wenren*; see also his "Yuren shu shiba" and "Yuren shu ershisi," in *Gu Tinglin shiwenji*, pp. 100, 102.

56. See Struve; and Peterson, pp. 1–17.

57. See Chen Xuewen.
58. Ping-ti Ho, "Salt Merchants," p. 130.
59. "Yufu zhi," in *Mingshi*, 11: 1671–72.
60. Ping-ti Ho, "Salt Merchants," p. 155n68.
61. *Luofan lou wenji, juan* 24; quoted in Yu Yingshi, "Zhongguo jinshi zongjiao lunli," p. 520.
62. Ping-ti Ho, "Salt Merchants," pp. 158–66; according to Ho (p. 165), from 1646 to 1802 the 300 or fewer transport and factory merchant families of the Liang-Huai area produced 139 *jinshi* and 208 *juren* degree holders. This is a very impressive success rate during that time; see also Xu Daling. For more recent discussions of social mobility in late imperial China, see Naquin and Rawski, pp. 123–27; and Clunas, pp. 141–65 (the latter focuses on the class anxiety caused by "commodity and consumption" but covers only the late Ming period).
63. Weinstein, pp. 148–49.
64. "Yu Jiang Bingu, Jiang Yujiu shu," in Zheng Xie, p. 191. Zheng Xie's remarks here are certainly related to the sense of moral inadequacy troubling many sensitive literati at that time (cf. Zheng's complaint about scholars' moral bankruptcy quoted earlier).
65. Weinstein, p. 149. For a discussion of Zheng Xie's well-known price list for his paintings, see Cheng-chi Hsü.
66. Though somewhat dated, Joseph R. Levenson's (pp. 15–43) discussion of the role of amateurism in Chinese literati tradition remains a convenient introduction on this issue.
67. Pohl, p. 32. This view seems to be shared by other students of Chinese art history. Nelson Wu ("Tung Ch'i-ch'ang," p. 275) notes that "by the seventeenth century, when the Southern school became decisively predominant, there were probably just as many professional amateurs as real amateurs." Cf. Weinstein's (p. 125) observation: "Thus Cheng Hsieh could see his painting as 'professional' because the distinction between scholar-amateur and professional was not a valid one for him."
68. Elman, *From Philosophy to Philology*, pp. 133, 135. In the field of literary writing, Li Yu was probably the first significant writer who could be considered a professional (who lived on his literary skill) in late imperial China. In the field of art, Chen Hongshou's (1598–1652) painting career may be considered one of the most telling cases of the dilemma faced by a seventeenth-century literati painter who had to struggle between the roles of the professional and the scholar-amateur; see Vinograd, esp. pp. 30–36.
69. Elman, *From Philosophy to Philology*, p. 67, and chap. 3, "The Professionalization of Lower Yangtze Academies," pp. 87–137.
70. Ibid., pp. 98–99.
71. See Du Weiyun.

72. The eighteenth-century scholar Zhang Xuecheng's (1738–1801) career is a case in point. Throughout his professional career as a scholar, he had to struggle constantly to seek patronage and to attain economic security. Even when he attained the *jinshi* degree at the age of 41, Zhang had to give up an official career largely because during that time a *jinshi* degree holder often had to wait as long as ten years before even a low-ranking position became available; for a study of his life, see Nivison, *Chang Hsüeh-ch'eng*.

73. See his poem "Bingzhong shugan," in Liu Dakui, p. 405. For a brief discussion of the history of *mufu* phenomenon, see Folson, pp. 33–57.

74. "Yu Xu Kejia" and "Yu Wang Yanru," in Gong Weizhai, pp. 44, 52.

75. Bol, p. 32.

76. Roddy (pp. 21, 22–27) finds a tension between what he considers the "diversification of social classifications" and the state-sponsored neo-Confucian concept of literati as "a harmonious and distinct group [potential servants of the throne]."

77. "Tongxin shuo," in Li Zhi, p. 99; quoted and trans. de Bary, "Individualism and Humanitarianism," p. 195; see also Li Zhi's criticism of those self-claimed "sages" and "mountain-men" (ibid., p. 206).

78. Vinograd, pp. 31–32, 36, 69.

79. Cahill, p. 124.

80. For a full translation of "Qijie" and detailed study, see Peterson, *passim*. Peterson (pp. 153–54) seems to believe that Baoshu Zi's final choice is to devote himself to the study of practical learning (*jingshi zhixue*): "Paoshu Tzu's resolution to 'recall times past, and consider the present situation of the world' implied the unambiguously Confucian aim of deriving guidance from history for moral conduct that has a social effect. More than that, it implied a life devoted to the scholarly pursuits that were to characterize the new orientation in thought in the seventeenth century."

81. Ibid., p. 150. Fang Yizhi's life has been characterized by another scholar as a constant process of negating his own past selves and of dealing with the ambiguities of his own self-identity (Jiang Guobao, chap. 3, pp. 33–79).

82. Plaks, *Four Masterworks*, p. 51. Here I consider Chen Hongshou and Fang Yizhi mainly late Ming figures. Hegel (*Novel in Seventeenth-Century China*, pp. 34–56, 105–6) discusses the issue of literati self-identity and self-expression in some seventeenth-century Chinese novels; see also his discussion (pp. 142–66) of Dong Yue's (1620–86) subtle psychological exploration of the issue of identity in *Xiyou bu*; Hegel (p. 147) also mentions Dong's fascination with names (he adopted more than twenty names for himself, a fascination shared by many of his contemporaries, such as the painter Bada shanren [1626–1705]).

Another related phenomenon, "gender fluidity" (the unstable boundaries between genders), that was becoming increasingly prevalent in the literati novel of the seventeenth and eighteenth centuries (as presented in *The Dream*) may also reflect this sense of the ambiguous self (see Chapter 3). Both Vinograd (pp. 28–67) and Zeitlin argue that "crossing boundaries" and an anxiety over such crossings characterize many works of art and literature in seventeenth- and eighteenth-century China; for other relevant discussions of gender fluidity in Ming-Qing China, see Furth; and Hinsch, pp. 118–61.

83. Elman (*From Philosophy to Philology*, pp. 29–32) argues that a "side-effect" of the "historicizing" approaches adopted by many eighteenth-century literati engaged in evidential study of the Classics was a general skepticism. Henderson (pp. 249–50) also detects among some Qing scholars an increasing awareness of the limitations of human knowledge. For example, Wang Xichan (1628–82) openly expressed doubts about men's ability to comprehend the rules of Heaven; see also Henderson's (pp. 227–56) discussions of what he has characterized as "anticosmological" worldview of the Qing literati. There was a particular attempt to deal with the "metaphysical crisis"—the traditional metaphysical system appeared to be losing its explanatory power in an increasingly complex and fragmented world.

84. Vinograd, p. 69. Vinograd (p. 70) further observes that "rather than the outspoken expression of anguish and resistance we find among seventeenth-century loyalists, however, the eighteenth-century response to the prevailing political and cultural climate of sham, grandiosity, and repression took the self-corrupting forms of cynicism and sycophancy."

85. "Xiti xiaoxiang ji Luo Liangfeng," in Yuan Mei, *Xiaocangshanfang chidu*, p. 290. Translation after Vinograd, p. 86; see also ibid., pp. 87–91. This fascination with one's own multiple selves and, furthermore, the willingness to play with this multiplicity were already anticipated by some seventeenth-century writers, such as Li Yu (e.g., in his various strategies of persona manipulation and self-invention; see the extensive discussion in Hanan, *Invention of Li Yu*); for a discussion of the rhetoric of the mask as a means for self-concealment as well as for self-expression in early Qing poetry, see Kang-i Sun Chang, "The Idea of the Mask"; see also Pei-yi Wu's (pp. 163–86) discussions of the strategies of self-invention of some late Ming autobiographers.

86. For other discussions of this emerging cynicism in the eighteenth century and its possible relation to the Qianlong emperor's various outrageous as well as cynical efforts at self-fashioning, see Nelson I. Wu, "Tolerance of the Eccentric"; Kahn; and Mote, "Intellectual Climate."

I believe this growing cynicism of the literati might also be related to their increasingly "depoliticization" (their exclusion from the political process) partly due to the power of the strong Manchu monarchs as well as the rapidly diminished opportunity for examination success and to their resulting sense of hopelessness. In this regard, *The Scholars* and *Humble Words* are very telling, as we will see later in this study.

87. Yang Maojian, 4.19; for an account of Huang's life, see Huang Yizhi. For a discussion of the literati passion for acting during that period, see Xu Fuming, pp. 150–58. It has been said that Cao Xueqin's grandfather Cao Yin (1658–1712) also shared this passion (Zhu Danwen, p. 35).

88. Cao Xueqin came from a family of Chinese bondservants (*baoyi*) attached to one of the Manchu banners (for the question of Cao's ethnic identity, see Chapter 3). His grandfather Cao Yin enjoyed special favors from the Kangxi emperor. For a study of Cao Yin's life, see Spence. Preston Torbert (pp. 69–77) has observed that because of the other advantageous avenues of social improvement available to those bondservants in the Imperial Household Department (Neiwu fu), though allowed to take the examinations, few of them really made this choice.

CHAPTER 2

EPIGRAPH, "The Critic as Artist," in Wilde, p. 389.

1. Pei-yi Wu, pp. 3–14, 71.
2. Ibid., p. 18.
3. "Zhuowu lunlüe," in Li Zhi, pp. 83–88. Here the last name of the narrator "kong" is an exact homophone in archaic Chinese of *kong* (empty). Thus his whole name "Kong Ruogu" may be read literally as "kong ruo gu" or "empty as a valley," calling attention to the fictional nature of this autobiographical narrative. See also Pei-yi Wu, p. 21.
4. Pei-yi Wu, p. 21. Wu (pp. 23–24) further observes that the "key to his success is the invention of the narrator-commentator K'ung, whose supposed closeness to Li made him privy to the domestic life of the biographical subject and afforded him an omnipresence seldom enjoyed by biographers. K'ung's professed insistence on writing a *lun* [comment] rather than a *chuan* [biography] relieved him of the necessity of relying on secondary sources and gave legitimacy to his narrative stance—reporting as an eyewitness and quoting at length from his subject. Li Chih himself . . . could then unabashedly employ the 'I' as long as he remained in the sanctuary of direct quotations. *This device, together with the persona of the Retired Gentleman Cho-wu, provides the autobiographer with sufficient distance that such a painful and personal story could be told without any effort to spare the protagonists, especially Li himself*" (my italics).
5. Cf. Stephen Owen's (*Traditional Chinese Poetry and Poetics*, p. 15) observations: "For Tu Fu's reader the poem is not a fiction: it is a unique, factual account of an experience in historical time, a human consciousness encountering, and responding to the world. And in his own turn the reader, at some later historical moment, encounters, interprets, and responds to the poem."

He (p. 15) further observes that "in the Chinese literary tradition, a poem is usually presumed to be nonfictional: its statements are taken as strictly true."

6. For the Chinese text and an English translation of the poem and the preface, see Wai-lim Yip, pp. 393–401.

7. In his discussion of autobiography in traditional Chinese poetry, Stephen Owen ("Self's Perfect Mirror," p. 72) points out that in traditional China "autobiography is not an easily recognizable literary form, but an intention, and for the reader, the intuition or the presumption of such an intention."

8. Pei-yi Wu, p. 19.

9. The new autobiographical possibilities that resulted from this masking strategy become more significant to the continued survival or even thriving of autobiographical sensibility in the genre of fictional narrative in a relatively more repressive cultural environment such as that of eighteenth-century China. This kind of sensibility had found its most successful expression in the self-writings of the late Ming, the golden age of traditional Chinese autobiography (see Pei-yi Wu, pp. 235–37). At the end of this chapter, I address a possible dilemma of the autobiographical enterprise in the novel that might be related to this masking strategy—the price the autobiographical self has to pay for relying too heavily on "others."

10. Cf. Peterson's (p. 20) observation about Fang's "Seven Solutions": "Because it was ostensibly fictional, Fang was released from the constraints of humility, but anyone who knew him easily understood whom the character Pao-shu Tzu represented." Despite the work's claim of fiction, several of Fang's friends felt, nevertheless, that Fang was too "overbearing" in "Seven Solutions" (ibid., pp. 14–15). Humility was supposed to be a main feature of autobiography in traditional China, although there were a few exceptions in the late Ming.

11. Peterson, p. 14.

12. In *Ciyuan* (p. 1403), one of the examples cited to illustrate the usage of *zikuang* is a passage from the biography of Tao Qian in the *Songshu* (The history of the Liu Song): "Tao Qian had been very proud even when he was very young. He wrote 'The Biography of Master Wuliu' for the sake of self-comparison (*zikuang*)." As mentioned earlier, Tao Qian was probably the first to write an autobiography in the guise of biography (self-presentation in the form of self-representation), and *zikuang* is the word to describe this kind of disguising strategy. In a postscript to an edition of *The Scholars*, Jin He described Du Shaoqing as an allegorical character referring to the author himself or as an example of self-comparison (*zikuang*; RLYZ, p. 129). Zhou Ruchang (*"Honglou meng" yu Zhonghua wenhua*, pp. 56–64) also finds *zikuang* a suitable word to describe the autobiographical features of *The*

Dream, although he seems to discern no difference between *zikuang* (self-comparison) and *zizhuan* (autobiography).

13. Robert Hegel (in the introduction to Hegel and Hessney, p. 3) uses the terms *revealed selves* and *created selves*. Of course, strictly speaking, a revealed self, in the sense used here, has to be a textual entity, already an other or created self, and the distinction between the two kinds of self is relative and at most heuristic.

14. Many scholars have noted the novel's indebtedness to the format of "linked biographies" (*liezhuan*) initiated by Sima Qian in his *Records of the Historian* and to the narrative structure of *The Water Margin*, although no one, as far as I know, has discussed how this structural format is employed in the novel for autobiographical purposes.

15. For a discussion of how traditional Chinese autobiographical writings suffered from the burden of the biographical convention in historiography, see Pei-yi Wu, pp. 3–14.

16. C. T. Hsia (*Classic Chinese Novel*, p. 246) complains that compared with Cao Xueqin's achievement Wu Jingzi manages only a "series of poses."

17. One of the main textual problems regarding *The Scholars* is the authenticity of chapter 56. Although the version used in this study contains 56 chapters, I tend to accept the theory that the novel originally had only 55 chapters.

18. See Tan Fengliang for a discussion of the possible relationship between the events in Wu's life and the writing of the novel.

19. Jin Liangming (fl. 1750), "He (Wu Qing) zuo" (*RLYZ*, p. 6).

20. In letters thought by some to be addressed to Wu Jingzi, the poet Yuan Mei (*XWJ*, 17.12a–13a) ironically calls the former a *shanren* (a man in the mountains) and laughs at him for "claiming himself to be a *wenren*" (*wenren ziming*). It is said that there were unpleasant incidents concerning the two. Once Yuan Mei even refused to receive Wu, and the abovementioned letters were part of a bitter correspondence between the two (*XWJ*, 17.12a–14a). One possible cause for this strained relationship was Yuan Mei's arrogance as a success in the examinations and Wu Jingzi's bitterness over his failures in the same field. For a discussion of this incident, see Meng Xingren and Meng Fanjing, pp. 273–78. In his most recent biography of the novelist, however, Chen Meilin (*Wu Jingzi pingzhuan*, pp. 309–13) expresses doubt that the addressee of these letters was Wu Jingzi and that there was any direct contact between the two, although he does not completely rule out the possibility. We do know (as Chen Meilin has also pointed out) that the description of the woman poet Shen Qiongzhi's experience with the magistrate in chapter 41 of the novel is based on an incident that happened to Yuan Mei when he was magistrate of Jiangning county, and thus, Wu must at least have

heard a lot about Yuan Mei. Furthermore, the two shared so many friends that it would be rather inconceivable that there were no direct contacts between them.

21. The fragmentation of the literati identity in *The Scholars* was vividly apparent to contemporary readers. After reading the novel, Yuan Mei deplored the tendency of this long narrative work to create, in an otherwise unified and harmonious literati world, a deep chasm between Confucian scholars (*rulin*) and men of culture (*wenren*). In a poem addressed to his friend Cheng Jinfang, who was also a friend of Wu Jingzi's, Yuan Mei (*xwj*, 6.2b) complained in an exaggerated fashion that since ancient times there had been no distinction between Confucian scholars and men of culture, but such a distinction had begun to appear only because of Wu Jingzi's novel. Yuan Mei's mention of the novel shows that he had read it, probably when its author was still alive or, at least, not long after he died. Of course, Yuan Mei was only too well aware of the ever-increasing chasm between *rulin* and *wenren*. In a letter to another friend, he (*xwj*, 19.6a) insisted that it was difficult to be both a scholar and a man of culture at the same time. It is apparent that Yuan Mei must have felt tremendous pressures to be a scholar since philology was becoming such a dominant trend in the eighteenth-century Chinese intellectual world.

22. The division of the novel into four sections is by no means absolute. Many obsessed examination candidates also appear in the second section, and different people try different means to achieve social success. Some of them may not be classified simply as *mingshi*. An important feature of the novel's narrative rhetoric is comparative juxtaposition (for example, the story of a relative authentic recluse will follow that of a fake one), a feature discussed below.

23. Here William C. Spengemann's (p. 130) observation on Charles Dickens's autobiographical strategy in *David Copperfield* is relevant: "Dickens's several past and present selves assume the guise of characters in a domestic novel and commune among selves in that invented world. Like Rousseau, Dickens saw in his past experiences not the tangled root-system of a single self but the seeds of many separate selves, all of whom had some ineffable kinship with each other but could be brought together only upon a fictive stage."

24. Most probably Wu Jingzi himself had never been to Beijing (Chen Ruheng, p. 88). He almost went there when he was recommended to take the Erudite Scholars examination, a factor that would have tremendous psychological impact on the author and a topic addressed below.

25. All these factors are certainly connected with Wu Jingzi's decision to exile himself to Nanjing.

26. He could never be an outsider in the true sense of the word, and his

stance is just as ambivalent as the implications of Nanjing are in the novel. At the symbolic level, as a pole opposite to the official world of Beijing, Nanjing seems to represent a place where unrecognized talents such as Du Shaoqing can find someone to appreciate them. However, the symbolic significances of the southern capital are sometimes ambivalent. For example, we are also told that Nanjing is place where "a man can easily starve to death" (*RLWS*, 28: 384; *S*, 308). During the last few years of his life, Wu Jingzi's stay in Nanjing was plagued by worries over poverty (Chen Meilin, *Wu Jingzi pingzhuan*, pp. 304–6). For a discussion of the significance of the travel motif in the novel, see Yue Hengjun.

27. "Ruyan fei," in Wu Jingzi, 4.6b. Cf. Timothy Wong's (p. 16) observation: "A central fact of Wu Ching-tzu's life is the high achievement and fame of his forebears, a fact which was to him at once a source of unceasing pride and, contrasted with his own failures in life, an eventual psychological burden." For relevant biographical information on Wu Jingzi, see Chen Meilin, *Wu Jingzi pingzhuan*.

28. Wu Linqi had always been thought to be Wu Jingzi's natural father since Hu Shi published his influential writings on Wu's life (see his "Wu Jingzi zhuan" and his "Wu Jingzi nianpu"). Recently, however, Chen Meilin has convincingly demonstrated that Wu Wenyan was Wu Jingzi's natural father and Wu Linqi was only his adoptive father. See Chen's relevant articles in his *Wu Jingzi yanjiu*, pp. 93–122. Later I return to the question of adoption and its relationship to some episodes in the novel.

29. Wu Jingzi, 1.7a–8a.

30. Hu Shi, "Wu Jingzi nianpu," p. 1088. Hu Shi (p. 1093) believed the novel was written between 1740 and 1750.

31. A few pieces of writing recovered more recently and believed to have been written by Wu Jingzi during his late years make no explicit references to these issues and thus are not helpful in determining Wu Jingzi's attitudes toward examinations and an official career after he was 40 (*RLYZ*, pp. 35–52).

32. See, e.g., Chen Xin; and Meng Xingren and Meng Fanjing, pp. 103–7.

33. See Tianmu shanqiao's relevant comment (*RLYZ*, 137–38): "Jin He in his postscript to *The Scholars* asserts that the author was no one else but the character who assumes the name of Du Shaoqing in the novel. However, in the novel Du Shaoqing is presented as rather a fool, and he hardly knows the world. Many readers have doubted this [autobiographical] claim. I would rather think this character is only Minxuan's [Wu Jingzi's] self-metaphor [*xingrongyu*] for his own self-allegorization [*zituo*] but not a direct autobiographical picture of himself." Obviously, Tianmu shanqiao objects to Jin He's "autobiographical" approach to the character of Du Shaoqing and to his view of the self-comparison (*zikuang*) relationship between Wu Jingzi

and this character. Tianmu shanqiao's comment here is relevant to my discussion of the hybrid nature of self-re/presentation, even though he is apparently not aware of the important distinction between autobiography and biography, which I am trying to call attention to.

34. C. T. Hsia, *Classic Chinese Novel*, p. 234.

35. See Du Shenqing's comment: "My cousin's weakness is this: anybody who claims to have known his father—even a dog—wins his respect. . . . Keep on harping on the fact that he is the only true patron in the world" (*RLWS*, 34: 421; *S*, 338).

36. Filiality as a phenomenon is generally presented in *The Scholars* as a moral virtue, although Du Shaoqing's case is more complicated.

37. In the novel, Shaoqing's father is said to be a palace graduate. However, Wu Jingzi's adoptive father, Wu Linqi, was actually only a *bagong* (an imperial student by selection), and he passed only the prefectural examination. Besides other possible implications, this subtle "elevation" may betray the novelist's anxiety or bitterness over his own failures in the examinations, especially in comparison with his family's glorious record of examination success. In chapter 44, the blind admiration and envy of the social status of provincial and palace graduates on the part of many vain people in Wuhe county are satirized (*RLWS*, 44: 600).

38. Both poems are entitled "The Song of a Poor Girl" ("Pinnü xing"). Wu Jingzi (3.1b–2a) compares himself to a poor girl resigned to her fate of being poor while her smug sister (representing his cousin Wu Qing) returns from the palace bragging about what she has seen there.

39. Ironically, it is in one of Wu Qing's poems, "On the Thirtieth Birthday of Minxuan," that we are told explicitly that Wu Jingzi once indulged in homosexual ventures, a way of life probably not uncommon among the *wenren* (men of culture) at that time. See especially the couplet "Drunk and wearing little, you slept with those charming boys,/ spending money like dust and sand" (*RLYZ*, p. 3). By describing homosexual romance as a central aspect of Shenqing's life in the novel, the author seems also to be criticizing his own past self in the form of re/presentation (presenting his own past self partly in the person of Shenqing).

40. What bothered Wu Jingzi was probably his cousin's success in the examinations.

41. For arguments that Wu Jingzi did feign illness, see Wu Xiaoru, "Wu Jingzi jiqi *Rulin waishi*"; He Manzi, p. 7; and Chen Xin. Their arguments are apparently biased by their refusal to see the difference between autobiography and biography and by their worry that a real illness would tarnish Wu Jingzi's image as a wholehearted satirist of traditional China. For a different view of this issue, see Chen Meilin, "Guanyu Wu Jingzi ying zhengbi

wenti." For studies in English that touch on this issue, see Ropp, *Dissent in Early Modern China*, pp. 262–63n53; and Wong, pp. 26–28.

42. James Olney, "Autobiography and the Cultural Movement," p. 19; cf. his remarks (p. 21): "It was this turning to *autos*—the 'I' that coming awake to its own being shapes and determines the nature of the autobiography and in so doing half discovers, half creates itself—that opened up the subject of autobiography specifically for literary discussion, for behind every work of literature there is an 'I' informing the whole and making its presence felt at every critical point, and without this 'I,' stated or implied, the work would collapse into mere insignificance."

43. The *Wenmushanfang ji* contains five poems with notes in which the honor of being recommended is duly mentioned. Since this collection must have been compiled by Wu Jingzi himself or by someone else with his consent, this fact testifies to the pride Wu took in this honor. Even as late as the year before his death, Wu Jingzi seemed to cherish the fact that he had once been recommended as a candidate for that examination; he mentioned this glory as one of his "official" titles on the first page of another collection of his poems (*RLYZ*, p. 51). See also Chen Meilin, "Guanyu Wu Jingzi ying zhengbi wenti"; and Rolston, "Theory and Practice," pp. 29–30.

44. Cf. Olney's ("Some Versions of Memory," p. 240) observation: "And to redeem the time is one of the autobiographer's prime motives, perhaps *the* prime motive—perhaps, indeed, the only real motive of the autobiographer."

45. See also Rolston, "Theory and Practice," pp. 692–93.

46. We know Yu Yude is modeled on one of Wu's friends, but the enormous pains Wu took to elevate and idealize this character tells us how much he invested in the creation of this character. For brief comparisons of Yu Yude in the novel and his real-life model, see He Zehan, "*Rulin waishi*" *renwu benshi kaolüe*, pp. 42–51; and *RLYZ*, pp. 200–202.

47. To a limited degree, the narrow-minded Miss Lu's claim that a man who has not passed the metropolitan examinations cannot be counted a romantic scholar (*mingshi*) is a valid observation (*RLWS*, 11:157). Yuan Mei (*XWJ*, 17.10b–11a) seems to have been quite aware of this. He advised one of his friends in a letter: "The worthlessness of writing examination essays is a fact that many people have long recognized. You are not the only person who would like to see them burned. However, my burning them is all right while your burning them is not. This is because I passed the examinations early in my life, and I am not an examination official. That's my luck. But since you have not got the *jinshi* degree, you mustn't give up the essays." Later in the same letter, Yuan Mei compared the examinations to a matchmaker and advised his friend that if he hated the "matchmaker" (writing eight-legged essays for the examinations), he should "get married" as quickly

as possible so that there would be no need to bother the matchmaker again. Besides adducing various practical reasons for passing the examinations (e.g., successes in the examination can bring economic security), Yuan Mei was trying to drive home the point that no matter how distasteful one finds the examinations, one must pass them in order to qualify as someone able to disparage them. Another interesting example is Wu Jingzi's friend Cheng Jinfang, who, though hating the eight-legged essays almost as much as Wu, tried all his life to pass the examinations and who later did become a *jinshi* (Chen Meilin, *Wu Jingzi pingzhuan*, p. 301).

48. Liu Xianxin (RLYZ, p. 294) has pointed out that Yu Huaxuan shares some important characteristics with Du Shaoqing. See also Ropp, *Dissent in Early Modern China*, pp. 111; and Rolston, "Theory and Practice," p. 747. Ropp (p. 276n78) also points out that Du Shaoqing is not the only autobiographical character in the novel.

49. Chen Meilin, *Wu Jingzi yanjiu*, pp. 101–6.

50. For a discussion of the function of ritual in the novel, see Shuen-fu Lin, "Ritual and Narrative Structure in *Ju-lin Wai-shih*."

51. This is reminiscent of the Qianlong emperor's posing as a hermit in a portrait, as discussed by art historians such as Nelson Wu and others.

52. The commentator of the *Woxian caotang* edition of the novel compares this autobiographical poem at the end of the novel to the famous "Self-preface" (*zixu*) that Sima Qian wrote for *The Records of the Historian* (RLWS, 56:761). Zbgniew Slupski (p. 46) notes that the poem forms "a special record of his changing attitude towards phenomena described" in the novel, and in it he discerns a "level of lyrical autobiography." In this article, Slupski argues that there are three levels of composition in the novel: the anecdotal, the biographical, and the autobiographical. He does not, however, address the question of autobiographical implications until the end of his article; his observations on this question, though interesting, are thus too brief to be persuasive.

CHAPTER 3

1. See Hu Shi, *Hu Shi "Honglou meng" yanjiu*; Yu Bingbo, *Yu Bingbo lun "Honglou meng"*; and Zhou Ruchang, *"Honglou meng" xinzheng*. The difficulties in reading *The Dream* as an autobiographical novel are partly due to the paucity of documented information about Cao Xueqin. Zhou Ruchang's monumental *"Honglou meng" xinzheng* has contributed tremendously to knowledge of the historical background of Cao Xueqin and his novel, although that knowledge still remains very limited. But Zhou tends to give people the impression that his strategy in this work is to use as imaginatively as possible the little information available to interpret the novel as

well as to use the novel to reconstruct Cao's life under the assumption that the novel is strictly (auto)biographical. There is a tautology involved here: the novel is proved to be autobiographical by establishing correspondences with data on the author's personal life even though these data are largely reconstructed from the novel under the presumption that the novel is autobiographical. What concerns Zhou Ruchang is probably not the "autobiographical" but the "biographical"—not how the fact that the author is the subject of his own writing transforms the writing of the novel but, rather, what is transmitted through the novel that actually happened to the author. Here William C. Spengemann's (p. 19) observation is pertinent: "The fictional detail we can trace back to some documented event in the writer's prior life is not more autobiographical than one whose source we cannot discover because the germinal experience was either too deeply personal to admit of documentation or too common to be noticed. For that matter, unless we take a writer's 'life' to include only those situations, actions, and experiences for which we have some independent evidence . . . everything a novelist puts into his fiction has a source somewhere in his 'life.'" This is not to deny the significance of studying the biographical facts of Cao Xueqin. The present discussion of *The Dream*, as will be seen later, is deeply indebted to the works by scholars such as Zhou Ruchang. In a recent letter to the author, Zhou Ruchang acknowledges that his *kaozheng* work on *The Dream* was aimed at the general historical background of the novel (literary trends, the nature of the Imperial Household Department [Neiwu fu], the life of the literati during that time, etc.) rather than at attempting to establish rigid correspondences between the novel and the author's life, and that *"Honglou meng" xinzheng* was a work conditioned by particular historical (especially political) circumstances. Indeed, in his more recent work (*"Honglou meng" yu Zhonghua wenhua*, pp. 56–64), Zhou Ruchang began to pay more attention to the question of *zikuang* (self-comparison) in the novel.

2. For a brief review in English of *The Dream*'s textual history, see Miller, pp. 257–77.

3. Basically, there are three theories about the authorship of the last 40 chapters: they were written by Gao E; they were written by Cao Xueqin and were edited by Gao E; they were written by someone other than Cao and Gao (Feng Qiyong and Li Xifan, pp. 1086–87). My decision to confine my discussion to the first 80 chapters is basically tactical or heuristic for the simple reason that a study of the autobiographical cannot afford uncertain authorship.

4. See, e.g., Feng Qiyong, *Lun gengchen ben*, esp. pp. 85–89; and Ying Bicheng, esp. pp. 111–12.

5. Feng Qiyong and others recently produced a single collated edition that

contains all eleven extant manuscript versions plus the first printed edition of the novel published by Cheng Weiyuan (the so-called Chengjia [1791] edition). This edition allows a comparison of all these versions line by line simultaneously. I refer to this collated edition (as ZHJ) whenever textual differences become significant to my analysis.

6. For example, Angela Jung Palandri (p. 227) considers it to be "fundamentally a novel about women."

7. Here I am basically following (with some modifications) the translation by Hsien-yi Yang and Gladys Yang (chap. 1, pp. 1–2), because theirs is more literal than that of Hawkes. In some manuscript versions of the novel the passage quoted is not included as a part of the novel proper (Hawkes translates and quotes this passage in his introduction to his translation rather than including it in the novel proper [SS, 1. 20–21]). See, e.g., the modern facsimile reprint of the *jiaxu* (1754) version of the manuscript, Cao Xueqin, *Zhiyan zhai chongping "Shitou ji,"* 2a–2b; and ZHJ, pp. 1–5. Some scholars consider it part of the commentary written by Zhiyan zhai or someone else. For example, Wu Shih-chang (pp. 63–72) thinks these remarks by Cao Xueqin were made by his brother, Cao Tangcun, in his preface to an earlier version of the novel. However, that these are Cao Xueqin's own words is beyond doubt. See also Miller, pp. 206–19.

8. HZJL, 1: 1 (the *Mengfu* manuscript version, interlinear comment). As to the identity of Zhiyan zhai and whether commentaries written under other names in these manuscripts, such as Jihu sou (Odd Tablet) were made by the same person, scholarly opinion is still divided. One thing that is certain is that he (or they) must have been very close to Cao Xueqin. For studies on this question, see Wu Shih-chang, pp. 50–102; Zhao Gang and Chen Zhongyi, pp. 73–138; and Sun Xun, pp. 43–77. For the sake of convenience, in this study, I will refer to Zhiyan zhai as the author of all the commentaries in the so-called Zhiyan zhai manuscript versions of the novel.

9. Scholars such as Zhao Gang (see Zhao Gang and Chen Zhongyi, pp. 171–72) and Wu Shih-chang (pp. 89–97) have speculated that Baoyu is a character modeled on the life of the author himself and that of Zhiyan zhai as well. Even if we find their observations persuasive, that the novel is autobiographical should not be doubted partly because the construction of the autobiographical self does not have to be modeled on the authorial self only. On the other hand, as I argue in the following pages, Cao also appropriates other characters in the novel for his autobiographical agenda, and Baoyu is not the author's only autobiographical character in the novel.

10. "Jiechao," quoted in Han Jingtai, p. 270. See also Wilhelm, for a discussion of expressions of this sentiment in many works of rhyme-prose written during the Han dynasty.

11. The rapidly increasing competition in the civil-service examinations

during late imperial China seemed to have further marginalized many literati (see Chapter 1 of this study). In *Male Anxiety and Female Chastity*, Ju-k'ang T'ien even points to the rising anxiety of male literati due to failure in the civil-service examinations as a direct cause of the increasingly popular practice during the Ming-Qing period of suicide among women for the purpose of acquiring a reputation for chastity.

12. Of interest is Julia Kristeva's definition of femininity as explained by Toril Moi (p. 166): "If 'femininity' has a definition at all in Kristevan terms, it is simply, as we have seen, as 'that which is marginalized by the patriarchal symbolic order.' This relational 'definition' is as shifting as the various forms of patriarchy itself, and allows her to argue that men can also be constructed as marginal by the symbolic order. . . . What is perceived as marginal at any given time depends on the position one occupies." The "relational" nature of this theory of femininity has caused some feminists to label it "antifeminist" feminism. For a brief discussion and defense of Kristeva, see Lechte, pp. 201–8. In *Gender Trouble*, Judith Butler (pp. 24–25, 134–141) has argued that "gender" should be understood as "performance" or "a process."

13. Needham and Wang, 2: 279–80. See also relevant discussions by Mundakata; and Pauline Yu, pp. 37–43.

14. Legge, p. 420; my italics.

15. *Chunqiu fanlu*, 12.5b–6a; English translation from Fung, 2: 42–43.

16. For a discussion of this phenomenon of seeking recognition, see Henry.

17. "Cike liezhuan," in Sima Qian, 8: 2519.

18. Kristeva considers *avant-garde* artists marginal and thus belonging to the same category of "feminine" (Moi, pp. 164–66).

19. For an excellent study of the ups and downs of the cult of Qu Yuan in Chinese history, see Schneider. See also You Guo'en, for a discussion of the gender question in Qu Yuan's poetry.

20. Pei Puxian.

21. Waley, pp. 6–7. For discussions of the psychology of traditional literati and the use of woman images in their poetry, see Lü Zhenghui, pp. 209–21; Ye Jiaying; and Fong, "Contextualization and Generic Codes." In *The Late-Ming Poet Ch'en Tzu-lung*, Kang-i Sun Chang discusses a number of tragic love poems by Chen Zilong (1608–47) as allegorical works mourning the fall of the Ming dynasty. Indeed, Pauline Yu (p. 123) has observed that "the categorical correspondence between wife and minister was a deeply rooted cultural assumption, so that any allusion to one would unavoidably implicate the other"; for an account of the ambivalent image of the feminine in the early Chinese poetic tradition, see Wai-yee Li, pp. 3–46.

22. See my "Dehistoricization and Intertextualization," p. 58. In that ar-

ticle, I interpret this development as a phenomenon of the privatization of the novel during that period.

23. McMahon (*Causality and Containment*, p. 34) notes that "male characters are shown as more sexually and sentimentally open to women and, at times, they assume feminine appearance." See also ibid., p. 51.

24. See Zhao Xingqin, "'Cai' yu 'mei.'"

25. Ibid., pp. 20–21.

26. Although there is evidence of more tolerant attitudes toward women during that period, some scholars have also observed that the cult of chaste widowhood reached a new height at approximately the same time. See Elvin; and Ju-k'ang T'ien, who argues that the cult of chastity was related to the anxieties of the male literati arising from their frustrations with the examinations. Some historians have noted the increasingly active presence of women poets in the Ming-Qing literary scene. This phenomenon might be reflected in the representation of female talents in contemporary literati fiction. Their findings, however, should not weaken my argument here that the fictional representation of women by some literati is problematized by their own male anxiety. For a review of recent studies on Ming-Qing women, see Bernhardt.

27. The most famous example is probably the case of the heroine Lu Mengli in *Yu jiao li*. Other *caizi jiaren* works where I have found cases of gender switching include *Liangjiao hun*, *Fenghuang chi*, *Chunliuying*, *Liner bao*, *Yuanyang zhen*, and *Yunxian xiao* (the last two works are collections of short stories, some of which do not belong to the *caizi jiaren* category). "Li Xiuqing Marries the Virtuous Huang," the twenty-eighth story in the *Yushi mingyan* by Feng Menglong (1574–1646) and Xu Wei's (1521–1593) famous play *Nü zhuangyuan* are based on this kind of gender switching or cross-dressing. Richard Hessney ("Beautiful, Talented, and Brave," p. 95) notes that "if the scholar and the beauty share their most vital characteristics, then they are essentially interchangeable" and that we can find "frequent use of disguises by both the scholars and the beauties in the romances."

28. In some of Pu Songling's stories the same strategy of gender switching is used. For example, in "Yanshi" the wife pretends to be her husband's brother and achieves the top honors in the examinations while the husband remains a miserable failure; for a discussion of gender questions in *Strange Stories from the Studio of Leisure* from a different perspective, see Zeitlin, pp. 98–131.

29. Yuanhu yanshui sanren, pp. 2–3. The exact authorship and date of this work are unresolved issues. It is generally considered to be an early Qing work (see Lin Chen, pp. 313–17). Compare the somewhat similar remarks made by Cao Xueqin at the beginning of *The Dream*, discussed above. The similar rhetoric (the celebration of female talent and virtue) is also employed

at the beginning of another Qing novel, *The Destinies of the Flowers in the Mirror* (*Jinghua yuan*) by Li Ruzhen (ca. 1763–1830).

30. Yuanhu yanshui sanren, *juan* 1, p. 1.

31. The three Chinese characters that make up the title of this novel, like those in the title of the famous Ming novel *The Plum in the Golden Vase* (*Jin Ping Mei*), denote three women characters who are all married to the same man in the novel. The title proves to be rather resistant to an accurate English rendering. Scholars have not been able to determine the exact date of this work and the identity of its author. Chen Hong argues that the novel was probably written during the Kangxi period. However, others have speculated that its author was probably a contemporary of Cao Xueqin (see, e.g., Lin Chen, p. 412).

32. *Lin Lan Xiang*, pp. 1, 495.

33. Ibid., p. 497. Some critics have argued that in many ways *Lin Lan Xiang* anticipated *The Dream*, especially in its fascinating depiction of female characters and domestic environment and in its fascination with the reality of dream. See, e.g., Zhang Jun.

34. Many of Shuangqing's poems as quoted in *Random Notes of Western Green* were later anthologized in various collections of Qing women poets. However, scholars have never been able to verify the existence of this poetess outside Shi Zhenlin's writing. Many have doubted whether this unrecognized female talent was a historical person and have suspected that she was a sheer fabrication by a male literatus who invented this other to relieve his own male anxiety (see, e.g., Hu Shi, "He Shuangqing kao"). Whether Shuangqing existed or not, that the Shuangqing we know from the *Random Notes of Western Green* is a "feminine" construction by a male literatus seems beyond doubt. For discussions of this memoir emphasizing the possible male literati anxieties implied, see Kang Zhengguo; and Fong, "Constructing a Feminine Ideal"; see also Ropp, "Shi Zhenlin and the Poetess Shuangqing" for a discussion from a slightly different perspective.

35. Shi Zhenlin, 2.28.

36. Ibid., 3.62–63.

37. For discussions of the "ethnic" (or "racial") identity of Cao Xueqin's ancestors, see Zhou Ruchang, "*Honglou meng*" *xinzheng*, pp. 122–40; Zhang Shucai; and Zhao Gang and Chen Zhongyi, pp. 1–7. In a recent study of the "racial" self-identity of the Manchus, Pamela Crossley (*Orphan Warriors*, pp. 13–30) has argued that "Manchu" as a "racial" or "ethnic" term was extremely ambiguous and "fluid" throughout Qing history, especially during the early Qing (see also Pei Huang, "New Light"; and Yang Xuechen). Elsewhere Crossley ("Qianlong Retrospect") discusses how the so-called *hanjun* or Chinese bannermen were caught between the "contradictions of the ideology of loyalty of the Qianlong period" and how their "racial am-

biguities" were exploited by the Qianlong court to promote its own political agenda by means of establishing new and more rigid "racial" criteria or vocabulary in order to maintain (the illusion of) the racial purity of the Manchus, which was being increasingly encroached on by the Han Chinese culture during that time (see also Chen Jiahua and Fu Kedong). Of course, the Caos were bondservants of Chinese origins that attached to the Manchu banner rather than Chinese bannermen (a subtle but significant fact that some scholars, such as Zhou Ruchang, have called attention to). Nevertheless, the new "racial atmosphere" during the Qianlong period must have made people like the Caos whose racial identity had always been a problem feel more vulnerable and confused. This unique case of racial ambiguities might be related to the seemingly confusing and sometimes contradictory "racial references" in *The Dream*. On the one hand, there are ample suggestions in the novel that the Jia family are Manchus, or at least, a family deeply influenced by Manchu culture (see Song Deyin), but, on the other hand, there are also many places where anti-Manchu sentiments are quite visible, though probably never so systematically or self-consciously represented as the "allegorists" (*suoyin pai*) have claimed (see Yu Yingshi, "Guanyu *Honglou meng*" and "Cao Xueqin").

38. See Zhou Ruchang, *"Honglou meng" xinzheng*, pp. 19–20. For studies of the phenomenon of bondservants, see Torbert; and Spence, pp. 1–41.

39. See Zhou Ruchang, *Cao Xueqin xiaozhuan*, pp. 103–4; according to Zhou (*"Honglou meng" xinzheng*, pp. 731–32), the Qianlong court had a very restrictive policy regarding the participation of Manchu bannermen in the examinations. Indeed, up until the late eighteenth century, the Qing monarchy's attitude toward Manchu bannermen's taking the civil-service examinations was rather ambivalent. The Manchu emperors, on the one hand, hoped that the Manchus could distinguish themselves with their traditional "military skills" (*wugong*) and thus retain their racial identity; on the other hand, they hoped that more Manchus could participate in the governing process by passing the civil-service examinations. See Teng Shaozhen, pp. 71–77. In any event, as a member of a family of bondservants attached to a Manchu banner receiving favors from the emperor, Cao would probably not consider himself a literatus (in the full sense of this word—as someone who depended on "learning" for his career or livelihood) till his family became bankrupt (see Torbert, pp. 69–77).

40. See Schneider, pp. 12–13, 24–26, 36, 44.

41. All of them are registered in the "Department of Ill-Fated Fair" (*SS*, 1.131).

42. See Zhiyan zhai's (*HZJL*, chap. 5, p. 94; the *jiaxu* manuscript version) interlinear comment on this couplet: "A line of lamentation and it refers to the author himself."

43. Ibid., chap. 1, p. 14 (marginal comment in the *jiaxu* version).
44. *HZJL*, chap. 2, p. 38 (the *jiaxu* manuscript version, marginal comment). For a brief discussion of the allusion in Zhiyan's comment here to some lines from the *Book of Songs*, see Wu Shih-chang, p. 119*n*4. Most scholars tend to follow strictly the meaning of the original lines from the *Book of Songs* in their factual interpretation of this allusion here in the novel—namely, that it refers to the strained relationship between brothers— and believe that Zhiyan zhai is hinting at the internal struggles among Cao Xueqin's male relatives (see, e.g., Zhu Danwen, pp. 111–14). I choose, however, to emphasize the more general implications of this gender juxtaposition, as clearly intended in Zhiyan zhai's comment. That is to say, the commentator is reminding us that the detailed description of many female characters in the novel can be read allegorically as referring to the anxiety among men. Another mention of this allusion can be found in chapter 15 (*H*, 15: 200; *SS*, 1.289): meeting Baoyu for the first time, the Prince of Beijing gave him a rosary called "the wagtail fragrance rosary" (*jiling xiangnian zhu*) (Hawkes translates this as "rosary made of the aromatic seeds of some Indian plant"). Erzhi daoren points out that Cao Xueqin tried to find relief for his frustrations and anger (*gufen*) through writing about romantic love; see his "*Honglou meng* shuomeng," in Yisu, p. 83.
45. This important passage regarding Baoyu's reasoning about why and how he should write this piece is missing from the printed editions published by Cheng Weiyuan; Hawkes also omits some sentences in his translation. See *ZHJ*, pp. 4689–92.
46. The figures referred to include Qu Yuan, Jia Yi (200–168 B.C.), Ji Kang (224–63), and Shi Chong (249–300), literati known for their political misfortunes.
47. Cf. Miller's (p. 232) relevant observation: "The irony inherent in Paoyu's elegy for Ch'ing-wen is that it is really about himself—it reveals that he is absorbed with the problem of writing and with fears about his personal mutability even more than he is concerned with Ch'ing-wen's death."
48. The beautiful goddess is described much in the fashion of Qu Yuan's *meiren xiangcao*. Cao Zhi stated in his preface to the *fu* that he was inspired by Song Yu's (probably a disciple of Qu Yuan) *fu* of the same title. There are controversies over the real allegorical intention behind this work. Some annotators, such as Li Shan (ca. 630–89), considered it as referring to his actual frustrated love for Zhen Mi (See Li Shan, 19.9a). However, considering the fact that Cao Zhi wrote a number of well-known allegorical poems (such as "Meinü") and the work's apparent indebtedness to Qu Yuan and Song Yu, most scholars agree that the *fu* is a political allegory. For example, see the Qing annotator Ding Yan (1794–1875), *juan* 2. Taking into consideration that the "Jinghuan xianzi fu" (the rhyme-prose on the Fairy Disenchantment)

in chapter 5 of the novel is clearly an emulation of Cao Zhi's "Luoshen fu," we will find that Baoyu's comment here on the goddess of the river Luo is all the more significant.

49. Thus, the stereotyped pattern of gender switching in "scholars and beauties" fiction, namely a girl is often raised (educated) like a boy because her parents have no male heir, is reversed here: a boy is raised like a girl even though he is considered the male heir.

50. This passage is omitted from the editions of the novel printed by Cheng Weiyuan; see *ZHJ*, pp. 4620–21.

51. Louise Edwards ("Gender Imperatives in *Honglou meng*, p. 77) notes that "[Baoyu's] social position as a young gentleman ensures that the sexual power he loses through the adoption of feminine traits is balanced by a general political power." Thus Baoyu's masculinity is guaranteed by the political structure of the Jia family.

52. Cf. Angelina C. Yee's (p. 623) observation that "the interweaving of the two worlds is accomplished through the mediation of two crucial characters, Xi-feng and Bao-yu." Zhou Ruchang (*"Honglou meng" yu Zhonghua wenhua*, pp. 195–205) also calls attention to the structural importance of the character of Xifeng.

53. "The role reversal between Xi-feng and Bao-yu is significant. Bao-yu is associated with qualities that the novel has implicitly identified as feminine: pacificity, poetry, and feeling, whereas Xi-feng's maleness consists in her ambition, greed and duplicity" (Yee, p. 641).

54. The storyteller's tale provokes a critique from Grandma Jia on the tradition of "scholars and beauties" fiction. The possible relationship between the character of Wang Xifeng and male anxiety is implicitly suggested by virtue of this reference to this tradition, which was to a certain degree an exercise in wish-fulfillment by some frustrated literati authors.

55. Cf. Louise Edwards's feminist reading of this episode, "Women in *Honglou meng*," pp. 419–20.

56. This "reversal" is later repeated by You Sanjie in her encounter with Jia Zhen and Jia Lian: "It was as though the roles had been reversed—as though she was the man and they were a pair of poor, simpering playthings whose service she had paid for" (*H*, 65: 931; *SS*, 3.283). See also Yee, p. 639.

57. There are some differences in the wording of this passage in different editions. Hawkes's translation here is probably based on the edition printed by Cheng Weiyuan (see also *H*, 77: 1109–10; and *ZHJ*, pp. 4589–90).

58. See Edwards's ("Gender Imperatives in *Honglou meng*," p. 76) remarks: "In actuality, Baoyu was placed in the reverse role by her aggression—that of sexualized Other rather than desiring Self."

59. Before being given to Xiangyun as a maid, Kuiguan is an actress specializing in the role of *hualian* (painted face, usually a male role). Here the

idea of "gender fluidity" is very much in the play. This long passage on changing maids' names is missing from the editions printed by Cheng Weiyuan and from some other manuscript versions, probably due to its risky references to the sensitive topic of race (see ZHJ, pp. 3551–58). Hawkes does not translate the whole passage as given in the *gengchen* edition (SS, 3.236–37). The translation here is mine.

60. A related detail is that Grandma Jia once mistakes Xiangyun for Baoyu and thinks that "she made a very good-looking boy" (H, 31.435–36; SS, 2.118); see also Daiyu's remarks: "If you were a man, you could go around like a knight-errant putting the world to rights; but a Jing Ke in skirts is just plain ridiculous!" (H, 57.815; SS, 3.115).

61. HZJL, chap. 34, p. 437 (the *jimao* [1759] and *jiaxu* manuscript versions, interlinear comment).

62. For a brief discussion of the implied "identifying" relationship between Daiyu and the novelist Cao Xueqin, see Yu Pingbo, "Cao Xueqin zibi Lin Daiyu."

63. See Cai Yijiang's "Preface" in *"Honglou meng" shi ci qu fu pingzhu*, p. 8. My discussion here is mainly based on Cai's analyses (pp. 7–8). See also his discussion of Tanchun's "Wearing the Chrysanthemums" and its relationship to one of Li Bai's poems (ibid.).

64. For another discussion of Baoyu's reluctance to grow up, see Zhu Xuequn; his approach and emphases are quite different from mine.

65. For discussions of the significance of the garden in the novel, see Plaks, *Archetype and Allegory*, pp. 178–211; Ying-shih Yü; C. Xiao; and my "Dilemma of Chinese Lyricism," pp. 56–73.

66. For discussions of the chronology of the novel and its possible implications, see Du Jinghua; Zhou Ruchang, *"Honglou meng" xinzheng*, pp. 183–212; and Pan Mingshen, *"Shitou ji" nianri kao*; see also Hawkes's relevant observations (SS, 2.17).

67. In chapter 25, when Baoyu becomes sick, the author goes out of his way to have the priest tell us that it has been thirteen years since he saw the jade under Green-sickness Peak (H, 25.357; SS, 1.505); on other occasions the author is reticent about Baoyu's age, and the reader never knows exactly when his birthday is.

68. Some scholars, such as Wu Shih-chang, have found Dai's theory of "rewriting" appealing despite serious doubts about his supporting evidence. However, most *Hongxue* students have found it too shaky to be persuasive. For Dai's theory on the authorship of the novel and various rebuttals from other *Hongxue* scholars, see the articles collected in *"Honglou meng" zhuzuoquan lunzhengji*.

69. For a detailed discussion of anachronism in *The Dream* and another possible chronology of the novel, see Dai Bufan. Zhu Danwen (pp. 195–259)

has tried to reconstruct the complicated process of Cao Xueqin's rewriting and editing of *The Dream* by analyzing various cases of anachronism in the novel.

70. For the Yongzheng emperor's decree, see *Guanyu Jiangning zhizao Caojia dang'an shiliao*, p. 185. The various official documents collected in this book make clear the dramatic decline of the fortunes of the Caos after Yongzheng ascended the throne in 1722. See also Zhu Danwen, pp. 74–120 (she tends to emphasize internal conflicts among the Cao family members as the main cause of the final collapse of the family); and Zhao Gang and Chen Zhongyi, pp. 24–34.

71. There are many theories about exactly when Cao Xueqin was born. The two most widely accepted dates are 1715 and 1724. The evidence for the former seems stronger to me. However, both theories agree that something terrible happened when Cao Xueqin was thirteen. According to Zhou Ruchang (*"Honglou meng" xinzheng*, pp. 676–84; *Cao Xueqin xiaozhuan*, pp. 48–53, esp. 51–52), who is the major scholar proposing that Cao Xueqin was born in 1724, the Cao family began to decline even more drastically when it suffered a second disgrace around 1736 during the reign of the Qianlong emperor (when Cao Xueqin was thirteen!). For a convenient review of the controversies over the dates of Cao Xueqin's birth and death, see Xiao Hai. Even though the idea that Cao Xueqin was exactly thirteen when his family experienced a dramatic downfall is only a hypothesis and might be invalidated by biographical evidence uncovered in the future (an unlikely possibility), the profound attachment to childhood and the persistent reluctance to grow up in the novel are worth special attention in the effort to discern an autobiographical structure of the novel.

72. This is certainly one of the best examples of the author's strategy of hiding truth (*zhenshi yin*). Persuaded by many clues provided in the first 80 chapters and the commentaries by Zhiyan zhai, many scholars believe that the final end of the Jia family planned by Cao Xueqin would have been much more tragic than what we have now in the last 40 chapters.

73. Even if we accept the ending of 120-chapter version of the novel in which Baoyu renounces the world and becomes a monk, we cannot conclude that this is a conversion, an experience often described in a Western autobiography. It is, rather, an ultimate gesture of refusal to take any positive literati roles. Cf. Stephen Owen's ("Self's Perfect Mirror," p. 73) observation: "Out of the Augustinian tradition, western narrative autobiography becomes possible: it recounts the essential changes of life between youth and maturity, a *Bildung* after which human nature grows steady. But such autobiography can have no place in the Chinese tradition: one may 'set one's mind on study at fifteen and be established at thirty,' but all the most interesting states of sagely development occur from the age of forty on. Given the

Confucian *Bildung* of late-flowering, it is hard to anticipate a final stasis from which to look back and write one's Life as a whole." In a note on the same page, Owen further observes that *The Dream* "would seem to be an interesting exception, but in its autobiographical dimension it is less a true *Bildung* than a case in which the world changes around the protagonist." Although Owen's generalization about the Chinese autobiographical tradition may need to be qualified somewhat (especially following Pei-yi Wu's study), his comment on *The Dream* is insightful; Wai-yee Li (pp. 202 and 219) presents a similar view on this issue.

74. See Yisu, p. 1.

75. See Dun Cheng's poem on his drinking with Cao, in Yisu, pp. 1–2; and Zhou Ruchang, *"Honglou meng" xinzheng*, p. 701.

76. In fact, for a period of time, Cao Xueqin probably did derive an income from selling his paintings (Zhou Ruchang, *Cao Xueqin xiaozhuan*, pp. 182–83).

77. C. T. Hsia, *Classical Chinese Novel*, p. 247; see also Chen Liao.

78. Confession of one's sin in written form was not a common practice in traditional China; the closest kind of writing is probably *zisong* (self-indictment). Having demonstrated that confession in the sense of disclosure of sin did exist in Chinese history, Pei-yi Wu (p. 233) is quick to point out that it was only a marginal phenomenon: "the insistence on self-disclosure" is a minor strain in the "complex fabric of intellectual and spiritual history of late Ming and early Ch'ing."

79. Zhou Ruchang, *"Honglou meng" yu Zhonghua wenhua*, pp. 137–38; and idem, *"Honglou meng" xinzheng*, pp. 829–31.

80. Cf. Owen, *Remembrances*, pp. 134–41.

81. Cf. Jean Starobinski's (p. 78) observation that "one would hardly have sufficient motive to write an autobiography had not some radical change occurred in his life—conversion, entry into a new life, the operation of Grace." See also John Henry Newman's remarks (quoted in Olney, *Metaphors of Self*, p. 41): "From the moment I became a Catholic, of course I have no further history of my religious opinion to narrate." What makes the autobiographical experience in *The Dream* so different is that Baoyu remains unchanged throughout the novel; it is his environment that changes in the course of the novel.

82. See Doody, pp. 18, 22. In chap. 2, "Confession's Rhetoric: Making a Confessor," Doody provides a convenient survey of various theories on confession in the West. Doody (esp. pp. 7, 21) tends to emphasize the role played the concept of "community" in the act of confession—the need to be readmitted or "validated" by the community (the confessor); according to him, the sense of guilt alone cannot account for all aspects of confession.

83. Zhou Ruchang (*"Honglou meng" yu Zhonghua wenhua*, p. 78n1)

seems careful to distinguish autobiography as practiced under the influence of traditional Chinese historiography from the Western autobiography written in the confessional mode that emphasizes the disclosure of sin and exploration of individual psyche. However, to support his own argument that *The Dream* is strictly autobiographical (or rather biographical), Zhou (ibid., pp. 82, 86) cites without qualification other critics' observations on this topic that apparently appeal to the Western concept of confession.

CHAPTER 4

1. Three editions of the novel published during the Guangxu reign period (1875–1907), approximately one hundred years after the death of the author, are still extant. The Piling huizhenlou edition (dated 1881) consists of 152 chapters with interlinear and chapter-end commentaries, but contains various lacunae. The Shenbaoguan edition, dated 1882, contains 154 chapters with only chapter-end commentaries similar to those of the 1881 edition; the Shiyinben edition (dated 1882) is identical to the Shenbaoguan edition. For a brief description of these editions, see ZMTY, p. 501. Most scholars believe that the Piling huizhenlou edition is closest to Xia's original manuscript, and the Shenbaoguan edition, despite (or because of) its completeness, was reedited by someone else. See, e.g., Sun Kaidi, "Xia Erming." In a recent article ("*Yesou puyan* banben bianxi"), however, Ouyang Jian argues that these two editions are both incomplete but equally authentic versions of Xia's completed manuscript. Ouyang Jian's argument seems partially supported by the existence of a manuscript version of the novel (dated 1878) identical to the Shenbaoguan edition. For a brief description of this manuscript version, see the entry on *Yesou puyan* in Liu Shide et al., p. 669.

The version of the novel used in this study is a modern typeset edition entitled *Wen Suchen* (referred to as W), which is apparently a reprint of the 154-chapter edition published by Shijie shuju (originally Shanghai, 1937) with all the explicit descriptions of sex expurgated; this edition is based on the 1882 version. However, the Piling huizhenlou edition will be referred to (as Y) whenever the expurgated passages or textual differences become significant to my discussion. For a comparison list of the chapter titles of the Piling huizhenlou, Shiyinben, and Shijie shuju editions, see the appendix in Wang Qiongling, pp. 165–83.

2. Cf. the statement in the "Editorial Principles" ("Fanli") section of the 1881 edition that the novel's title "indicates that the author considers himself to be an old rustic giving a 'pure talk' (*qingtan*) while enjoying the sunshine in his leisure."

3. Yan Jie and Yan Beiming, pp. 187–88.

4. *Ciyuan*, pp. 786, 1092, 1715.

5. Other English translations of the novel's title include *A Rustic's Idle*

Talk (Lu Hsun, p. 301) and *A Country Codger Puts His Word out to the Sun* (McMahon, "Case of Confucian Sexuality," p. 32).

6. This is probably why the title of the edition used in this study was changed to *Wen Suchen* after the name of the protagonist.

7. See Lu Xun, *Zhongguo xiaoshuo shilüe*, p. 244. For a discussion of the possible correspondences between the novel and the author's own personal experiences, see Zhao Jingshen.

8. Zhao Jingshen, p. 446.

9. Ibid., pp. 446–47. For a discussion of the date Xia attempted to present his work to the emperor, see Luan Xing, "Xinjiaoben *Yesou puyan* xu," pp. 102–3.

10. Zhao Jingshen, p. 434.

11. Sun Kaidi, "Xia Erming," p. 241.

12. Zhao Jingshen, pp. 434, 443–44. I later return to the significance of the resemblance of this episode to events in the novel *The Fortunate Union* (*Haoqiu zhuan*).

13. Besides Li Yu's candid remarks quoted at the beginning of this chapter, the observation by a student of modern Western autobiography may be helpful here: "Healing is completed in transformation. As a writer gains distance from personal crisis, the opportunities for artful revision of autobiographical material become clearer. In autobiographical fiction, an author can actually finish an experience, reach a conclusion, reclaim the past and build on it" (Chandler, p. 40).

14. See "Zhenzhong ji," in *Tangren xiaoshuo*, pp. 37–39. This story was later rewritten or adapted by many writers and dramatists and became extremely popular.

15. For a brief discussion of *Humble Words* as a frustrated literatus's fantasy-dream of wish-fulfillment, see Lu Xingji.

16. Originally *suwang* referred to a sage who has the virtue of a king but does not actually occupy that position. The earliest use of this term can be found in *Zhuangzi* (see Chen Guying, p. 337). This title began to be associated with Confucius in the Former Han dynasty.

17. This trend to apotheosize Confucius as a divine prophet (rather than a "transmitter" or "teacher," the image people of later ages are more accustomed to) began among Confucians in the Former Han dynasty but lost momentum during later dynasties. However, this messianic aspect of Confucius came to be re-emphasized by many Confucian scholars of the so-called New Text School (*jinwen xue*), which began in the late eighteenth century. For a study of the revival of this particular trend of Han Confucianism in the Qing dynasty, see Elman, *Classicism, Politics, and Kinship*. Accurately characterizing the connections between this novel and Qing New Text Confucianism (which probably flourished after the novel was already completed) is not

easy, but I offer my observations on this matter later in this chapter. In the novel Madame Shui displays particular resentment against the Han Confucians (W, 9.85), but it is difficult to know whether she is referring to the New Text School or the Old Text School of Han Confucianism or whether it reflects the author's general antagonism toward *kaozheng* scholars. McMahon ("Case for Confucian Sexuality," p. 51n33) seems to have also noted the possible connection between the novel and New Text Confucianism, although he does not elaborate.

18. The novel contains numerous elaborate accounts describing in detail how the crown prince, who later becomes the emperor Xiaozong, insists on treating Wen Suchen as a teacher or a superior rather than a subject or a minister and how this makes the latter particularly uneasy (W, 115.996–97).

19. Leo Ou-fan Lee (p. 286) also uses the term *wenxia* to describe Lao Can in Liu E's *Travels of Lao Can* (*Lao Can youji*). But he uses this term in a slightly different way, to mean "civilian knight-errant" (a knight-errant who does not engage himself in physical fighting).

20. The four arts (zither, chess, calligraphy, and painting), traditionally considered to be essential to the cultivation of a literatus and the subject of so much emphasis in *The Scholars* and *The Dream*, are replaced in *Humble Words* with another set of four arts: poetry, archery, mathematics, and medicine. Whereas Suchen is said to be the master of all these four arts, each of his four concubines is good at one of them. Besides many other implications, this replacement signifies a much more activist (statecraft-oriented) trend in the novel, a topic I discuss later in the chapter.

21. Struve, p. 332.

22. Although differing considerably in their respective strategies for relieving their male anxiety, Cao Xueqin and Xia Jingqu shared the same frustrations as emasculated literati. In their novels the two male characters Wen Suchen and Jia Baoyu are surrounded by women and probably are admired by many of them. But whereas Wen Suchen is a fantastic attempt to rejuvenate the image of a traditional literatus, Jia Baoyu is a symbolic questioning of that very image. However, both authors seem deeply bothered by their problematic identity as literati. For a discussion of the implications of sexuality as described in the novel, see McMahon, "Case for Confucian Sexuality."

23. In his discussion of *Haoqiu zhuan*, Richard Hessney ("Beyond Beauty and Talent," pp. 231–32) relates the tendency toward knight-errantry exhibited in the character of Tie Zhongyu to the "marked preference for a more martial brand of heroism" that Struve detects in some of the literati writings of the mid-Kangxi period. *The Fortunate Union*'s emphasis on physical prowess and knight-errantry is rather unique among works in the genre of

caizi jiaren fiction, which is characterized by feminized male protagonists and various symbolic incidents of gender masquerading (or reversals of gender roles). A frustrated male literatus's impulse to empathize (and to identify) with a woman in distress and the reversed desire to reassert masculinity are, in fact, two sides of the same coin, a literary phenomenon resulting from the literati author's anxiety caused by his experience of marginality. Cf. Hessney's (p. 223) observation that "this difference from the typical *ts'ai-tzu* perhaps can be accounted for by 'activist' trends among the frustrated K'ang-hsi period scholars."

24. Cf. James Liu's (pp. 7–8) relevant discussion of the relationship between the practice of knight-errantry and Confucianism: "Thus, by Confucian standards, the knights-errant often went beyond the call of duty. This, to the Confucian way of thinking, was not only unnecessary but also undesirable, for if one died for a stranger, what would one do for one's parents?"

25. Of course, the most celebrated example of the Confucian idea of "expediency" can be found in *Mengzi* (7.17):

> Ch'un-yu K'un said, "Is it prescribed by the rites that, in giving and receiving, man and woman should not touch each other?"
> "It is," said Mencius.
> "When one's sister-in-law is drowning, does one stretch out a hand to help her?"
> "Not to help a sister-in-law who is drowning is to be a brute. It is prescribed by the rites that, in giving and receiving, man and woman should not touch each other, but in stretching out a helping hand to the drowning sister-in-law one uses one's discretion [*quan*]." (D. C. Lau, p. 124; Yang Bojun, p. 177)

26. There are many passages where the idea of *quan* and *jing* is important (W, 40.391, 42.410, 55.530–31, 70–649, 121.1184). However, Madame Shui often warns others that the strategy of expediency should be employed with caution (9.85, 38.376). In fact, the idea of *quan* and *jing* is not immune to controversy within neo-Confucianism itself; see Cheng-t'ung Wei. For a discussion of how this idea of expediency finds expression in fictional works of the seventeenth century, see Zhao Xingqin, "'Jing' yu 'quan'."

27. The idea of *quan* also figures prominently in *The Fortunate Union*. Tie Zhongyu specifically refers to the idea at the beginning of the novel (Mingjiaozhongren, chap. 1, p. 3). When the virtuous heroine Shui Bingxin decides to take care of the sick Tie Zhongyu, she apparently considers it a case of expediency. This episode must have inspired Xia Jingqu to write the much more bizarre romance between Suchen and Su'e while Suchen is sick, though the case in *Humble Words* is much more dramatic as well as more exaggerated. In fact, chapter 31 of the novel mentions *The Fortunate Union*

(W, 31.315). The possibility of parody (the conventions of "scholars and beauties" fiction are extensively parodied in the novel) is always there, although a full exploration of this issue has to await another occasion.

28. See McMahon ("Case of Confucian Sexuality," pp. 44–47) for an interesting discussion of the relationship between this Confucian idea of expediency and Xia Jingqu's justification for explicit description of sex in the novel.

29. For a relevant discussion, see Hou Jian, who tries to read the novel from a psychoanalytical perspective. According to him, the novel reflects the imbalance in the author's psyche (death wish, neurosis, oedipus complex, mother fixation, megalomania, etc.).

30. For an attempt to discuss the relationship between Suchen and Madame Shui in terms of the oedipus complex, see Hou Jian.

31. Zhao Jingshen (pp. 441–42) points out that Hong Changqing is modeled on the author's best friend, Zhang Tianyi. There are many references to him in Xia's poems.

32. Roddy (pp. 260–61) attempts to discuss the question of "recognition" (*yu*, or "encounter") in terms of what he calls the "Confucian-feminist utopias" in the novel: "Mme. Shui brings about a domestic environment wherein women not only escape the degradation and dangers of the outside world, but achieve an intellectual fulfillment enviable even from a male point of view. Her charges may be regarded as counterparts of, and perhaps proxies for, the unrecognized male talent of the political world, yet they also delineate a distinctly novel adaptation to a world of narrowed and uncertain possibilities."

33. The character of Shigong is apparently based on Xia's famous contemporary Yang Mingshi, who unsuccessfully recommended Xia to the imperial government as a participant in the compiling of *A General Record of the Members of the Eight Banners* (*Baqi tongzhi*) (Sun Kaidi, "Xia Erming," p. 241). The brief but significant appearance in the novel of this thinly veiled reference to a personal acquaintance betrays Xia's haunting memory of his frustrated career.

34. In Ming examination terminology, both *huiyuan* and *huikui* referred to the same thing—first place in the metropolitan examination (*huishi*). The metropolitan examination was the first among the three examinations that constituted the series of exams at the highest level, which were conducted to select *jinshi* (palace graduates), the other two being *fushi* (re-examination) and *dianshi* (palace examination). See "Xuanju" in *Mingshi*, p. 1693. Translating *huiyuan* here as "first place in metropolitan examination" would not make any sense, since *huikui* is later used to mean the same thing. I suspect that the author probably used the term *huiyuan* by mistake for *zhuangyuan*, which is the title given to the top-ranking candidate in the palace examina-

tion or, more likely, this mistake is due to a corruption of the text (this confusion of *huiyuan* with *huikui* also appears in the 1881 ed. [Y, 121.5a]). As we will see later, Madame Shui properly uses *huiyuan* to refer to the rank of first place in the metropolitan examination and *zhuangyuan* to the rank of first place in the palace examination.

35. This was certainly a burden shared by Wu Jingzi, the author of *The Scholars*; see Chapter 2 for a discussion of Wu's attempt to come to terms in his novel with his history of being an examination failure.

36. Here the author might have been inspired by the famous erotic novel *The Carnal Prayer Mat* (*Rou putuan*) in which the game of finger guessing is used to decide who among the girls will have an opportunity to have sex with the male protagonist (who is also known for his sexual potency); the winner is given the title of *zhuangyuan* and the advantage of choice. See Hanan, *Carnal Prayer Mat*, chap. 17, pp. 266–75.

Literati frustrated in the examinations seem to have had a penchant for relieving their anxiety by having women succeed in the examinations (these examinations can be "real" or "game-like"), as I mentioned in discussing cases of gender-switching in "scholars and beauties" novels. For example, in the seventeenth-century novel *A Tale of the Female Examinees* (*Nü kaike zhuan*), a young literatus and his friends stage an elaborate examination for their favorite female prostitutes. Through the comic description of this staged "examination," the author is able to satirize various unfair practices such as cheating in the examinations (a candidate's vagina is searched because he [or rather she] is being suspected of cheating [*Nü kaike zhuan*, chap. 3, pp. 28–29]). For a brief discussion of this interesting novel, see Lin Chen, pp. 378–83. Of course, the most famous fictional treatment of women taking the civil-service examinations can be found in the nineteenth-century novel *The Destinies of the Flowers in the Mirror* (*Jinghua yuan*).

37. For a discussion of these two important schools of neo-Confucianism and the relationships between them, see Fung Yu-lan, 2: 531–629, esp. pp. 605–10. Some scholars have detected a break between the kind of orthodox Cheng-Zhu neo-Confucianism promoted by the imperial court and the Confucianism envisioned by many literati in the mid-Qing;. see, e.g., Elman, *From Philosophy to Philology*, pp. 3–4, 26–36. The feverish defense of orthodoxy by Suchen and his people as described in the novel may reflect a more general anxiety on the part of contemporary orthodox Confucians.

38. The novel implicitly refers to Yang's death; Suchen travels to the capital only to find Shigong has died after recommending him to the government (W, 11.103). Furthermore, Yang Mingshi's mentor happened to be Li Guangdi (1642–1718), one of the most influential neo-Confucians of the early Qing (Li Yuandu, 12.6a.). Li probably played an important role in the Kangxi emperor's ardent promotion of Cheng-Zhu neo-Confucianism. On

Kangxi's orders, he compiled the well-known *Xingli jingyi* (Essential Ideas of [the Cheng-Zhu school of] Nature and Principle; see Wing-Tsit Chan, "Hsing-li ching-i" and the entry on Li Guangdi in ECCP, pp. 473–75). Li Guangdi was once a student of Wu Guodui, Wu Jingzi's great-grandfather (Chen Meilin, *Wu Jingzi pingzhuan*, p. 47).

39. Apparently, the anonymous commentator on the novel had no qualms about showing his support for the author's criticism of the *xinxue* school of neo-Confucianism by explicitly mentioning Wang Yangming together with Lu Xiangshan ("Lu-Wang") as is common in discussing that school. For example, see his chapter-end comment on chapter 60 (Y, 60.14b). So far the commentator's identity remains unknown. In the preface to the 1882 edition, Ximin shanqiao (the supposed owner of the manuscript version on which this printed edition was based) claims that his great-great-grandfather, Taosou, was a close friend of Xia Jingqu's. At Xia's request, Taosou wrote a commentary on the novel and at the same time copied the novel for himself (W, p. 18). There is no documented evidence to support this claim, but the tone of the commentaries suggests that the commentator was very likely someone other than the author.

40. See Qian Dehong, 32.1b; hereinafter cited in the text as "Nianpu." For a detailed English account of Wang's political life based largely on Qian's "Nianpu," see Yü-chüan Chang. See also Wang's biography in *Mingshi*, pp. 5159–72.

41. Yü-chüan Chang, p. 11; and Qian Dehong, 32.5a–b.

42. In fact, many readers have pointed out that the name Jin Zhi combines two Chinese characters from the names of two powerful eunuchs, Wang Zhi (fl. 1476–81) and Liu Jin (d. 1510), during the reign of the emperor Wuzong (see Sun Kaidi, "Xia Erming," p. 242). This further confirms that the author must have Wang Yangming in his mind when he wrote this episode.

43. For a list of similarities between the life of Suchen and that of Wang Yangming, see Wang Qiongling, pp. 58–60.

44. For a discussion of the controversy over the recognition of Wang Yangming, see Hung-lam Chu.

45. See Zhao Jingshen, p. 441.

46. Li Yuandu, 15.1a. For an English account of Sun's life, see ECCP, pp. 673–74.

47. Zhao Jingshen (pp. 435, 442–43) also calls attention to the resemblance between this experience of Suchen in the novel and that of Sun. Apparently, Xia also considered himself "courageous" in daring to disagree with those superior to him.

48. For example, his request to return home to attend to his seriously ill

grandmother was denied as was his later request to attend her funeral (see Qian Dehong, 33.1a, 33.8b; and Yü-chüan Chang, p. 51).

49. Li Yuandu, 15.1a.

50. See Wang Qiongling, pp. 60–70. The commentator specifically praises Suchen's ability in managing the defense of the border areas of the Ming monarchy as much greater than those of Qi Jiguang and others (Y, 36.13b).

51. The year *gengchen* (1520) is mentioned in chapter 153 (W, 153.1494) and in the last chapter, chapter 154, the worship ceremony is conducted on the first day of the next year (*yuandan* or the new year; W, 154.1508). Hou Jian's (p. 40) calculation that the novel ends in 1519 is inaccurate. Wang Qiongling (p. 149) seems to accept Hou's calculation.

52. This incident described in the novel must have been inspired by the historical rumor that Wan Gueifei (Lady An in the novel), the favorite of Xianzong, took steps to ensure that the emperor's other wives failed to produce a son that could become the heir apparent, and she probably had a hand in the death of Lady Ji, the mother of Xiaozong. See Wang Qiongling, pp. 66–68; for an account of how Wan Gueifei was able to manipulate Xianzong and persecute her various enemies, see Chaoying Fang's article on her in *DMB*, pp. 1335–37.

53. Mote and Twichett, p. 352. See also Chaoying Fang's article on Xiaozong in *DMB*, pp. 375–80. Fang (p. 376) even speculates that Xiaozong might have been the only monogamous emperor in China's imperial history.

54. Hucker, p. 200. In the section on the "function of remonstration," Hucker discusses various cases of remonstrations in the Ming and traces them to the possible ideological background of Confucianism.

55. *Yichuan wenji*, in *Er Cheng quanshu*, 2.2a–b, 3b; quoted and trans. in Nivison, "Ho-shen and His Accusers," p. 230. Xia Jingqu must have had Cheng Yi's words in mind when he wrote the novel because "royal concubines" (or their associates the eunuchs) and "monks" are exactly the two elements Suchen considers most harmful to the monarchy.

56. *Yichuan wenji*, 2:6a; quoted and trans. in Nivison, "Ho-shen and His Accusers," p. 231.

57. Quoted and trans. in Nivison, "Ho-shen and His Accusers," p. 231.

58. See Nivison, "Ho-shen and His Accusers."

59. Elman, *Classicism, Politics, and Kinship*, pp. 275–90.

60. In the novel, Suchen is said to be twenty-four years old (24 *sui*) in the third year of the Chenghua reign (1467) and thus he would have been born in 1444. The novel ends in 1521 when Suchen is 77. Xia Jingqu probably finished *Humble Words* at around that age. Zhao Jingshen (pp. 444–45) also points out the account of the celebration of Suchen's seventieth birthday in

the novel may actually refer to his own seventieth birthday, and he speculates that the novel was finished around 1779.

61. It is indeed amazing to see the re-emergence of a literati hero in the person of Hong Liangji (1746–1809) just a decade or so after the death of Xia Jingqu, who had "prophesied" in his novel the coming of such a messiah-like figure. In 1799 Hong Liangji presented a several-thousand-character-long letter to a certain prince (his official status was too low to allow him to present it directly to the Jiaqing emperor) detailing his criticisms of the contemporary state of the country. The letter was forwarded to the emperor, who flew into rage after reading it. Hong was first sentenced to death; later the punishment was changed to exile. Hong became a national hero and almost a martyr: "Hung went not to the executioner, but to Ili; not into oblivion but on to acclaim (crowds greeted him at every step along the way, and one obscure Manchu even paid his passage); not into silence but on to a bigger and better travelogue. . . . Hung's letter marks the beginning of the shift of the balance, away from the throne and out into the ranks of the bureaucracy" (Jones, pp. 159–60).

62. For general discussions of the intellectual background of the late Qing period, see Fairbank and Liu, pp. 274–338; and Wakeman, pp. 101–14.

63. If we accept the credibility of the preface attached to the 1882 (Shenbaoguan) edition of the novel, then we have reason to believe that Xia Jingqu was well aware of the "dangerous" nature of his novel and was probably reluctant to have it published while he was alive (W, p. 17). The popularity of *Humble Words* in the late Qing is attested by the publication of a sequel, *Xin Yesou puyan*, in 1909. For a summary of the plot of this interesting sequel, see ZMTY, p. 1146.

64. Jack Dull, "History and the Old Text / New Text Controversy in the Han," p. 29; quoted in Wakeman, p. 107.

65. Pei-yi Wu, p. 165.

66. Ibid., p. 169.

67. Ibid., p. 165.

68. No matter how strange it may sound, the heightened individual consciousness of the late Ming probably does share something with the New Text Confucianism of the late Qing; cf. Wakeman's (p. 111) relevant observation: "Thus, the New Text *chün-tzu*'s martyrdom was an apotheosis of the self—an expression of individuality which was anathema to restrained conservatives of the nineteenth century."

69. To a degree, the craving for cultural immortality and tactics of exaggeration on the part of Xia Jingqu resemble various grandiose acts of self-dramatization of the Qianlong emperor, to whom Xia tried to present one of his works (Xia wished that Qianlong could appreciate his talents just as Xiaozong did those of his autobiographical protagonist in the novel). Harold

Kahn ("Matter of Taste") uses terms to characterize Qianlong's artistic tastes, such as "monumental" and "exotic," that would be equally applicable to *Humble Words* (despite the apparent humility claimed in the novel's title).

CONCLUSION

1. Bock, pp. 7–8.
2. Manning, p. 74; quoted by Bock, p. 133.
3. Plaks ("Towards a Critical Theory of Chinese Narrative," p. 329) notes a similar paradoxical phenomenon in classical Chinese short stories: "It appears that as the author in the classical medium must dispense with the narrative devices that signal the simulated context of oral storytelling, his focus turns *ipso facto* from an essentially public exposure of private lives (e.g., the ribaldry of *P'ai-an Ching-ch'i*) to a more intensely personal, introspective revelation of the inner world of fantasy. Thus we observe the paradox that the more the Chinese author 'refines himself out of existence,' the more intimate—personal—is the final aesthetic effect." Plaks's observation is especially relevant to *The Scholars*, where the detached narrator always keeps a careful distance from his characters, a narrative rhetoric that can be traced to the classic medium of historiography.
4. For discussions of their autobiographical writings, see Pei-yi Wu, pp. 163–86.
5. For a discussion of the phenomenon of the "liminal" in *The Dream*, see Jing Wang, pp. 198–208.
6. For discussions of the implications of dream in *The Dream*, see Shuen-fu Lin, "Chia Pao-yü's First Visit"; for the possible Buddhist influence on the presentation of dream in the novel, see Anthony Yu.
7. Wai-yee Li (pp. 152–230) offers some interesting observations on the relationship between the two realms of existence in *The Dream* (the supernatural and the mundane) and on the question of self-knowledge through what she has termed the dialectics of "enchantment and disenchantment."
8. Cf. Plaks's ("Towards a Critical Theory of Chinese Narrative," p. 329) pertinent observation on the Qing novel: "The important point here is that transparent, unabashed treatment of the self as a fitting subject of public transmission through narrative (rather than lyric) almost inevitably leads to a transcending of the narrow sphere of personal sensitivity to move towards some broader, more public range of meaning—typically allegory and satire. Hence we observe the striking coincidence of autobiographical fiction and the rise of what Professor Hsia has termed the 'scholar-novelist' in the Ch'ing period. As in the case of Fielding and Sterne, the self-conscious introversion of conventional narrative rhetoric begins by making the narrator himself the object of public view, but soon turns to the author's overall *erudition* as the principal focus of narrative, so that in the end it is the entire cultural heritage

and no longer the private world of the individual writer that is at issue." If Plaks in his more recent *Four Masterworks* is correct that what is at issue in these Ming novels is the entire cultural heritage, then this is hardly a striking coincidence because the ambitious concern with "some broader, more public range of meaning" has always been a hallmark of the traditional Chinese novel. What is significant about these Qing novels is that these concerns are now related more intimately to their authors' own personal agenda.

9. For an exploration of how this idea of the relational shapes the characterization strategies in *The Dream*, see my "Poetics of Characterization."

10. See, e.g., Jing Wang, pp. 144–46.

11. For a discussion of Wu Jingzi's yearning to return to a "purified" Confucianism characterized by an emphasis on ritual, see Shuen-fu Lin, "Ritual and Narrative Structure in *Ju-lin wai-shih*." C. T. Hsia (*Classic Chinese Novel*, p. 209) also claims that *The Scholars* was "consciously written from the Confucian point of view." This tendency of Wu Jingzi can also be related to a larger intellectual movement in the mid-Qing—what has been termed the "purist" reading of the Confucian classics (see Chow).

12. For a more detailed discussion of this topic, see my "Stylization and Invention."

13. Tu Shen's (1744–1801?) novel in literary language, *A History of White Fish* (*Yinshi*), may be an exception in a limited sense. Another eighteenth-century novel I briefly discussed early in this study, *The Footsteps of an Immortal in the Mundane World* (*Lüye xianzong*), may be another exception, although a more careful study is needed before anything definite can be said about this interesting work in terms of its autobiographical implications. One is sometimes tempted to speculate that a literati novelist's tendency to claim encyclopedic coverage for his work (his concern for the whole literati culture) and the sometimes excessive reliance on the narrative strategy of self-re/presentation (masking) may have contributed to the dilution of the autobiographical intensity of some novels of the period.

14. See Hu Shi's "*Ernü yingxiong zhuan* xu." A full exploration of the autobiographical significance of these two novels is beyond the scope of this study.

15. Another interesting fact about *Six Records of a Floating Life* is that it can be classified as a writing falling between the genres of autobiography and memoir, mainly because the autobiographer's wife occupies such a prominent place in the narrative. It has been classified as *yiyu ti* (prose recollection or memoir) because, judging from its style and content, *Six Records of a Floating Life* may have been influenced by the seventeenth-century writer Mao Xiang's (1611–93) famous memoir (or biography) of his lover, Dong Xiaowan (a well-known courtesan, 1624–51), *Memoirs of the Plum Shadow Hut* (*Yingmei'an yiyu*) (Zhao Tiaokuang, p. 40). Zhou Ruchang

("*Honglou meng*" *yu Zhonghua wenhua*, p. 98) speculates that *Six Records of a Floating Life* may have been influenced by *The Dream*. He notes that the Qing dramatist and official Shi Yunyu (1750–1837) was a great fan of *The Dream* and even wrote a play based on the novel and that Shen Fu once served as a private secretary on his staff. Thus, the chance that Shen Fu had read *The Dream* is great.

16. For relevant discussions, see C. T. Hsia, "*The Travels of Lao Ts'an*," p. 40; and Leo Ou-fan Lee, p. 287.

17. Consider Peterson's (pp. 167–68) remarks: "One of the central problems for twentieth-century Chinese intellectuals, and a problem which seems to me to remain unresolved, has been, and apparently is, the formulation of a 'new' alternative to government service that will satisfy the requirements of being a morally justifiable endeavor which promotes and defends 'our culture' as well as the general good of 'our nation.'" In her reading of modern Chinese autobiographical writings (*Literary Authority and the Modern Chinese Writer*), Wendy Larson appears to have found a somewhat similar problem troubling many writers—how to justify their continued endeavor of *wen* (or "textual labor" in her terms) while it becomes increasingly difficult, it seems to them, to find such endeavor relevant to the practical demands of contemporary society (especially following the drastic demotion of textual labor that resulted from the abolition of the civil-service examination system).

Selected Bibliography

SOURCES IN ENGLISH

Barr, Allan. "Pu Songling and the Qing Examination System." *Late Imperial China* 7.1 (1986): 87–109.

Bernhardt, Kathryn. "A Ming-Qing Transition in Chinese Women's History?" Paper presented at the Rethinking Chinese Women's History conference, UCLA, Nov. 1993.

Bock, Carol Ann. "Narrative and Symbolic Displacement in the Victorian Mask Confession." Ph.D. diss., University of Wisconsin-Madison, 1982.

Bol, Peter. *"This Culture of Ours": Intellectual Transitions in T'ang and Sung China*. Stanford: Stanford University Press, 1992.

Brandauer, Frederick. *Tung Yüeh*. New York: Twayne, 1978.

Brokaw, Cynthia. "Review of *The Confucian's Progress: Autobiographical Writings in Traditional China* by Pei-yi Wu." *HJAS* 53.1 (1993): 174–85.

Butler, Judith. *Gender Trouble: Feminism and the Subversion of Identity*. New York: Routledge, 1990.

Cahill, James. *The Compelling Image: Nature and Style in Seventeenth-Century Chinese Painting*. Cambridge, Mass.: Harvard University Press, 1982.

Chan, Wing-tsit. "The *Hsing-li ching-i* and the Ch'eng-Chu School of the Seventeenth Century." In de Bary, *The Unfolding of Neo-Confucianism*, 543–79.

Chan, Wing-tsit, trans. and comp. *A Source Book in Chinese Philosophy*. Princeton: Princeton University Press, 1963.

Chandler, Marilyn R. *A Healing Art: Regeneration Through Autobiography*. New York: Garland Publishing, 1990.

Chang, Chun-shu, and Shelley Hsueh-lun Chang. *Crisis and Transformation in Seventeenth-Century China: Society, Culture, and Modernity in Li Yü's World*. Ann Arbor: University of Michigan Press, 1992.

Chang, Kung-i Sun. "The Idea of the Mask in Wu Wei-yeh (1609–1671)." *HJAS* 48.1 (1988): 289–320.

———. *The Late-Ming Poet Ch'en Tzu-lung: Crises of Love and Loyalism.* New Haven: Yale University Press, 1990.
Chang, Yü-chüan. *Wang Shou-jen as a Statesman.* Arlington: University Publications of America, 1973 (1st published in *Chinese Social and Political Science Review* 23 [1939–40]).
Chow, Kai-wing. "Purist Hermeneutics and Ritualist Ethics in the Mid-Ch'ing Thought." In Richard J. Smith and D. W. Y. Kwok, eds., *Cosmology, Ontology and Human Efficacy: Essays in Chinese Thought,* 170–204. Honolulu: University of Hawaii Press, 1993.
Chu, Hung-lam. "The Debate over Recognition of Wang Yang-ming." *HJAS* 48.1 (1988): 47–70.
Clunas, Craig. *Superfluous Things: Material Culture and Social Status in Early Modern China.* Cambridge, Eng.: Polity Press, 1991.
Crossley, Pamela Kyle. *Orphan Warriors: Three Manchu Generations and the End of the Qing World.* Princeton: Princeton University Press, 1990.
———. "Qianlong Retrospect on the Chinese-Martial (*hanjun*) Banners." *Late Imperial China* 10 (1989): 63–107.
de Bary, Wm. Theodore. "Individualism and Humanitarianism in Late Ming Thought." In idem, *Self and Society in Ming Thought,* 145–247.
———. *The Message of the Mind in Neo-Confucianism.* New York: Columbia University Press, 1989.
———. "Neo-Confucian Cultivation and the Seventeenth-Century 'Enlightenment.'" In de Bary, *The Unfolding of Neo-Confucianism,* 141–216.
de Bary, Wm. Theodore, ed. *Self and Society in Ming Thought.* New York: Columbia University Press, 1970.
———. *The Unfolding of Neo-Confucianism.* New York: Columbia University Press, 1975.
de Man, Paul. "Autobiography as De-facement." *MLN* 94 (1979): 919–30.
Doody, Terrence. *Confession and Community in the Novel.* Baton Rouge: Louisiana State University Press, 1980.
Eakin, Paul John. *Fictions in Autobiography: Studies in the Art of Self-invention.* Princeton: Princeton University Press, 1985.
Edwards, Louise. "Gender Imperatives in *Honglou meng*: Baoyu's Bisexuality." *CLEAR* 12 (1990): 69–81.
———. "Women in *Honglou meng*: Prescriptions of Purity in the Femininity of Qing Dynasty China." *Modern China* 16 (1990): 407–29.
Elman, A. Benjamin. *Classicism, Politics, and Kinship: The Ch'ang-chou School of New Text Confucianism in Late Imperial China.* Berkeley: University of California Press, 1990.
———. *From Philosophy to Philology: Intellectual and Social Aspects of Change in Late Imperial China.* Cambridge, Mass.: Harvard University, Council on East Asian Studies, 1984.

Elvin, Mark. "Female Virtue and the State in China." *Past and Present* 104 (1984): 111–52.
Fairbank, John, and Kwang-ch'ing Liu, eds. *Cambridge History of China*, vol. 10, *Late Ch'ing, 1800–1911, Part 2*. Cambridge, Eng.: Cambridge University Press, 1980.
Fleishman, Avrom. *Figures of Autobiography: The Language of Self-writing in Victorian and Modern England*. Berkeley: University of California Press, 1983.
Folson, Kenneth E. *Friends, Guests, and Colleagues: The Mu-fu System in the Late Ch'ing Period*. Berkeley: University of California Press, 1968.
Fong, Grace S. "Constructing a Feminine Ideal in the Eighteenth Century: *Random Records of West-Green* and the Story of Shuangqing." Paper presented at the conference "Women and Literature in Ming-Qing China," Yale University, June 1993.
———. "Contextualization and Generic Codes in the Allegorical Reading of *Tz'u* Poetry." *Tamkang Review* 19 (1989): 663–79.
Fung, Yu-lan. *A History of Chinese Philosophy*. Trans. Derk Bodde. Princeton: Princeton University Press, 1953.
Furth, Charlotte. "Androgynous Men and Deficient Females: Biology and Gender Boundaries in Sixteenth- and Seventeenth-Century China." *Late Imperial China* 9.2 (1988): 1–31.
Goodrich, Luther Carrington. *The Literary Inquisition of Ch'ien-lung*. New York: Paragon Books, 1966 (1935).
Goodrich, L. Carrington, and Chaoying Fang, eds. *Dictionary of Ming Biography, 1368–1644*. New York: Columbia University Press, 1976.
Guy, R. Kent. *The Emperor's Four Treasuries: Scholars and the State in the Late Ch'ien-lung Era*. Cambridge, Mass.: Harvard University, Council on East Asian Studies, 1987.
Hanan, Patrick. *The Chinese Vernacular Story*. Cambridge, Mass.: Harvard University Press, 1981.
———. *The Invention of Li Yu*. Cambridge, Mass.: Harvard University Press, 1988.
Hanan, Patrick, trans. *The Carnal Prayer Mat*. New York: Ballantine Books, 1990.
Hawkes, David, trans. *Ch'u Tz'u: The Song of the South*. Oxford: Oxford University Press, 1959.
Hawkes, David, and John Minford, trans. *The Story of the Stone*. 5 vols. Harmondsworth, Eng.: Penguin, 1973–86.
Hegel, Robert E. *The Novel in Seventeenth-Century China*. New York: Columbia University Press, 1981.
Hegel, Robert E., and Richard C. Hessney, eds. *Expressions of Self in Chinese Literature*. New York: Columbia University Press, 1985.

Henderson, John. *The Development and Decline of Chinese Cosmology.* New York: Columbia University Press, 1984.
Henry, Eric. "The Motif of Recognition in Early China." *HJAS* 47 (1987): 5–30.
Hessney, Richard C. "Beautiful, Talented, and Brave: Seventeenth-Century Chinese Scholar-Beauty Romances." Ph.D. diss., Columbia University, 1978.
——. "Beyond Beauty and Talent: The Moral and Chivalric Self in *The Fortunate Union.*" In Hegel and Hessney, *Expressions of Self in Chinese Literature,* 214–50.
Hinsch, Bret. *Passions of the Cut Sleeve: The Male Homosexual Tradition in China.* Berkeley: University of California Press, 1990.
Ho, Ping-ti. *The Ladder of Success in Imperial China: Aspects of Social Mobility, 1368–1911.* New York: Columbia University Press, 1962.
——. "The Salt Merchants of Yang-chou: A Study of Commercial Capitalism in Eighteenth-Century China." *HJAS* 17 (1954): 130–68.
Hsia, C. T. *The Classic Chinese Novel.* New York: Columbia University Press, 1968.
——. "The Scholar-Novelist and Chinese Culture: A Reappraisal of *Ching-hua Yuan.*" In Plaks, *Chinese Narrative,* 266–305.
——. "*The Travels of Lao Ts'an:* An Exploration of Its Art and Meaning." *Tsing Hua Journal of Chinese Studies,* n.s. 7.2 (1969): 40–66.
Hsu, Cheng-chi. "Zheng Xie's Price List: Painting as a Source of Income in Yangzhou." *Phoebus* 6.2 (1990): 261–71. Special issue: Ju-hsi Chou and Claudia Brown, eds., *Chinese Painting Under the Qianlong Emperor, 1735–1795.*
Huang, Martin W. "Author(ity) and Reader in Traditional Chinese *Xiaoshuo* Commentary." *CLEAR* 16 (1994), forthcoming.
——. "Dehistoricization and Intertexualization: The Anxiety of Precedents in the Evolution of the Traditional Chinese Novel." *CLEAR* 12 (1990): 45–68.
——. "The Dilemma of Chinese Lyricism and the Qing Literati Novel." Ph.D. diss., Washington University, 1991.
——. "Notes Towards a Poetics of Characterization in the Traditional Chinese Novel: *Hung-lou meng* as Paradigm." *Tamkang Review* 21 (1990): 1–27.
——. "Stylization and Invention: The Burden of Self-Expression in *The Scholars.*" Paper presented at the conference "The Symbolic Self in China, Japan and India," East-West Center, Honolulu, Aug. 1990.
Huang, Pei. *Autocracy at Work: A Study of the Yung-cheng Period, 1723–1735.* Bloomington: Indiana University Press, 1974.

———. "New Light on the Origins of the Manchus." *HJAS* 50.1 (1990): 239–82.
Huang, Ray. *1587, A Year of No Significance: The Ming Dynasty in Decline*. New Haven: Yale University Press, 1981.
Hucker, Charles O. "Confucianism and the Chinese Censorial System." In David S. Nivison and Arthur F. Wright, eds., *Confucianism in Action*, 108–208. Stanford: Stanford University Press, 1959.
Hummel, Arthur H., ed. *Eminent Chinese of the Ch'ing Period*. 2 vols. Washington, D.C.: U.S. Government Printing Office, 1944.
Idema, W. L. *Chinese Vernacular Fiction*. Leiden: E. J. Brill, 1974.
Johnstone, Henry W., Jr. *The Problem of the Self*. University Park: Pennsylvania State University Press, 1970.
Jones, Susan Mann. "Hung Liang-chi (1746–1809): The Perception and Articulation of Political Problems in Late Eighteenth Century China." Ph.D. diss., Stanford University, 1972.
Kahn, Harold L. "A Matter of Taste: The Monumental and Exotic in the Qianlong Reign." In Ju-hsi Chen and Claudia Brown, eds., *The Elegant Brush: Chinese Painting Under the Qianlong Emperor, 1735–1795*, 288–302. Phoenix: Phoenix Art Museum, 1985.
Kant, Immanuel. *Immanuel Kant's "Critique of Pure Reason."* Ed. and trans. Norman Kemp Smith. New York: St. Martin's Press, 1965 (1929).
Kao, Yu-kung. "Lyric Vision in Chinese Narrative: A Reading of *Hong-lou meng* and *Ju-lin wai-shi*." In Plaks, *Chinese Narrative*, 227–43.
Larson, Wendy. *Literary Authority and the Modern Chinese Writer*. Durham, N.C.: Duke University Press, 1991.
Lau, D. C., trans. *Mencius*. Harmondsworth, Eng.: Penguin, 1970.
Lechte, John. *Julia Kristeva*. London: Routledge, 1990.
Lee, Leo Ou-fan. "The Solitary Traveler: Images of the Self in Modern Chinese Literature." In Hegel and Hessney, *Expressions of Self in Chinese Literature*, 282–307.
Legge, James, trans. *The Sacred Books of China: The Texts of Confucianism*. Part II. *The Yi King*. Oxford: Clarendon Press, 1899.
Levenson, Joseph R. *Confucian China and Its Modern Fate: The Problem of Intellectual Continuity*. Berkeley: University of California Press, 1958.
Li, Wai-yee. *Enchantment and Disenchantment: Love and Illusion in Chinese Literature*. Princeton: Princeton University Press, 1993.
Lin, Lien-hsiang. "Examination Syndrome in Ch'ing Fiction." *Tamkang Review* 15:1–4 (Autumn 1984–Summer 1985): 495–507.
Lin, Shuen-fu. "Chia Pao-yü's First Visit to the Land of Illusion: An Analysis of a Literary Dream in an Interdisciplinary Perspective." *CLEAR* 14 (1992): 77–106.

———. "Ritual and Narrative Structure in *Ju-lin wai-shih*." In Plaks, *Chinese Narrative*, 244–65.
Lin, Shuen-fu, and Stephen Owen, eds. *The Vitality of the Lyric Voice: Shih Poetry from the Late Han to the T'ang*. Princeton: Princeton University Press, 1986.
Lin, Yutang, ed. *The Wisdom of China and India*. New York: Random House, 1942.
Liu, James J. Y. *The Chinese Knight-Errant*. Chicago: University of Chicago Press, 1967.
Lu Hsun. *A Brief History of the Chinese Novel*. Trans. Hsien-yi Yang and Gladys Yang. Peking: Foreign Languages Press, 1982 (1959).
Ma, Y. W. "Fiction." In William Nienhauser, Jr., et al., eds., *The Indiana Companion to Traditional Chinese Literature*, 31–48. Bloomington: Indiana University Press, 1986.
Manning, Sylvia. "Masking and Self-Revelation: Dickens's Three Autobiographies." *Dickens Studies Newsletter* 7 (1977): 69–74.
McMahon, Keith. "A Case of Confucian Sexuality: The Eighteenth-Century Novel *Yesou puyan*." *Late Imperial China* 9.2 (1988): 32–55.
———. *Causality and Containment in Seventeenth-Century Chinese Fiction*. Leiden: E. J. Brill, 1988.
Metzger, Thomas. *Escape from Predicament: Neo-Confucianism and China's Evolving Political Culture*. New York: Columbia University Press, 1977.
Miller, Lucien. *Masks of Fiction in "Dream of the Red Chamber": Myth, Mimesis, and Persona*. Tucson: University of Arizona Press, 1975.
Moi, Toril. *Sexual/Politics: Feminist Literary Theory*. London and New York: Methuen, 1985.
Mote, Frederick W. "Confucian Eremitism in the Yuan Period." In Arthur F. Wright, ed., *The Confucian Persuasion*, 202–40. Stanford: Stanford University Press, 1960.
———. "The Intellectual Climate in Eighteenth-Century China." *Phoebus* 6.1 (1988): 25–29. Special issue: Ju-hsi Chen and Claudia Brown, eds., *Chinese Painting Under the Qianlong Emperor, 1735–1795*.
Mote, Frederick W., and Denis Twitchett, eds. *Cambridge History of China*, Vol. 7, *The Ming Dynasty, 1368–1644, Part I*. Cambridge, Eng.: Cambridge University Press, 1988.
Mundakata, Kiyohiko. "Concepts of *Lei* and *Kanlei* in Early Chinese Art Theories." In Susan Bush and Christian Murch, eds., *Theories of the Arts in China*, 105–31. Princeton: Princeton University Press, 1983.
Naquin, Susan, and Evelyn S. Rawski. *Chinese Society in the Eighteenth Century*. New Haven: Yale University Press, 1987.

Needham, Joseph, and Wang Ling. *Science and Civilization in China*, vol. 2. Cambridge, Eng.: Cambridge University Press, 1954.
Nivison, David S. "Ho-shen and His Accusers: Ideology and Political Behavior in the Eighteenth Century." In David S. Nivison and Arthur F. Wright, eds., *Confucianism in Action*, 209–243. Stanford: Stanford University Press, 1959.
———. *The Life and Thought of Chang Hsüeh-ch'eng (1738–1801)*. Stanford: Stanford University Press, 1966.
Olney, James. "Autobiography and the Cultural Movement: A Thematic, Historical, and Bibliographical Introduction." In idem, *Autobiography: Essays Theoretical and Critical*, 3–27.
———. *Metaphors of Self: The Meaning of Autobiography*. Princeton: Princeton University Press, 1972.
———. "Some Versions of Memory/Some Versions of Bios: The Ontology of Autobiography." In idem, *Autobiography: Essays Theoretical and Critical*, 236–67.
Olney, James, ed. *Autobiography: Essays Theoretical and Critical*. Princeton: Princeton University Press, 1980.
Organ, Troy Wilson. *Philosophy and the Self: East and West*. London and Toronto: Associated University Press, 1987.
Owen, Stephen. *Remembrances: The Experience of the Past in Classical Chinese Literature*. Cambridge, Mass.: Harvard University Press, 1986.
———. "The Self's Perfect Mirror: Poetry as Autobiography." In Lin and Owen, *The Vitality of the Lyric Voice*, 71–102.
———. *Traditional Chinese Poetry and Poetics*. Madison: University of Wisconsin Press, 1985.
Palandri, Angela Jung. "Women in *Dream of the Red Chamber*." *Literature East and West* 12.2–3 (1968): 226–38.
Peterson, J. Willard. *Bitter Gourd: Fang I-chih and the Impetus for Intellectual Change*. New Haven: Yale University Press, 1979.
Plaks, Andrew H. "After the Fall: *Hsing-shih yin-yüan chuan* and the Seventeenth-Century Chinese Novel." *HJAS* 45 (1985): 543–80.
———. *Archetype and Allegory in the "Dream of the Red Chamber."* Princeton: Princeton University Press, 1976.
———. *The Four Masterworks of the Ming Novel*. Princeton: Princeton University Press, 1987.
———. "Full-length *Hsiao-shuo* and the Western Novel: A Generic Reappraisal." In William Tay et al., eds., *China and West: Comparative Literature Studies*, 163–76. Hong Kong: Chinese University Press, 1980.
———. "Towards a Critical Theory of Chinese Narrative." In Plaks, *Chinese Narrative*, 309–52.

Plaks, Andrew H., ed. *Chinese Narrative: Critical and Theoretical Essays.* Princeton: Princeton University Press, 1977.
Pohl, Karl-Heinz. *Cheng Pan-ch'iao: Poet, Painter and Calligrapher.* Netteal, Ger.: Steyler Verlag, 1990.
Průšek, Jaroslav. "Subjectivism and Individualism in Modern Chinese Literature." *Archiv Orientální* 25 (1957): 261–86.
Qian, Zhongshu. "Poetry as a Vehicle of Grief." Trans. Siu-kit Wong. In Stephen Soong, ed., *A Brotherhood in Song: Chinese Poetry and Poetics*, 21–40. Hong Kong: Chinese University Press, 1985.
Renza, Louis A. "The Veto of the Imagination: A Theory of Autobiography." In Olney, *Autobiography: Essays Theoretical and Critical*, 268–95.
Roddy, Stephen. "*Rulin waishi* and the Representation of Literati in Qing Fiction." Ph.D. diss. Princeton University, 1990.
Rolston, David L. "Theory and Practice: Fiction, Fiction Criticism, and the Writing of the *Ju-lin wai-shih*." Ph.D. diss., University of Chicago, 1988.
Rolston, David L., ed. *How to Read the Chinese Novel.* Princeton: Princeton University Press, 1990.
Ropp, Paul S. *Dissent in Early Modern China.* Ann Arbor: University of Michigan Press, 1981.
——— . "Shi Zhenlin and the Poetess Shuangqing: Gender, Class, and Literary Talent in an Eighteenth-Century Memoir." Paper presented at the Harvard-Wellesley conference "Engendering China," Feb. 1992.
——— . "Vehicles of Dissent in Late Imperial Chinese Culture." Paper presented at the symposium "State Vs. Society in East Asian Traditions," Paris, May 1991.
Schneider, Laurence A. *A Madman of Ch'u: The Chinese Myth of Loyalty and Dissent.* Berkeley: University of California Press, 1980.
Schwartz, Benjamin. *The World of Thought in Ancient China.* Cambridge, Mass.: Harvard University Press, 1985.
Slupski, Zbigniew. "Three Levels of Composition of the *Rulin waishi*." *HJAS* 49.1 (1989): 5–53.
Smith, J. Handlin. Review of *The Confucian's Progress* by Pei-yi Wu. *Journal of Asian Studies* 50.1 (1991): 149–51.
Spacks, Patricia M. *Imagining a Self: Autobiography and Novel in Eighteenth-Century England.* Cambridge, Mass.: Harvard University Press, 1976.
Spence, Jonathan D. *Ts'ao Yin and the K'ang-hsi Emperor.* New Haven: Yale University Press, 1966.
Spengemann, William C. *The Forms of Autobiography: Episodes in the History of a Literary Genre.* New Haven: Yale University Press, 1980.
Starobinski, Jean. "The Style of Autobiography." In Olney, *Autobiography: Essays Theoretical and Critical*, 73–83.

Starr, G. A. *Defoe and Spiritual Autobiography*. Princeton: Princeton University Press, 1965.
Stewart, Philip. *Imitation and Illusion in the French Memoir-Novel, 1700–1750: The Art of Make-Believe*. New Haven: Yale University Press, 1976.
Struve, Lynn. "Ambivalence and Action: Some Frustrated Scholars of the K'ang-hsi period." In Jonathan D. Spence and John E. Wills, Jr., eds., *From Ming to Ch'ing: Conquest, Region, and Continuity in Seventeenth-Century China*, 321–65. New Haven: Yale University Press, 1979.
T'ien, Ju-k'ang. *Male Anxiety and Female Chastity: A Comparative Study of Chinese Ethical Values in Ming-Ch'ing Times*. Leiden: E. J. Brill, 1988.
Torbert, Preston M. *The Ch'ing Imperial Household Department: A Study of Its Organization and Principal Functions, 1662–1796*. Cambridge, Mass.: Harvard University Press, 1977.
Vinograd, Richard. *The Boundaries of the Self: Chinese Portraits, 1600–1900*. Cambridge, Eng.: Cambridge University Press, 1992.
Wakeman, Frederic, Jr. *History and Will: Philosophical Perspectives of Mao Tse-tung's Thought*. Berkeley: University of California Press, 1973.
Waley, Arthur. *A Hundred and Seventy Chinese Poems*. London: Constable, 1918.
Wang, Jing. *The Story of the Stone: Intertextuality, Ancient Chinese Folklore, and the Stone Symbolism of "Dream of the Red Chamber," "Water Margin," and "The Journey to the West."* Durham, N.C.: Duke University Press, 1992.
Watson, Burton. *Ssu-ma Ch'ien: Grand Historian of China*. New York: Columbia University Press, 1958.
Wei, Cheng-t'ung. "Chu Hsi on the Standard and the Expedient." In Wing-tsit Chan, ed., *Chu Hsi and Neo-Confucianism*, 255–72. Honolulu: University of Hawaii Press, 1986.
Weinstein, Vicki Frances. "Painting in Yang-chou, 1710–1765: Eccentricity or the Literati Tradition?" Ph.D. diss., Cornell University, 1972.
Widmer, Ellen. *The Margins of Utopia: "Shui-hu hou-chuan" and the Literature of Ming Loyalism*. Cambridge, Mass.: Harvard University Press, 1987.
Wilde, Oscar. *The Artist as Critic: Critical Writings of Oscar Wilde*. Ed. Richard Ellmann. New York: Vintage, 1969.
Wilhelm, Hellmut. "The Scholar's Frustration: A Note on a Type of 'fu.'" In John K. Fairbank, ed., *Chinese Thought and Institutions*, 310–19. Chicago: University of Chicago Press, 1957.
Wong, Timothy C. *Wu Ching-tzu*. Boston: Twayne, 1978.
Wu, Nelson I. "The Tolerance of the Eccentric." *Art News* 56.3 (1957): 27–29, 52–54.
———. "Tung Ch'i-ch'ang (1555–1636): Apathy in Government and Fer-

vor in Art." In Arthur F. Wright and Denis Twitchett, eds., *Confucian Personalities*, 260–93. Stanford: Stanford University Press, 1962.

Wu, Pei-yi. *The Confucian's Progress: Autobiographical Writings in Traditional China*. Princeton: Princeton University Press, 1990.

Wu, Shih-chang. *On the "Red Chamber Dream."* Oxford: Clarendon Press, 1961.

Wu, Yenna. "Marriage Destinies to Awaken the World: A Literary Study of *Xingshi yinyuan zhuan*." Ph.D. diss., Harvard University, 1986.

Xiao, Chi. "Garden as Lyric Enclave: A Generic Study of *The Dream of the Red Chamber*." Ph.D. diss., Washington University, 1993.

Yang, Hsien-yi, and Gladys Yang, trans. *The Dream of Red Mansions*. Beijing: Foreign Languages Press, 1978.

———. *The Scholars*. Beijing: Foreign Languages Press, 1957.

Yee, Angelina. "Counterpoise in *Honglou meng*." *HJAS* 50 (1990): 613–50.

Yip, Wai-lim, ed. and trans. *Chinese Poetry: Major Modes and Genres*. Berkeley: University of California Press, 1976.

Yoshikawa, Kōjirō. *Five Hundred Years of Chinese Poetry, 1150–1650*. Trans. John Timothy Wixted. Princeton: Princeton University Press, 1989.

Yu, Anthony. "The Quest of Brother Amor: Buddhist Intimations in *The Story of the Stone*." *HJAS* 49 (1989): 55–92.

Yu, Pauline. *The Reading of Imagery in the Chinese Poetic Tradition*. Princeton: Princeton University Press, 1987.

Yü, Ying-shih. "The Two Worlds of *Hung-lou meng*." Trans. Diana Yu. *Renditions* 2 (1974): 5–22.

Zeitlin, Judith T. *Historian of the Strange: Pu Songling and the Chinese Classical Tale*. Stanford: Stanford University Press, 1993.

SOURCES IN CHINESE

Cai Yijiang 蔡義江. *"Honglou meng" shi ci qu fu pingzhu* 紅樓夢詩詞曲賦評注. Beijing: Beijing chubanshe, 1979.

Cao Xueqin 曹雪芹. *Honglou meng* 紅樓夢. 3 vols. Ed. Zhongguo yishu yanjiu yuan Honglou meng yanjiu suo 中國藝術研究院紅樓夢研究所. Beijing: Renmin wenxue chubanshe, 1982.

———. *Zhiyan zhai chongping "Shitou ji"* 脂硯齋重評石頭記 (facsimile reprint of the *jiaxu* 甲戌 or 1754 edition). Shanghai: Shanghai renmin chubanshe, 1975.

———. *Zhiyan zhai chongping "Shitou ji"* 脂硯齋重評石頭記 (facsimile reprint of the *gengchen* 庚辰 or 1760 edition). Beijing: Renmin wenxue chubanshe, 1975.

Chen Dakang 陳大康. "Lun Ming Qing zhiji de shishi xiaoshuo" 論明清之際的時事小說. *Huadong shifan daxue xuebao* 華東師範大學學報 1991.1, 470–76; reprinted in *Zhongguo gudai jindai wenxue yanjiu* (Renmin

daxue fuyin ziliao) 中國古代近代文學研究（人民大學複印資料）1991.11, 303-9.
———. *Tongsu xiaoshuo de lishi guiji* 通俗小說的歷史軌跡. Changsha: Hu'nan chubanshe, 1993.
Chen Guying 陳鼓應. *Zhuangzi jinzhu jinyi* 莊子今注今譯. Hong Kong: Zhonghua shuju, 1990.
Chen Hong 陳洪. "*Lin Lan Xiang* chuangzuo niandai xiaokao" 林蘭香創作年代小考. *MXYJ* 9 (1988): 151–55.
Chen Jiahua 陳佳華 and Fu Kedong 傅克東. "Baqi Hanjun kaolüe" 八旗漢軍考略. In Wang Zhonghan 王鍾翰, ed., *Manzu shi yanjiu ji* 滿族史研究集, 281–306. Beijing: Zhongguo shehui kexue chubanshe, 1988.
Chen Lang 陳朗. *Xue Yue Mei* 雪月梅; reprinted in *Ming Qing yanqing xiaoshuo daguan* 明清言情小說大觀, vol. 3, Beijing: Huaxia chubanshe, 1993.
Chen Liao 陳遼. "*Honglou meng*: yibu teshu de chanhuilu" 紅樓夢：一部特殊的懺悔錄. *MXYJ* 16 (1990): 111–21.
Chen Meilin 陳美林. "Guanyu Wu Jingzi yingzhengbi wenti" 關於吳敬梓應徵辟問題. In idem, *Wu Jingzi yanjiu* 吳敬梓研究, 123–34.
———. "Nanjing Xianxianci de xingfei jiqi yu Wu Jingzi de guanxi" 南京先賢祠的興廢及其與吳敬梓的關係. In idem, *Wu Jingzi yanjiu*, 135–142.
———. *Wu Jingzi pingzhuan* 吳敬梓評傳. Nanjing: Nanjing daxue chubanshe, 1990.
———. *Wu Jingzi yanjiu* 吳敬梓研究. Shanghai: Shanghai guji chubanshe, 1984.
Chen Ruheng 陳汝衡. *Wu Jingzi zhuan* 吳敬梓傳. Shanghai: Shanghai wenyi chubanshe, 1981.
Chen Wanyi 陳萬益. *Wan Ming xiaopinwen yu Mingji wenren shenghuo* 晚明小品文與明季文人生活. Taipei: Da'an chubanshe, 1988.
Chen Xin 陳新. "Ping Hu Shi 'Wu Jingzi nianpu'" 評胡適吳敬梓年譜. *Rulin waishi xuekan* 儒林外史學刊 1 (1988): 190–205.
Chen Xuewen 陳學文. "Mingdai zhongye yilai qinong qiru congshang fengqi he zhongshang sichao de chuxian" 明代中葉以來棄農棄儒從商風氣和重商思潮的出現. *Jiuzhou xuekan* 九州學刊 3.4 (1990): 56–66.
Ciyuan 辭源. Rev. ed. Beijing: Shangwu yinshuguan, 1988.
Dai Bufan 戴不凡. "Shixu cuoluan pian: qian bashi hui shixu de maodun" 時序錯亂篇：前八十回時序的矛盾. In idem, *Hongxue pingyi waipian* 紅學評議外篇, ed. Dai Yun 戴雲, 269–331. Beijing: Wenhua yishu chubanshe, 1990.
Dai Zhen 戴震, ed. *Qu Yuan fu zhu* 屈原賦注. Taipei: Shijie shuju, 1970.
Ding Yan 丁晏, ed. *Cao Zhi quanzhu* 曹植全注. Taipei: Guangwen shuju, 1961.
Dong Zhongshu 董仲舒. *Chunqiu fanlu* 春秋凡露. *SBBY*.

Du Jinghua 杜景華. "*Honglou meng* de xushi liunian jiqi yinyu tankao" 紅樓夢的敘事流年及其隱寓探考. *HXK* 1991.4, 165–86.
Du Weiyun 杜維運. "Qingdai Qian Jia shidai liuxing yu zhishi fenzi jian de yintui sixiang" 清代乾嘉時代流行於知識分子間的隱退思想. *Guoli zhengzhi daxue lishi xuebao* 國立政治大學歷史學報 7 (1990): 63–71.
Fang Zhengyao 方正耀. *Zhongguo xiaoshuo piping shilüe* 中國小說批評史略. Beijing: Zhongguo shehui kexue chubanshe, 1990.
Feng Qiyong 馮其庸. *Lun gengchen ben* 論庚辰本. Shanghai: Shanghai wenyi chubanshe, 1978.
Feng Qiyong 馮其庸 and Li Xifan 李希凡, eds. *"Honglou meng" da cidian* 紅樓夢大辭典. Beijing: Wenhua yishu chubanshe, 1990.
Feng Qiyong 馮其庸 et al., eds. *Zhiyan zhai chongping "Shitou ji" huijiao* 脂硯齋重評石頭記彙校, 5 vols. Beijing: Wenhua yishu chubanshe, 1987–89.
Gong Weizhai 龔未齋. *Xuehong xuan chidu* 雪鴻軒尺牘. Ed. Yu Jun 余軍. Changsha: Hu'nan wenyi chubanshe, 1987.
Gu Yanwu 顧炎武. *Gu Tinglin shiwenji* 顧亭林詩文集. Hong Kong: Zhonghua shuju, 1976.
———. *Rizhilu jishi* 日知錄集釋. *SBBY*.
Guanyu Jiangning zhizao Caojia dang'an shiliao 關於江寧織造曹家檔案史料. Ed. Gugong bowuyuan Ming Qing dang'anbu 故宮博物院明清檔案部. Beijing: Zhonghua shuju, 1975.
Guo Dengfeng 郭登峯, ed. *Lidai zixuzhuan wenchao* 歷代自敘傳文鈔. Shanghai: Shanghai shangwu yinshuguan, 1937.
Guo Yingde 郭英德. *Ming Qing wenren chuanqi yanjiu* 明清文人傳奇研究. Beijing: Beijing shifan daxue chubanshe, 1992.
Han Jingtai 韓經太. "Lun Zhongguo gudian shige de beijuxing mei" 論中國古典詩歌的悲劇性美. *Zhongguo shehui kexue* 中國社會科學 1990.1, 183–99; reprinted in *Zhongguo gudai jindai wenxue yanjiu* 中國古代近代文學研究 1990.7, 263–79.
Han Yu 韓愈. *Han Changli quanji* 韓昌黎全集. *SBBY*.
He Manzi 何滿子. *Lun "Rulin waishi"* 論儒林外史. Rev. ed. Beijing: Zhonghua shuju, 1981.
He Zehan 何澤翰. *"Rulin waishi" renwu benshi kaolüe* 儒林外史人物本事考略. Rev. ed. Shanghai: Shanghai guji chubanshe, 1985.
"Honglou meng" zhuzuo quan lunzheng ji 紅樓夢著作權論爭集. Ed. Beifang luncong bianjibu 北方論叢編輯部. Taiyuan: Shanxi renmin chubanshe, 1985.
Hou Hui 侯會. "*Honglou meng* yu Zhang Dai" 紅樓夢與張岱. *HXK* 1991.1, 219–41.
Hou Jian 侯健. "*Yesou puyan* de biantai xinli" 野叟曝言的變態心理. In idem,

Zhongguo xiaoshuo bijiao yanjiu 中國小說比較研究, 433–48. Taipei: Dongda dushu kongsi, 1983.

Hu Shi 胡適. "*Ernü yingxiong zhuan* xu" 兒女英雄傳序. In *Hu Shi gudian wenxue yanjiu lunji* 胡適古典文學研究論集, 1156–73. Shanghai: Shanghai guji chubanshe, 1988.

———. "He Shuangqing kao" 賀雙卿考. In *Hu Shi gudian wenxue yanjiu lunji*, 600–603 (see preceding entry).

———. *Hu Shi "Honglou meng" yanjiu lunshu quanbian* 胡適紅樓夢研究論述全編. Shanghai: Shanghai guji chubanshe, 1988.

———. "Wu Jingzi nianpu" 吳敬梓年譜. In *Hu Shi gudian wenxue yanjiu lunji*, 1070–104 (see above).

———. "Wu Jingzi zhuan" 吳敬梓傳. In *Hu Shi gudian wenxue yanjiu lunji*, 1060–64 (see above).

Huang Lin 黃霖, ed. *"Jin Ping Mei" ziliao huibian* 金瓶梅資料彙編. Beijing: Zhonghua shuju, 1987.

Huang Lin 黃霖 and Han Tongwen 韓同文, eds. *Zhongguo lidai xiaoshuo lunzhu xuan* (shang) 中國歷代小說論著選(上). Nanchang: Jiangxi renmin chubanshe, 1982.

Huang Yizhi 黃逸之. "Huang Zhongze nianpu" 黃仲則年譜. In Huang Baoshu 黃葆樹 et al., eds., *Huang Zhongze yanjiu ziliao* 黃仲則研究資料, 23–90. Shanghai: Shanghai guji chubanshe, 1986.

Jiang Guobao 蔣國寶. *Fang Yizhi zhexue sixiang yanjiu* 方以智哲學思想研究. Hefei: Anhui renmin chubanshe, 1987.

Jin Xingyao 金性堯. *Qingdai bihuo lu* 清代筆禍錄. Hong Kong: Zhonghua shuju, 1989.

Kang Zhengguo 康正果. "Bianyuan wenren de cainü qingjie jiqi chuanda de shiyi: *Xiqing sanji* chutan" 邊緣文人的才女情結及其傳達的詩意：西清散記初探. Paper presented at the conference "Women and Literature in Ming-Qing China," Yale University, June 1993.

Li Baichuan 李百川. *Lüye xianzong* (baihui ben) 綠野仙踪(百回本). Ed. Hou Zhongyi 侯忠義. Beijing: Beijing daxue chubanshe, 1986.

———. *Lüye xianzong* 綠野仙踪 (facsimile reprint of the Qianlong 100-chapter manuscript version). Beijing: Beijing daxue chubanshe, 1986.

Li Hanqiu 李漢秋, ed. *"Rulin waishi" Huang Xiaotian pingben* 儒林外史黃小田評本. Hefei: Huangshan shushe, 1986.

———. *"Rulin waishi" huijiao huipingben* 儒林外史會校會評本. Shanghai: Shanghai guji chubanshe, 1984.

———. *"Rulin waishi" yanjiu lunwen ji* 儒林外史研究論文集. Beijing: Zhonghua shuju, 1987.

———. *"Rulin waishi" yanjiu ziliao* 儒林外史研究資料. Shanghai: Shanghai guji chubanshe, 1984.

Li Lüyuan 李綠園. *Qilu deng* 歧路燈. Zhengzhou: Zhongzhou shuhuashe, 1980.
Li Ruzhen 李汝珍. *Jinghua yuan* 鏡花緣. Hong Kong: Zhonghua shuju, 1965 (Beijing, 1951).
Li Shan 李善. *"Wenxuan" Li Shan zhu* 文選李善注. *SBBY*.
Li Yu 李漁. *Li Yu quanji* 李漁全集. Hangzhou: Zhejiang guji chubanshe, 1992.
Li Yuandu 李元度. *Guochao xianzheng shilüe* 國朝先正事略. *SBBY*.
Li Zhi 李贄. *Fenshu, Xufenshu* 焚書續焚書. Beijing: Zhonghua shuju, 1975.
Liao Yan 廖燕. *Chaizhou bieji sizhong* 柴舟別集四種; reprinted in *Qingren zaju erji* 清人雜劇二集. Ed. Zheng Zhenduo 鄭振鐸. Changle, 1934 (private publication).
Lin Chen 林辰. *Mingmo Qingchu xiaoshuo xulu* 明末清初小說敘錄. Shenyang: Chunfeng wenyi chubanshe, 1988.
Lin Lan Xiang 林蘭香. Shenyang: Chunfeng wenyi chubanshe, 1985.
Liu Dakui 劉大櫆 *Liu Dakui ji* 劉大櫆集. Ed. Wu Mengfu 吳孟復. Shanghai: Shanghai guji chubanshe, 1990.
Liu Shide 劉世德 et al., eds. *Zhongguo gudai xiaoshuo baike quanshu* 中國古代小說百科全書. Beijing: Zhongguo dabaike quanshu chubanshe, 1993.
Lu Xingji 盧興基. "Dushu ren zuole liangqian nian de meng: cong wenhua xinli kan *Yesou puyan*" 讀書人做了兩千年的夢：從文化心理看野叟曝言. *MXYJ* 14 (1989): 114–28.
Lu Xun 魯迅. "Zhongguo xiaoshuo de lishi de bianqian" 中國小說的歷史的變遷. In *Lu Xun quanji* 魯迅全集 9: 301–40. Beijing: Renmin chubanshe, 1982.
———. *Zhongguo xiaoshuo shilüe* 中國小說史略. In *Lu Xun quanji* 9: 1–297 (see preceding entry).
Lü Xiong 呂熊. *Nüxian waishi* 女仙外史. Tianjin: Baihua wenyi chubanshe, 1985.
———. *Nüxian waishi* 女仙外史 (facsimile reprint of the Kangxi edition). In *Guben xiaoshuo jicheng* 古本小說集成. Shanghai: Shanghai guji chubanshen, 1990.
Lü Zhenghui 呂正惠. *Shuqing chuantong yu zhengzhi xianshi* 抒情傳統與政治現實. Taipei: Da'an chubanshe, 1989.
Luan Xing 欒星. *"Qilu deng" yanjiu ziliao* 歧路燈研究資料. Zhengzhou: Zhongzhou shuhuashe, 1982.
———. "Xinjiaoben *Yesou puyan* xu" 新校本野叟曝言序. *Zhongzhou xuekan* 中州學刊 1990.6: 101–4.
Luo Gang 羅鋼 and Chen Qing 陳慶. "Weida xinling de yishu touying: cong zizhuan xiaoshuo xingshi laikan *Honglou meng* de meixue yiyi" 偉大心靈的藝術投影：從自傳小說形式來看紅樓夢的美學意義. *HXK* 1987.2: 9–43.

Meng Xingren 孟醒仁. *Wu Jingzi nianpu* 吳敬梓年譜. Hefei: Anhui renmin chubanshe, 1981.
Meng Xingren 孟醒仁 and Meng Fanjing 孟凡經. *Wu Jingzi pingzhuan* 吳敬梓評傳. Zhengzhou: Zhongzhou guji chubanshe, 1987.
Mingjiaozhongren 名教中人. *Haoqiu zhuan* 好逑傳. Zhengzhou: Zhongzhou guji chubanshe, 1980.
Ming Qing xiaoshuo xuba xuan 明清小說序跋選. Ed. Dalian dushuguan cankaobu 大連圖書館參考部. Changchun: Chunfeng wenyi chubanshe, 1983.
Mingshi 明史. Beijing: Zhonghua shuju, 1974.
Nü kaike zhuan 女開科傳. Shenyang: Chunfeng wenyi chubanshe, 1983.
Ouyang Jian 歐陽健. "*Yesou puyan* banben bianxi" 野叟曝言版本辯析. *MXYJ* 7 (1988): 181–95.
Ouyang Xiu 歐陽修. *Ouyang wenzhong quanji* 歐陽文忠全集. *SBBY*.
Pan Mingshen 潘銘燊. "*Shitou ji* nianri kao" 石頭記年日考. Hong Kong: Zhongguo xueshe, 1988.
Pei Puxian 裴普賢. "Meiren xiangcao xiangzheng zhuyi de suyuan" 美人香草象征主義的溯源. In idem, "*Shijing*" *bijiao yanjiu yu xinshang* 詩經比較研究與欣賞, 44–53. Taipei: Xuesheng shuju, 1983.
Pingshan lengyan 平山冷燕. Shenyang: Chunfeng wenyi chubanshe, 1982.
Pu Songling 蒲松齡. "*Liaozhai zhiyi*" *huijiao huizhu huipingben* 聊齋誌異會校會注會評本. Ed. Zhang Youhe 張友鶴. Shanghai: Shanghai guji chubanshe, 1978.
Qi Yukun 齊裕焜. "Mingmo Qingchu shishi xiaoshuo shuping" 明末清初時事小說述評. *Fujian shifan daxue xuebao* 福建師範大學學報 1989.2, 44–49; reprinted in *Zhongguo gudai jindai wenxue yanjiu* 中國古代近代文學研究 1989.8, 219–25.
Qian Dehong 錢德洪. "Nianpu" 年譜. In Wang Shouren 王守仁, *Yangming quanshu* 陽明全書, 32.1a–36.17b. *SBBY*.
Qian Zhongshu 錢鍾書. "Shi keyi yuan" 詩可以怨. *Wenxue pinglun* 文學評論 1981.1, 16–21.
Qing Sanxiang 卿三祥. "*Lüye xianzong* sanlun" 綠野仙踪散論. *MXYJ* 20 (1991): 139–51.
Shen Xinlin 沈新林. "Lun Li Yu xiaoshuo zhong de ziwo xingxiang: jianlun ziwo jituo de chuangzuo fangfa" 論李漁小說中的自我形象：兼論自我寄托的創作方法. *MXYJ* 14 (1989): 103–14.
Shi Zhenlin 史震林. *Xiqing sanji* 西青散記. Beijing: Guoji shudian, 1987 (1907).
"*Shuihu zhuan*" *huipingben* 水滸傳會評本. Ed. Chen Xizhong 陳曦鍾 et al. Beijing: Beijing daxue chubanshe, 1981.
Sima Qian 司馬遷. *Shiji* 史記. Beijing: Zhonghua shuju, 1972.

Song Deyin 宋德胤. "*Honglou meng* zhong de Mansu chutan" 紅樓夢中的滿俗初探. *HXK* 1984.4, 269–92.
Sun Kaidi 孫楷弟. *Cangzhou ji* 滄州集. Beijing: Zhonghua shuju, 1965.
———. "Li Liweng yu *Shi'er lou*" 李立翁與十二樓. In idem, *Cangzhou houji* 滄州後集, 151–205. Beijing: Zhonghua shuju, 1985.
———. "Xia Erming yu *Yesou puyan*" 夏二銘與野叟曝言. In idem, *Cangzhouji*, 236–48 (see preceding entry).
Sun Xun 孫遜. "*Honglou meng*" *Zhiping chutan* 紅樓夢脂評初探. Shanghai: Shanghai guji chubanshe, 1981.
Tan Fengliang 談風梁. "*Rulin waishi* chuangzuo shijian guocheng xintan" 儒林外史創作時間過程新探 In Li Hanqiu, ed. "*Rulin waishi*" *yanjiu lunwen ji*, 229–47.
Tangren xiaoshuo 唐人小說. Ed. Wang Bijiang 汪辟彊. Shanghai: Shanghai guji chubanshe, 1978.
Teng Shaozhen 騰紹箴. *Qingdai baqi zidi* 清代八旗子弟. Beijing: Zhongguo huaqiao chuban gongsi, 1989.
Wang Qiongling 王瓊玲. "*Yesou puyan*" *yanjiu* 野叟曝言研究. Taipei: Xuehai chubanshe, 1988.
Wang Xianpei 王先霈 and Zhou Weimin 周偉民. *Ming Qing xiaoshuo lilun piping shi* 明清小說理論批評史. Guangzhou: Huacheng chubanshe, 1988.
Wang Yingzhi 王英志. "'Fafen zhushu' shuo pingshu" 發憤著書說評述. *Gudai wenxue lilun yanjiu* 古代文學理論研究 11 (1986): 125–56.
Wang Zhong 汪中. *Shuxue* 述學. *SBBY*.
Wu Jingzi 吳敬梓. *Wenmushanfang ji* 文木山房集. Shanghai: Shanghai yadong dushuguan, 1931.
Wu Xiaoru 吳小如. "Wu Jingzi jiqi *Rulin waishi*" 吳敬梓及其儒林外史. In Zuojia chubanshe bianjibu 作家出版社編輯部, ed., "*Rulin waishi*" *pinglun ji* 儒林外史評論集, 105–29. Beijing: Zuojia chubanshe, 1955.
Xia Jingqu 夏敬渠. *Wen Suchen* 文素臣 (*Yesou puyan* 野叟曝言). Taipei: Wenyuan shuju, 1982.
———. *Yesou puyan* 野叟曝言. 20 vols. (facsimile reprint of the 1881 edition). Taipei: Tianyi chubanshe, 1985.
———. *Yesou puyan* 野叟曝言. Changchun: Changchun chubanshe, 1993.
Xiao Hai 逍海. "Cao Xueqin shengzu nian yanjiu shuyao" 曹雪芹生卒年研究述要. *HXK* 1991.1, 239–51.
Xu Daling 徐大齡. *Qingdai juanna zhidu* 清代捐納制度. Beijing: Harvard Yenching Institute, 1950.
Xu Fuming 徐扶明. "*Honglou meng*" *xiqu bijiao yanjiu* 紅樓夢戲曲比較研究. Shanghai: Shanghai guji chubanshe, 1984.
Xue Hongji 薛洪勣. "Mingmo Qingchu xiaoshuo manyi" 明末清初小說漫議. *MXLC* 1 (1984): 17–33.

Yan Jie 嚴捷 and Yan Beiming 嚴北溟, trans. and annot. *Liezi yizhu* 列子譯注. Hong Kong: Zhonghua shuju, 1987.
Yang Bojun 楊柏峻, trans. and annot. *Mengzi yizhu* 孟子譯注. Beijing: Zhonghua shuju, 1960.
Yang Maojian 楊懋建. *Jingchen zalu* 京塵雜錄. In *Biji xiaoshuo daguan* 筆記小說大觀, vol. 18. Yangzhou: Jiangsu guangling guji keyinshe, 1984.
Yang Xuechen 楊學琛. "Lüelun Qingdai Man Han guanxi de fazhan he bianhua" 略論清代滿漢關係的發展和變化. In Wang Zhonghan 王鍾翰, ed., *Manzu shi yanjiu ji* 滿族史研究集, 209–27. Beijing: Zhongguo shehui kexue chubanshe, 1988.
Ye Jiaying 葉嘉瑩. "Lun cixue zhong zhi kunhuo yu *Huajian* ci zhi nüxing xuxie jiqi yinxiang" (shang) 論詞學中之困惑與花間詞之女性敘寫及其影響 (上). *Zhongwai wenxue* 中外文學, 20.8 (1992): 4–30.
Yisu 一粟, ed. "*Honglou meng*" *juan* 紅樓夢卷. Beijing: Zhonghua shuju, 1963.
Ying Bicheng 應必誠. *Lun "Shitouji" gengchen ben* 論石頭記庚辰本. Shanghai: Shanghai guji chubanshe, 1983.
You Guo'en 游國恩. "*Chuci* nüxing zhongxin shuo" 楚辭女性中心說. In idem, "*Chuci*" *lunwenji* 楚辭論文集, 191–204. Hong Kong: Wenchang shuju, 1966 (Shanghai, 1955).
Yu Pingbo 俞平伯. "Cao Xueqin zibi Lin Daiyu" 曹雪芹自比林黛玉. In idem, *Yu Pingbo lun "Honglou meng,"* 717–21.
———. *Yu Pingbo lun "Honglou meng"* 俞平伯論紅樓夢. Shanghai: Shanghai guji chubanshe, 1988.
Yu Yingshi (Ying-shih Yü) 余英時. "'Cao Xueqin de Hanzu rentonggan' bulun" 曹雪芹的漢族認同感補論. In idem, *Honglou meng de liangge shijie* 紅樓夢的兩個世界, 197–210. Taipei: Lianjing chuban gongsi, 1981 (1978).
———. "Guanyu *Honglou meng* de zuozhe he sixiang wenti de shangque" 關於紅樓夢的作者和思想問題的商榷. In Hu Wenbin 胡文彬 and Zhou Lei 周雷, eds., *Haiwai Hongxue lunji* 海外紅學論集, 233–44. Shanghai: Shanghai guji chubanshe, 1982.
———. "Gudai zhishi jieceng de xingqi yu fazhan" 古代知識階層的興起與發展. In idem, *Shi yu Zhongguo wenhua* 士與中國文化, 1–83. Shanghai: Shanghai renmin chubanshe, 1987.
———. "Zhongguo jinshi zongjiao lunli yu shangren jingshen" 中國近世宗教倫理與商人精神. In idem, *Shi yu Zhongguo wenhua*, 441–579 (see preceding entry).
Yuan Mei 袁枚. *Xiaocangshanfang chidu* 小倉山房尺牘. Ed. Fan Yinzheng 范寅錚. Changsha: Hu'nan wenyi chubanshe, 1987.
———. *Xiaocangshanfang shiwenji* 小倉山房詩文集. *SBBY*.
Yuanhu yanshui sanren 鴛湖煙水散人. *Nücaizi shu* 女才子書. Shenyang: Chunfeng wenyi chubanshe, 1983.

Yue Hengjun 樂衡軍. "Shiji de piaobo zhe" 世紀的飄泊者. In Ke Qingming 柯慶明 and Lin Mingde 林明德, eds., *Zhongguo gudian wenxue yanjiu congkan: xiaoshuo zhipu* (3) 中國古典文學研究叢刊: 小說之部(三), 175–91. Taipei: Juliu dushu gongsi, 1970.

Zhang Dai 張岱. *Zhang Dai shiwen ji* 張岱詩文集. Ed. Xia Xianchun 夏咸淳. Shanghai: Shanghai guji chubanshe, 1991.

Zhang Jun 張俊. "Lun *Lin Lan Xiang* yu *Honglou meng*: jiantan lianjie *Jin Ping Mei* yu *Honglou meng* de 'lianhuan'" 論林蘭香與紅樓夢: 兼談聯結金瓶梅與紅樓夢的鏈環. *MXLC* 5 (1987): 63–84.

Zhang Shucai 張書才. "Cao Xueqin qiji kaobian" 曹雪芹旗籍考辨 *HXK* 1982.3, 287–310.

Zhao Gang 趙岡 and Chen Zhongyi 陳仲毅. *"Honglou meng" yanjiu xinbian* 紅樓夢研究新編. Taipei: Lianjing chuban gongsi, 1975.

Zhao Jingshen 趙景深. "*Yesou puyan* zuozhe Xia Erming nianpu" 野叟曝言作者夏二銘年譜. In idem, *Zhongguo xiaoshuo congkao* 中國小說叢考. Ji'nan: Qi Lu shushe, 1980.

Zhao Tiaokuang 趙苕狂. "*Yingmei'an yiyu* kao" 影梅庵憶語考. In *Yingmei'an yiyu, Fusheng liuji, Xiangwan lou yiyu, Qiudeng suoyi,* 影梅庵憶語, 浮生六記, 香畹樓憶語, 秋燈瑣憶, 40–62. Changsha: Yuelu shushe, 1991.

Zhao Xingqin 趙興勤. "'Cai' yu 'mei': Ming Qing xiaoshuo chutan" 才與美: 明清小說初探. *MXLC* 4 (1986): 14–23.

———. "'Jing' yu 'quan': Mingmo Qingchu yanqing xiaoshuo tantao zhiyi" 經與權: 明末清初言情小說探討之一. *MXYJ* 4 (1986), 279–88.

Zheng Xie 鄭燮. *Zheng Banqiao ji* 鄭板橋集. Shanghai: Shanghai guji chubanshe, 1979.

Zheng Zhenduo 鄭振鐸. "Qingchu dao zhongye de changpian xiaoshuo de fazhan" 清初到中葉的長篇小說的發展. In idem, *Zheng Zhenduo gudian wenxue lunwenji* 鄭振鐸古典文學論文集, 453–72. Shanghai: Shanghai guji chubanshe, 1984.

———. "Zhongguo gudian wenxue zhong de xiaoshuo chuantong" 中國古典文學中的小說傳統. In idem, *Zheng Zhenduo gudian wenxue lunwenji*, 287–302 (see preceding entry).

Zhongguo tongsu xiaoshuo zongmu tiyao 中國通俗小說總目提要. Ed. Jiangsu sheng shehui kexue yuan Ming Qing xiaoshuo yanjiu zhongxin 江蘇省社會科學院明清小說研究中心. Beijing: Zhongguo wenlian chuban gongsi, 1990.

Zhou Ruchang (Ju-ch'ang Chou) 周汝昌. *Cao Xueqin xiaozhuan* 曹雪芹小傳. Tianjin: Baihua wenyi chubanshe, 1980.

———. "*Honglou meng* xinzheng" 紅樓夢新証. Beijing: Renmin wenxue chubanshe, 1976 (Shanghai, 1953).

———. *"Honglou meng" yu Zhonghua wenhua* 紅樓夢與中華文化. Beijing: Gongren chubanshe, 1989.

Zhu Danwen 朱淡文. *"Honglou meng" lunyuan* 紅樓夢論源. Nanjing: Jiangsu guji chubanshe, 1992.

Zhu Xuequn 朱學羣. "Mishi zai chengnian shehui menkan de Jia Baoyu" 迷失在成年社會門檻的賈寶玉. *HXK* 1991.1, 47–66.

Zhu Yixuan 朱一玄, ed. *"Honglou meng" Zhiping jiaolu* 紅樓夢脂評校錄. Ji'nan: Qi Lu shushe, 1986.

Character List

Personal names and titles given in the Bibliography are not listed here. Entries are alphabetized letter by letter, ignoring word and syllable breaks with the exception of personal names, which are ordered first under the surname and then under the given name.

anfu zunrong 按富尊榮
An Guifei 安貴妃
aoshi 傲世

Bada shanren 八大山人
bagong 拔貢
bagu wen 八股文
Bai Juyi 白居易
bangyan 榜眼
Bao Tingxi 鮑亭璽
Baoshu zi 抱蜀子
baoxi 抱膝
baoyi 包衣
Baqi tongzhi 八旗通誌
Bingxian 冰絃
"Bingzhong shugan" 病中抒感
Boxue hongci 博學鴻詞
butian 補天
"Buyi" 補遺
buyi 布衣
buyu zhi shi 不遇之士

caizi jiaren xiaoshuo 才子佳人小說
Cao Fu 曹頫
Cao Pi 曹丕
Cao Tangcun 曹棠村

Cao Xueqin 曹雪芹
Cao Yin 曹寅
Cao Zhi 曹植
Chaizhou bieji sizhong 柴舟別集四種
chaoben 抄本
chaodai nianji wukao 朝代年紀無考
chen 臣
Chen Chen 陳忱
Chen Hongshou 陳洪綬
Chen Jiru 陳繼儒
Chen Zilong 陳子龍
Cheng Jinfang 程晉芳
Cheng Weiyuan 程偉元
Cheng Yi 程頤
Chenghua 成化
Chengjia 程甲
Chi Hengshan 遲衡山
chuanchao 傳抄
chuanxi 串戲
Chu bawang 楚霸王
Chunliuying 春柳鶯
chushan 出山
"Cike liezhuan" 刺客列傳

da Baoyu 大寶玉
Daguan yuan 大觀園

Dai Mingshi 戴名世
Dai Xian 戴銑
da laoguan 大老官
danbo 淡泊
Dao 道
daoxue 道學
daoxue xiansheng 道學先生
Da Qing huidian 大清會典
da tiaokan yuyi chu 大調侃寓意處
Daxue 大學
dianshi 殿試
Dong Xiaowan 董小宛
Dong Yue 董說
Dong Zhongshu 董仲舒
Du Shaoqing 杜少卿
Du Shenqing 杜慎卿
Dun Cheng 郭誠

Er Cheng quanshu 二程全書
Ernü yingxiong zhuan 兒女英雄傳
Erzhi daoren 二知道人

fafen 發憤
fafen zhushu 發憤著書
Fan Jin 范進
fan'an 翻案
Fang Xiaoru 方孝孺
Fang Yizhi 方以智
Fangguan 芳官
fanli 凡例
"Fanxian shu zhong ji shedi Mo disishu" 范縣署中寄舍弟墨第四書
fei'e touhuo 飛蛾投火
Feixiong 飛熊
Feng 鳳
Feng Menglong 馮夢龍
Feng'ge 鳳哥
Fenghuang chi 鳳凰池
fengshi 諷世
fu 賦
"Furong nüer lei" 芙蓉女兒誄

Fusheng liuji 浮生六記
fushi 復試

Gai Kuan 盖寬
Gangmu juzheng 綱目舉正
gengchen (1760) 庚辰
gong 工
gongye baoguo 功業報國
Gu Dashao 顧大韶
Gu Yanwu 顧炎武
Guangxu 光緒
Gufen 孤憤
guige tingwei zhi zhuan 閨閣庭闈之傳
guige zhaozhuan 閨閣昭傳
Guo Moruo 郭沫若
guotiao mingjue nanzi 果條明決男子
Guxin 古心

Hai Rui 海瑞
haoju 豪舉
Heshen 和珅
"He (Wu Qing) zuo" 和(吳檠)作
Hong Changqing 洪長卿
Hong Liangji 洪亮吉
"*Honglou meng* shuomeng" 紅樓夢說夢
Hongniang 紅娘
Hongxue 紅學
Hongzhi 弘治
hu 唬
hualian 花臉
Huang Jingren 黃景仁
Huang Longzi 黃龍子
Huang Zhongze 黃仲則
hui (chapter) 回
hui (regret) 悔
huikao 會考
huikui 會魁
huishi 會試
huiyuan 會元

Ji En 紀恩
Ji Kang 嵇康
Ji Shufei 紀淑妃
Ji Weixiao 季葦簫
jia 假
Jia Baoyu 賈寶玉
Jia Jing 賈敬
Jia Lan 賈蘭
Jia Lian 賈璉
Jia Rong 賈蓉
Jia Rui 賈瑞
Jia She 賈赦
Jia Yi 賈誼
Jia Yucun 賈雨村
Jia Zhen 賈珍
Jia Zheng 賈政
Jiahui 佳惠
Jiangning 江寧
Jiangyin 江陰
jiaogou hui 交媾會
Jiaqing 嘉慶
jiayu cun 假語存
jiaxu (1754) 甲戌
"Jiechao" 解嘲
Jihu sou 畸笏叟
Jiling xiangnianzhu 鶺鴒香念珠
Jiling zhi bei, tangli zhi wei 鶺鴒之悲，棠棣之威
jimao (1759) 己卯
Jin He 金和
Jin Liangming 金兩銘
Jin Shengtan 金聖歎
Jin Zhi 瑾直
jing 經
Jing Ke 荊苛
Jinghu yisou 鏡湖逸叟
Jinghua ting 鏡花亭
"Jinghuan xianzi fu" 警幻仙子賦
Jingshi 京師
jingshi 經世
jingshi zhixue 經世之學

"Jing Tan changhe shi xu" 荊潭唱和詩序
Jingting 敬亭
Jin Ping Mei 金瓶梅
jinshi 進士
jinwen xue 今文學
jituo 寄托
juren 舉人
jushi 居士

Kang Youwei 康有為
Kangxi 康熙
kaoguan 考官
kaozheng 考證
keming 科名
ketou 科頭
kong 空
Kong Ruogu 孔若谷
kong ruo gu 空若谷
Kuang Chaoren 匡超人
kuangshi (audacious man) 狂士
kuangshi (social reform) 誆世
Kuiguan 葵官
kun 昆
"Kuxiao shuo" 苦孝說

Lao Can youji 老殘遊記
Leng Yubing 冷於冰
Leng Zixing 冷子興
Li Bai 李白
Li Guangdi 李光地
Li Wan 李紈
Li Xiang 李詳
Li Youquan 李又全
liancai pi 憐才癖
Liangjiao hun 兩交婚
Liao Yan 廖燕
liezhuan 列傳
Lin Daiyu 林黛玉
Liner bao 麟兒報
Lingguan 齡官

Liu Bei 劉備
Liu Dalang 劉大郎
Liu E 劉鶚
Liu Jin 劉瑾
Liu Xianxin 劉咸炘
Liu Xiaobiao 劉孝標
lixue 理學
lixue mingchen 理學名臣
liyan 立言
li yue nong bing 禮樂農兵
Lu Mengli 盧夢梨
Lu Xiangshan 陸象山
luandao huoshi 亂道惑世
lunluo ren 淪落人
Luo Pin 羅聘
Luo Siju 羅思舉
Luofan lou wenji 落帆樓文集
"Luoshen fu" 洛神賦
Luo Zhuangyong gong nianpu 羅壯勇公年譜

Ma Chunshang 馬純上
Mao Qiling 毛奇齡
Mao Xiang 冒襄
maoming 冒名
"Meinü" 美女
meiren xiangcao 美人香草
"*Mei Shengyu shiji* xu" 梅聖俞詩集序
Mengfu 蒙府
Mengqing 夢卿
Mengruan 夢阮
Mingyan 茗煙
Minxuan 敏軒
mingshi 名士
mufu 幕府
muyou 幕友

neisheng waiwang 內聖外王
Neiwu fu 內務府
nianpu 年譜
Niu Buyi 牛布衣
Niu Pulang 牛浦朗

nong 農
Nüwa 女媧
nüzhong daru 女中大儒
Nü zhuangyuan 女狀元

panci 判詞
Piling huizhenlou 毗陵匯珍樓
"Pinnü xing" 貧女行
pipa 琵琶
"Pipa xing" 琵琶行
pu 曝
pufu qishou 匍匐乞受

qi 妻
Qi Jiguang 戚繼光
qianci 謙辭
Qianlong 乾龍
Qidiao 漆雕
"Qijie" 七解
Qin Keqing 秦可卿
Qin Zhong 秦鍾
qing 情
qingtan 清談
Qingwen 晴雯
qiong er hougong 窮而後工
Qiuxiang 秋香
Qu Gongsun 蘧公孫
Qu Yuan 屈原
quan 權

Ren Luanchui 任鶯吹
Rijing 日景
Rou putuan 肉圃團
Ruan Ji 阮籍
rulin 儒林
"Ruyan fei" 乳燕飛

san 散
san'gang 三綱
Sanguo yanyi 三國演義
Sanjiao kaimi guizheng yanyi 三教開迷歸正演義

Character List 227

"Sanyu lou" 三與樓
shang 商
shanren 山人
Shen Fu 沈復
Shen Qiongzhi 沈瓊枝
Shen Yao 沈垚
Shenbaoguan 申報館
sheng bu fengshi 生不逢時
sheng yu moshi 生於末世
shenwei 神位
shi (literatus) 士
shi (service to the state) 仕
shi (timing) 時
Shi Chong 石崇
Shi Xiangyun 史湘雲
Shi Yunyu 石韞玉
shidafu 士大夫
Shigong 時公
shipin 士品
shiqi 士氣
shishi xiaoshuo 時事小說
shiyin 仕隱
Shiyinben 石印本
shizu 士族
Shuangqing 雙卿
Shui 水
Shui Bingxin 水冰心
Shuihu houzhuan 水滸後傳
Shuihu zhuan 水滸傳
Shuinan 說難
shuren 庶人
simin 四民
simin zhishou 四民之首
Song Yu 宋玉
Su Shi 蘇軾
Suchen 素臣
Su'e 素娥
Sufu 素父
suikao 歲考
Sui Tang yanyi 隨唐演義
Sui Yangdi yanshi 隋煬帝艷史
Sun Jiagan 孫嘉淦

Sun Shaozu 孫紹祖
suoyin pai 索隱派
Su pipa 訴琵琶
suwang 素王

Tanchun 探春
tanhua 探花
Tang 湯
Tang Yin 唐寅
tangtang xumei 堂堂鬚眉
Tao Qian 陶潛
"*Tao'an mengyi zixu*" 陶庵夢憶自序
Taosou 韜叟
Tianhuazang zhuren 天花藏主人
Tianmu shanqiao 天目山樵
Tie Zhongyu 鐵中玉
"Ti Wang Shushan zuomaoyou-
  jiang du" 題王朔山左茅右蔣圖
tongcai 通才
"Tongxin shuo" 童心說
toucuo tai 投錯胎
Tu Shen 屠申

waishishi 外史氏
Wan Guifei 萬貴妃
Wang Anshi 王安石
Wang Jie 汪价
Wang Mian 王冕
Wang Wei 王維
Wang Xichan 王錫闡
Wang Xifeng 王熙鳳
Wang Yangming 王陽明
Wang Zhi 汪直
Wang Zhong 汪中
Wei Daying 韋大英
Wei Zhongxian 魏忠賢
weici 微辭
Wen Bai 文白
Wen Kang 文康
Wen Lin 文麟
Wen Long 文龍
Wen Ruyu 溫如玉

Wen Suchen 文素臣
"Wenguo lou" 聞過樓
wenren 文人
wenren hua 文人化
"Wenren zhiduo" 文人之多
wenren ziming 文人自命
wen sijian 文死諫
"Wenyan" 文言
wenwu 文武
wenxia 文俠
wenxing chuchu 文行出處
wenzhang baoguo 文章報國
Woxian caotang 臥閑草堂
Wu Guodui 吳國對
Wu Jingzi 吳敬梓
Wu Linqi 吳霖起
Wu Qing 吳檠
Wu Wenyan 吳文延
wudao zeyin 無道則隱
wugong 武功
wu jinshi qi 無進士氣
"Wuliu xiansheng zhuan" 五柳先生傳
wuwei zhe 無位者
Wuzong 武宗

Xia 夏
Xia Jingqu 夏敬渠
xian 仙
Xiang Yu 項羽
Xiangling 湘靈
Xiangling 香菱
Xiangru 相如
Xiangyun 湘雲
xianjue 先覺
xiankao 縣考
xianpu 獻曝
Xianqing ouji 閒情偶記
xianqin wulu 獻芹無路
Xianzong 憲宗
xiao Baoyu 小寶玉
Xiaohong 小紅

xiaolaopo qingjie 小老婆情結
xiaoshuo 小說
Xiaozong 孝宗
Xichun 惜春
Ximin shanqiao 西岷山樵
Xinchuan dian 薪傳殿
Xingli jingyi 性理經義
xingrong yu 形容語
Xingshi yinyuan zhuan 醒世姻緣傳
xinxue 心學
Xin Yesou puyan 新野叟曝言
Xiren 襲人
"Xiti xiaoxiang ji Luo Liangfeng"
  戲題小像寄羅兩峯
xiucai 秀才
xiushen 修身
xiushen, qijia, zhiguo, ping tianxia
  修身、齊家、治國、平天下
Xixiang ji 西廂記
Xiyou bu 西遊補
Xiyou ji 西遊記
Xu Wei 徐渭
Xuangu 璇姑
"Xuanju" 選舉
Xue Pan 薛潘
Xue Yue Mei 雪月梅
Xu Jin Ping Mei 續金瓶梅
Xu Su pipa 續訴琵琶
Xun Mei 荀玫

yang 陽
Yang Dingjian 楊定見
Yang Mingshi 楊名時
Yang Xiong 楊雄
Yang Zhu 楊朱
"Yanshi" 顏氏
yelü xiongnu 耶律雄奴
yeren qinpu 野人芹曝
yeren xianpu 野人獻曝
yeren xianri 野人獻日
yeshi zhuren 野史主人
yesou 野叟

yibao zhiji 以報知己
Yichuan wenji 伊川文集
yidai wenren 一代文人
"Yijia fu" 移家賦
Yijing 易經
yin (feminine principle) 陰
yin (withdrawal) 隱
Yingchun 迎春
Yinglian 英蓮
Yingmei'an yiyu 影梅庵憶語
Yinshi 蟫史
yinwei zhuanta, bingke zhuanwo 因爲傳他, 並可傳我
yixia 義俠
Yixing 一行
yiyu ti 憶語體
yong 咏
yonghuai shi 咏懷詩
yongshi shi 咏史詩
Yongzheng 雍正
You Sanjie 尤三姐
youming wuyun 有命無運
youshi 遊士
Youshi 尤氏
yu 遇
Yu Dafu 郁達夫
Yu Huaxuan 噓華軒
Yu Yude 虞育德
"Yu Jiang Bingu, Jiang Yujiu shu" 與江賓谷, 江禹九書
Yu jiao li 玉嬌梨
"Yu Wang Yanru" 與王言如
"Yu Xu Kejia" 與徐克家
Yuan Wuya 袁無涯
yuandan 元旦
yuanqi 緣起
Yuanyang 鴛鴦
Yuanyang zhen 鴛鴦針
yueji zhe 悅己者
"Yufu zhi" 與服誌
Yunxian xiao 雲仙笑
"Yuqiu xiaosi" 語求肖似

"Yuren shu shiba" 與人書十八
"Yuren shu ershisi" 與人書二十四
Yushi mingyan 喻世明言
"Yuwei zizhiming' 預爲自誌銘

"Zaida Tao Guancha shu" 再答陶觀察書
zaju 雜劇
Zeng Guofan 曾國番
Zhang Dai 張岱
Zhang Junmin 張俊民
Zhang Tianyi 張天一
Zhang Wenhu 張文虎
Zhang Xuecheng 張學誠
Zhang Zhupo 張竹坡
Zhao Yi 趙翼
Zhen Baoyu 甄寶玉
Zhen Mi 甄宓
Zheng Banqiao 鄭板橋
Zhengde 正德
zhenshi yin 眞事隱
"Zhenzhong ji" 枕中記
zhiguo ping tianxia 治國平天下
zhiji zhe 知己者
Zhiyan zhai 脂硯齋
zhiyin 知音
Zhong Xing 仲惺
Zhongjing 仲景
Zhongyi Shuihu quanzhuan 忠義水滸全傳
Zhou Jin 周進
Zhu Youtang 朱祐樘
Zhu Xi 朱熹
Zhuang Shaoguang 莊紹光
zhuangyuan 狀元
Zhuge Liang 諸葛亮
Zhuo Wenjun 卓文君
"Zhuowu lunlüe" 卓吾論略
zhushu ziyu 著書自娛
ziba 自跋
Zihan 紫函
Zijuan 紫娟

zikuang 自況
zisong 自訟
zituo 自託
"Ziwei muzhiming" 自爲墓誌銘
zixu (self-account) 自敘
zixu (self-written preface) 自序
"Zixu" 自敘
zizhi 自誌

zizhuan 自傳
Zou Shan 鄒善
Zui huatu 醉畫圖
"Zuiyin xiansheng zhuan" 醉吟先生傳
Zuo Guangdou 左光斗
Zuo Si 左思

Index

In this index an "f" after a number indicates a separate reference on the next page, and an "ff" indicates separate references on the next two pages. A continuous discussion over two or more pages is indicated by a span of page numbers, e.g., "57–59." *Passim* is used for a cluster of references in close but not consecutive sequence.

Allegorical tradition, 81f; in fiction, 82ff; in *Honglou meng*, 85–88. See also Gender; Literati; Qu Yuan; Self-re/presentation
Aunt Zhao, 91
Autobiographical writing, 1f, 10f; and the novel, 7f, 11f; paradoxical nature of, 9f; compared with the West, 157–58n23. See also Self-re/presentation; *Zikuang*; *Zixu*

Bada shanren, 169n82
Bai Juyi, "The Biography of Master Drunken Singer" ("Zuiyin xiansheng zhuan"), 45; "The Song of the *Pipa*" ("Pipa xing"), 46–48, 78
Bao Tingxi, 67
Baoyu, see Jia Baoyu
Barthes, Roland, 159n31
Bingxian, 130
Bol, Peter, 165n41
Brokaw, Cynthia, 156n12
Butler, Judith, 181n12

Cahill, James, 37, 158n24
Cai Yijiang, 96, 187n63
Caizi jiaren xiaoshuo ("scholars and beauties" fiction), 20ff, 25f, 82ff, 162n26, 186n49, 192–93n23, 193–94n27, 195n36
Cao Fu, 101
Cao Pi, 88

Cao Xueqin, 41f, 75, 84ff, 101–5 passim, 171n87, 178–79n1, 184n39, 185n44, 188n70; birth and death dates, 101, 188n71; and *wenren* (men of culture), 104f; ethnic identity of, 183–84n37. See also *Honglou meng*
Cao Yin, 171n87
Cao Zhi, 88, 185–86n48
Censorship, 1ff, 9, 21, 136, 155–56n9
Chang, Chun-shu, and Chang, Shelley, 165n39
Chang, Kang-i Sun, 170n85, 181n21
Chen Chen, 16, 18
Chen Dakang, 160n6
Chen Hong, 183n31
Chen Hongshou, 36f, 168n68, 169n82
Chen Jiru, 5
Chen Meilin, 165n36, 173–74n20, 175nn27–28, 176–77n41
Chen Zilong, 181n21
Cheng Jinfang, 178n47
Cheng Yi, 116, 139, 197n55. See also Cheng-Zhu neo-Confucianism
Cheng-Zhu neo-Confucianism, 2f, 121, 129ff, 133, 141f, 166–67n47, 195n37, 196n39. See also Cheng Yi; *Lixue*; Zhu Xi
Chi Hengshan, 42f, 62, 67, 114
Chuanxi (amateur acting), 39, 171n87
Clunas, Craig, 168n62
Confession, 106ff, 189n78, 189n82

Index

Confucius, 115f; as a messiah, 191n16, 191–92n17
Crossley, Pamela, 183–84n37
Cynicism, 38f, 42, 102f, 114, 170–71n86

Dai Bufan, 100f, 187n68
Dai Mingshi, 155n91
Dai Xian, 132
Daiyu, *see* Lin Daiyu
de Bary, Wm. Theodore, 156n11
Dickens, Charles, 50, 143f
Dong Xiaowan, 200n15
Dong Yue, 169n82
Dong Zhongshu, 79
Doody, Terrence, 189n82
Du Shaoqing, 49–53, 68; as Wu Jingzi's alter ego, 56–66, 175–76n33; relationship with Du Shengqing, 60, 176n39; as Wu Jingzi's self-vindication, 61f. *See also Rulin waishi*; Wu Jingzi
Du Shengqing, 51, 54, 57, 60, 70, 79, 176n35, 176n39. *See also* Du Shaoqing; Wu Qing
Dun Cheng, 104, 189n75

Edwards, Louise, 186n51, 186n55, 186n58
Elman, Benjamin, 27, 33f, 140, 170n83
Ernü yingxiong zhuan (A tale of heroic lovers), 150
Erzhi daoren, 185n44
Expediency (*quan*), 120, 193nn25–26, 193–94n27

Fan Jin, 50, 54
Fang Chaoying, 197n53
Fang Xiaoru, 138
Fang Yizhi, 169n82; and "Seven Solutions" ("Qijie"), 37, 40, 48, 169nn80–81, 172n10
Fangguan, 93
Feixiong, 115
Feng Menglong, 182n27
Feng Qiyong, 179–80n5
Fictionality, 158–59n29
Fusheng liuji (Six records of a floating life), 108, 150f, 200–201n15

Gai Kuan, 66f
Gender, 169–70n82, 182n28; in *Honglou meng*, 88–97. *See also* Allegorical tradition; Jia Baoyu; Literati; Wang Xifeng
Grandmother Jia, 89ff, 186n54, 187n60
Gong Weizhai, 34f
Gu Yanwu, 156n10, 167n55
Guy, Kent, 155n9
Guxin, 120, 134

Hai Rui, 138
Hanan, Patrick, 170n85
Han Yu, 17
Haoqiu zhuan (The fortunate union), 82; and *Yesou puyan*, 119, 192–93n23, 193–94n27
He Manzi, 176n41
Hegel, Robert E., 160n4, 161n20, 163n27, 165n39, 169n82
Heshen, 140
Hessney, Richard, 182n27, 192–93n23
Ho, Ping-ti, 31
Hong Changqing, 122
Hong Liangji, 198n61
Honglou meng (The dream of the red chamber), 41ff, 73, 143, 145–49; textual problem of, 76, 179–80nn2–5, 180n7; and the autobiographical, 77, 88–97; growing up in, 97–106; garden in, 99ff, 187n65; anachronism in, 100f, 187n66, 187–88n69; and confession, 106ff. *See also* Cao Xueqin; Jia Baoyu
Hou Jian, 197n51
Hsia, C. T., 57, 106, 160n4
Hu Shi, 56, 75
Huang Longzi, *see* Yellow Dragon
Huang, Pei, 155n5
Huang Zhongze (Huang Jinren), 39
Hucker, Charles, 197n54

Idema, L. W., 159n4

Ji En, 110
Ji Kang, 185n46
Ji Weixiao, 70
Jia Baoyu, 41f, 77; attitudes toward women, 89, 97; femininity of, 89f; and Wang Xifeng, 90ff; male deficiency of, 93; fear of growing up, 97–100; split personalities of, 100f; cynicism of, 102f; and *wenren* (men of culture), 104f; ambivalence of, 105f;

and *qing*, 149. See also Cao Xueqin;
  Honglou meng; Literati
Jia Jing, 93
Jia Lan, 101
Jia Lian, 88, 93
Jia Rong, 90
Jia Rui, 92
Jia She, 91
Jia Tanchun, see Tanchun
Jia Yi, 185n46
Jia Yingchun, see Yingchun
Jia Yucun, 104
Jia Zhen, 88
Jiahui, 98
Jihu sou, 180n8. See also Zhiyan zhai
Jin He, 156n9, 172n12, 175n33
Jin Ping Mei (The plum in the golden vase), 15ff, 19f
Jin Shengtan, 17f, 160n11
Jin Zhi, 132, 196n42
Jinghua yuan (The destinies of the flowers in the mirror), 150, 182–83n29, 195n36
Jingting, 116
Jituo, 11, 48. See also Allegorical tradition; *Zikuang*
Joyce, James, 50

Kangxi, 2, 85, 129, 195–96n38
Kant, Immanuel, 10
Knight-errantry, 118–21, 134, 192n19, 192–93nn23–24. See also Literati
Kong Youwei, 140
Kristeva, Julia, 181n12
Kuang Shaoren, 53
Kuiguan, 93, 186n59

Lady An, 137, 197n52
Lady Ji, 137, 197n52
Lady Wang, 99
Lao Can, 151
Lao Can youji (The travels of Lao Can), 151, 192n19
Larson, Wendy, 201n17
Lee, Leo Ou-fan, 192n19
Lee, Wai-yee, 189n73, 199n7
Leng Yubing, 20
Leng Zixing, 92
Levenson, Joseph, 168n66
Li Baichuan, see *Lüye xianzong*
Li Lüyuan, see *Qilu deng*

Li Ruzhen, 150. See also *Jinghua yuan*
Li Wan, 99
Li Xiang, 10f
Li Youquan, 120, 128
Li Yu, 22, 25, 160n9, 164n35, 168n68, 170n85. See also *Rou putuan*
Li Zhi: and individualism, 1, 3, 155n2, 156n10, 166n45; and fiction, 8, 158n27; commentary on *Shuihu zhuan*, 18, 161n17; on "phoniness" (*jia*), 36, 169n77; "A Brief Comment on Zhuowu" ("Zhuowu lunlüe"), 45f, 171nn3–4; on women, 82
Liao Yan, 22f
Liaozhai zhiyi (Strange stories from the Studio of Leisure), 22, 160n9, 163–64n31, 182n28
Liezi, 109
Lin Daiyu, 93f, 97ff, 102, 187n60, 187n62
Lin Lan Xiang (The fragrance of forest and orchid), 83f, 183n31, 183n33
Lin, Shuen-fu, 178n50
Lingguan, 90
Literati (*shi*): identity crisis of, 9, 35f, 145ff, 174n21; origins of, 26; and government service, 26f, 165n41, 169nn72–73; and self-cultivation 27f, 166n44; as *wenren* (men of culture), 29ff, 105, 165n41, 167nn51–53, 167n55, 168n66; and merchants, 31ff; professionalization of, 33ff, 168nn67–69, 169n73; autobiographical strategies of, 36–40; and autobiographical fiction, 40–44; in *Yesou puyan*, 42f, 114–22, 135, 138–41; in *Rulin waishi*, 51–54, 66–74 *passim*, 174n21; and marginality, 78ff, 112, 119; in *Honglou meng*, 78–84, 96f, 104f
Literati novel, 15f, 159–60n4, 163n30; and high literati tradition, 17ff, 163–64n31; authorship of, 19f, 23f; contemporaneity in, 20f; inward turning of, 21; and the novel of the literati, 22; circulation of, 23f; healing potential of, 24ff; feminization in, 82, 181–82nn22–23, 182–83nn26–29; and autobiographical writing, 148ff
Liu Bei, 138
Liu Dakui, 34

Liu Dalang, 118
Liu E, 151
Liu, James J. Y., 193n24
Liu Jin, 132f, 196n42
Liu Xianxin, 178n48
Liu Xiaobiao, 10
Lixue (school of principle), 129, 131, 195n37, 196n39. See also Cheng-Zhu neo-Confucianism
Liyan (seeking cultural immortality), 18f, 142
Lu Xiangshan, 130, 136
Lu-Wang neo-Confucianism, 2f, 129ff, 195n37, 196n39. See also Wang Yangming; Wang Yangming school of neo-Confucianism; *Xinxue*
Lü Xiong: "Authorial Preface" ("Zixu") and "Authorial Postscript" ("Ziba") to *Nüxian waishi*, 161–62n21
Luo Pin, 38f
Luo Siju, 156n13
Lüye xianzong (The footsteps of an immortal in the mundane world), 19f, 161n21

Ma Chunshang, 54
Ma, Y. M., 162–63n26
McMahon, Keith, 182n23, 192n17, 194n28
Madame Shui, 110, 113, 119ff, 124, 130, 134, 192n17
Mao Qiling, 2f, 8, 144f, 158n28
Mao Xiang, 200n15
Marginality, see Gender; Literati
Mask, 11, 41, 71ff, 143ff, 150, 152f, 170n85, 172n9. See also under *Rulin waishi*; Self-re/presentation
Meiren xiangcao ("beauty and flower" allegorical tradition), see Allegorical tradition
Memory: and forgetfulness, 22, 55f, 103, 147, 175n27. See also Autobiographical writing; Self-re/presentation
Merchants, 31f. See also Literati
Metzger, Thomas, 166n44
Miller, Lucien, 179n2, 185n47
Mingyan, 89
Miss Lu, 59, 177n47
Moi, Toril, 181n12
Mufu, 34f, 169n73. See also Literati
Muyou, see *Mufu*

Naquin, Susan, and Rawski, Evelyn, 165n39
Neisheng waiwang (sage within, king without), 27; in *Yesou puyan*, 42, 115, 121f, 131, 135, 166nn43–44
New Text Confucianism (*jinwen xue*), 140ff, 191–92n17, 198n68
Niu Buyi, 51, 69
Niu Pulang, 69
Nivison, David, 155n6
Nü caizi shu (A book of female talents), 83, 182–83n29
Nü kaike zhuan (A tale of female examinees), 195n36
Nüwa: in *Honglou meng*, 85f; in *Yesou puyan*, 123
Nüxian waishi (An unofficial history of a female immortal), see Lü Xiong

Olney, James, 11, 61, 159n34, 177n42, 177n44
Ouyang Jian, 190n1
Ouyang Xiu, 17
Owen, Stephen, 157n17, 171–72n5, 172n7, 188–89n73

Peterson, Willard, 166n44, 167n51, 169n80, 172n10
Plaks, Andrew, 15f, 37f, 158n27, 159–60n4, 163n28, 164n34, 199n3, 199–200n8
Pingshan lengyan (The flat mountain and the cold swallow), 25f
Pu Songling, 163n31. See also *Liaozhai zhiyi*

Qi Jiguang, 135, 197n50
Qianlong, 39, 111, 134, 138ff, 155n6, 170n86, 178n51, 198–99n69
Qilu deng (The warning light at the crossroads), 23f, 162n21
Qin Keqing, 90
Qin Zhong, 92
Qingwen, 87, 92, 185n47
Qiuxiang, 130
Qu Yuan, 81, 83, 86ff, 185n46, 185–86n48

Recognition, 80, 83; in *Rulin waishi*, 54; in *Honglou meng*, 94f; in *Yesou puyan*, 110f, 122ff, 127f, 138, 194n32. See also Literati

Ren Luanchui, 112, 118, 123
Renza, Louis A., 159*n*31
Rijing, 125
Roddy, Stephen, 163*n*29, 166*n*47, 169*n*76, 194*n*32
Rolston, David, 158*n*27
Ropp, Paul, 156*n*10, 165*n*39, 166*n*47, 177*n*41, 178*n*48, 183*n*34
Rou putuan (The carnal prayer mat), 160*n*9, 195*n*36
Ruan Ji, 104f
Rulin waishi (The scholars), 42ff, 143–49; structure and autobiographical pattern of, 49–54 *passim*, 68, 114, 174*n*22; masquerading in, 67–70; dilemma of satire in, 73f; and *Yesou puyan*, 114f; textual problem of, 173*n*17. *See also* Wu Jingzi

Sagehood, 27. *See also Neisheng waiwang*
Sanguo yanyi (The romance of the Three Kingdoms), 19f
Sanjiao kaimi guizheng yanyi (A tale of redemption due to the teachings of the three religions), 21
Self-cultivation, 27f. *See also* Cheng-Zhu neo-Confucianism; *Neisheng waiwang*
Self-re/presentation: advantages of, 8f, 48, 144, 147, 172*n*9; examples of, 46–48, 143f, 150f; definition of, 48f; in *Rulin waishi*, 57, 63, 72f; dilemma of, 71–74, 145, 200*n*13; in *Honglou meng*, 77f; in *Yesou puyan*, 135. *See also* Autobiographical writing; *Jituo*; Mask; *Zikuang*; *Zixu*
Shen Qiongzhi, 173*n*20
Shen Yao, 31f
Shi, see Literati
Shi Chong, 185*n*46
Shi Xiangyun, 93, 95f, 187*n*60
Shi Yunyu, 201*n*15
Shi Zhenlin, 84
Shidafu (scholar-official), 29. *See also* Literati
Shigong, 123, 130f, 194*n*33. *See also* Yang Mingshi
Shuangqing, *see Xiqing sanji*
Shuihu houzhuan (A supplement to The Water Margin), 16. *See also* Chen Chen

Shuihu zhuan (The water margin), 17ff, 173*n*14
Sima Qian, 17f, 78, 80, 173*n*14, 178*n*52
Slupski, Zbgniew, 178*n*52
Song Yu, 185*n*48
Spengemann, William, 158*n*25, 179*n*1
Starobinski, Jean, 189*n*81
Su Shi, 29
Suchen, *see* Wen Suchen
Su'e, 112, 123
Sui Tang yanyi (The romance of the Sui and the Tang), 21
Sui Yangdi yanshi (The romantic tale of Emperor Yang of the Sui), 160*n*9
Sun Jiagan, 112; and Wen Suchen, 133f

Tan Fenglian, 173*n*18
Tanchun, 12, 86, 94ff, 102f
Tang Yin, 104
Tao Qian, 104; "The Biography of Master Five Willows" ("Wuliu xiansheng zhuan"), 45, 172*n*12
Tianhuacang zhuren, *see* Pingshan lengyan
Tianmu shanqiao (Zhang Wenhu), 57, 175*n*33
T'ien, Ju-k'ang, 181*n*11, 182*n*26
Tousou, 196*n*39
Tu Shen, 200*n*13

Vinograd, Richard, 38, 170*n*82, 170*n*84

Waley, Arthur, 81
Wang Jie, 141, 144
Wang, Jing, 199*n*5
Wang Mian, 52, 66
Wang Qiongling, 190*n*1, 196*n*43, 197*n*51
Wang Wei, 96
Wang Xianpei and Zhou Weiming, 160*n*10
Wang Xichan, 170*n*83
Wang Xifeng, 90–93, 95ff, 103, 107, 186*n*52
Wang Yangming, 1ff, 129; in *Yesou puyan*, 131–36, 138, 146, 196*n*39, 196*n*43. *See also* Lu-Wang neo-Confucianism; Wang Yangming school of neo-Confucianism; *Xinxue*
Wang Yangming school of neo-

Confucianism, 2f. *See also* Lu-Wang neo-Confucianism; Wang Yangming
Wang Zhi, 196*n*42
Wang Zhong, 10f
Wei Zhongxian, 140
Weinstein, Vicki, 32f, 168*n*67
Wen Bai, 110. *See also* Wen Suchen
Wen Kang, *see Ernü yingxiong zhuan*
Wen Lin, 125f
Wen Long, 43, 125ff
Wen Ruyu, 19f, 162*n*22
Wen Suchen, 42f, 143; meaning of his name, 110, 116; compared to Confucius, 115f; as a super literatus, 117; and knight-errantry, 118ff; and examinations, 123–28; compared with Jia Baoyu, 192*n*22; age of, 197–98*n*60. *See also* Xia Jingqu; *Yesou puyan*
Wenren (men of culture), *see* Literati
Wong, Timothy, 175*n*27, 177*n*41
Wu Guodui, 55, 196*n*38
Wu Jingzi: ancestors of, 55; failures in life, 55f, 58, 176*n*37; motivation for writing, 56, 60f; and adoption, 67, 175*n*28; and Erudite Scholarship Examination, 174*n*24, 175*n*31, 176*n*37, 176–77*n*41, 177*n*43. *See also* Du Shaoqing; *Rulin waishi*; Wu Linqi
Wu Linqi, 55, 67, 175*n*28, 176*n*37
Wu, Nelson, 168*n*67
Wu, Pei-yi: on the golden age of Chinese autobiography, 1; on the envoi of Chinese autobiography, 1f, 13, 156*n*13; on the underdevelopment of Chinese autobiography, 45, 157*n*16; on autobiography disguised as biography, 45ff, 48, 67f; on self-invention in autobiography, 141f, 144; on *Honglou meng*, 157*n*20; on historiography, 158*n*26; on confession, 163*n*27, 189*n*78; on *zixu*, 162*n*21
Wu Qing: and Du Shengqing, 60, 176*n*39
Wu, Shih-chang, 180*n*9, 187*n*68

Xia Jingqu, 35, 43, 111ff, 133, 198–99*n*69; compared with Cao Xueqin, 119, 192*n*22. *See also* Wen Suchen; *Yesou puyan*
Xiang Yu, 92

Xiangling (in *Honglou meng*), 86
Xiangling (in *Yesou puyan*), 122f
Xiangyun, *see* Shi Xiangyun
Xianzong, 115f, 132–39 *passim*, 197*n*52
Xiaohong, 98
Xiaozong, 118, 137ff, 192*n*18, 197*nn*52–53
Ximin shangqiao, 196*n*39
Xingshi yinyuan zhuan (A marriage that awakens the world), 19, 21
Xinxue (school of the mind or the study of the mind), 129, 131, 195*n*37. *See also* Lu-Wang neo-Confucianism; Wang Yangming school of neo-Confucianism
Xiqing sanji (Random notes of western green), 84, 183*n*34
Xiren, 90, 94, 99
Xiyou bu (A supplement to *The Journey to the West*), 21, 169*n*82
Xiyou ji (The journey to the west), 15, 19
Xu Wei, 182*n*27
Xuangu, 118, 120, 122
Xue Pan, 88
Xue Yue Mei (The plum under the snowy moon), 18f, 183*n*31
Xun Mei, 54

Yang Dingjian, 160*n*9
Yang Mingshi, 112, 130f, 194*n*33, 195–96*n*38. *See also* Shigong
Yang Xiong, 78
Yellow Dragon, 151
Yesou puyan (The humble words of an old rustic), 42ff, 143–49 *passim*; meaning of the title, 109ff, 191*n*6; irony in, 113f, 128f, 164*n*34; structure of, 115; as autobiographical vindication, 119, 122–29, 142; and historiography, 136ff; and Wang Yangming, 131–36; as prophecy, 140f; textual history of, 190*n*1. *See also* Literati; Recognition; Self-re/presentation; Wen Suchen; Xia Jingqu
Yijing (Book of changes), 79
Yingchun, 93, 99
Yinshi (A history of white fish), 200*n*13
Yongzheng, 188*n*70

Yoshikawa Kōjirō, 29
Yu Dafu, 152
Yu Huaxuan, 65f, 178*n*48
Yu, Pauline, 181*n*21
Yu Pingbo, 75
Yu Yingshi, 165*n*40
Yu Yude, 51f, 54, 62ff, 70f, 73, 104, 177*n*46
Yuan Mei, 34; on *wenren* (men of culture), 30, 174*n*21; on self-identity, 38f, 170*n*85; and Wu Jingzi, 173–74*n*20; and examinations, 177–78*n*47
Yuan Wuyai, 160*n*9
Yuanyang, 91

Zeitlin, Judith, 163–64*n*31, 170*n*82
Zeng Guofan, 156*n*13
Zhang Dai, "Self-Written Tomb Inscription" ("Ziwei muzhiming"), 4f; and *Honglou meng*, 6f, 106f, 157*n*21; "Self-Written Preface to *Tao'an's Dream Memories*" ("*Tao'an mengyi zixu*"), 107, 157*n*17
Zhang Junming: "Ziwei muzhiming," 5f
Zhang Xuecheng, 169*n*72
Zhang Zhupo, 17
Zhao Jingsheng, 194*n*31, 196*n*47, 197–98*n*60
Zhao Kang, 180*n*9
Zhao Yi, 34
Zhen Baoyu, 87
Zheng Xie (Zheng Banqiao), 28, 32, 39f, 168*nn*64–65
Zhiji (the one who appreciates), *see* Recognition
Zhiyan zhai, 77, 86f, 94, 106, 180*nn*8–9, 184*n*42, 185*n*44, 188*n*72

Zhiyin (the one who understands the music), *see* Recognition
Zhong Xing, 156*n*10
Zhou Jin, 50, 54
Zhou Ruchang (Zhou Ju-ch'ang): on the autobiographical in *Honglou meng*, 75, 172–73*n*12, 178–79*n*1, 189–90*n*83; on *Honglou meng*'s chronology, 100, 187*n*66; on Cao Xueqin's ethnic identity, 183–84*n*37; on Qing examinations, 184*n*39; on the dates of Cao Xueqin's birth and death, 188*n*71; on *Fusheng liuji*, 200–201*n*15
Zhu Danwen, 187–88*n*69, 188*n*70
Zhu Xi, 1f, 3, 116, 130f, 133. *See also* Cheng-Zhu neo-Confucianism
Zhu Xuejun, 187*n*64
Zhuang Shaoquang, 51, 54, 62ff, 70
Zhuge Lian, 117, 138
Zhuo Wenjun, 156*n*10
Zijuan, 97f
Zikuang (self-comparison), 11, 48, 51, 172–73*n*12, 175–76*n*33. *See also* Autobiographical writing; *Jituo*; Mask; Self-re/presentation; *Zituo*; *Zixu*; *Zizhuan*
Zisong (self-indictment), *see* Confession
Zituo, 175*n*33
Zixu (self-account), 162*n*21
Zixu (self-written preface or authorial preface), 19, 161–62*n*21, 178*n*52. *See also* Autobiographical writing; Self-re/presentation
Zizhuan, 173*n*12. *See also* Autobiographical writing
Zou Shan, 166*n*45
Zuo Guangdou, 138
Zuo Si, 47

Library of Congress Cataloguing-in-Publication Data
Huang, Martin W., 1960–
   Literati and self-re/presentation : autobiographical sensibility in the eighteenth-century Chinese novel / Martin W. Huang
   p. cm.
   Includes bibliographical references and index.
   ISBN 0-8047-2462-8 (acid-free paper) :
   1. Chinese fiction—Ch'ing dynasty, 1644–1912—History and criticism.   2. Autobiographical fiction, Chinese.   I. Title.
PL2437.H83   1995
895.1'34809—dc20   94-33002
                                                        CIP